STRUCTURAL ADJUSTMENT, RECONSTRUCTION AND DEVELOPMENT IN AFRICA

Structural Adjustment, Reconstruction and Development in Africa

Edited by
KEMPE RONALD HOPE, Sr.
Faculty of Social Sciences
University of Botswana, Gaborone

Routledge
Taylor & Francis Group
LONDON AND NEW YORK

First published 1997 by Ashgate Publishing

Reissued 2018 by Routledge
2 Park Square, Milton Park, Abingdon, Oxon, OX14 4RN
52 Vanderbilt Avenue, New York, NY 10017

Routledge is an imprint of the Taylor & Francis Group, an informa business

A Library of Congress record exists under LC control number:

ISBN 13: 978-1-138-39345-5 (hbk)
ISBN 13: 978-0-429-40174-9 (ebk)

Contents

List of contributors

Arnon Bar-On is a Senior Lecturer in Social Work, University of Botswana.

Ben C. Chikulo is Associate Professor of Development Studies, University of the North West, South Africa.

Kwame Frimpong is Associate Professor of Law, University of Botswana.

Kempe Ronald Hope, Sr. is Professor of Development Studies at the University of Botswana.

Gloria Jacques is a Lecturer in Social Work, University of Botswana.

Ben Kaluwa is Professor of Economics, Chancellor College, University of Malawi.

Gladson Kayira is an Economist in the Ministry of Finance and Development Planning, Government of Botswana.

Gwen N. Lesetedi is a Lecturer in Sociology, University of Botswana.

Dave Macdonald is a Senior Lecturer in Sociology, University of Botswana.

Dumisani Magadlela is a Lecturer in Sociology, University of Zimbabwe.

G.S. Maipose is a Senior Lecturer in Political and Administrative Studies, University of Botswana.

The Honourable Themba N. Masuku is Minister for Economic Planning and Development, Government of Swaziland.

S.N-A. Mensah is a Senior Lecturer in Economics, University of Swaziland.

H.P.B. Moshi is a Senior Research Fellow at the Economic Research Bureau, University of Dar es Salaam, Tanzania.

Kwaku Osei-Hwedie is Professor of Social Work, University of Botswana.

Pacharo H. Simukonda is a Lecturer in Political and Administrative Studies, University of Botswana.

Preface

The chapters contained in this book are the revised proceedings of the 18th Southern African Universities Social Science Conference (SAUSSC) held in Mbabane, Swaziland, December 4-7, 1995 on the theme 'Structural Adjustment, Reconstruction and Development'. They represent a rich mixture of analytical views and ideas with a wide range of country and sector case study coverage.

This book is intended to make a contribution to both the literature and debate on the relationship between structural adjustment and reconstruction and development in Africa, as seen from the perspective of academics and practitioners working in Africa on African development problems and issues, using multidisciplinary approaches.

The implementation of structural adjustment in Africa has spawned a considerable, and still on-going, debate with vociferous advocates on both sides of the issue, particularly with respect to the efficacy of structural adjustment programmes (SAPs) as an antidote to Africa's development crisis. Much of the debate is centred around the impact (real or perceived) of structural adjustment programmes on the populaces of the African countries. That African countries needed to adjust to policy failure is no longer a contentious issue. What is, however, still being contended, are some of the elements of SAPs and their sequencing.

One of the factors giving rise to criticisms of SAPs is that they (SAPs) did not yield the expected results over the short- nor medium-term. The benefits of SAPs are now seen as a long-term accomplishment and much empirical evidence is now emerging which indicate that in those African countries that were committed to staying the course of structural adjustment, for example, Ghana, there is a growth dividend which has generally benefited the poor. On the other hand, in African countries, such as Kenya and Côte d'Ivoire, that were ambivalent about the reform agenda or that delayed implementing SAPs, the poor have become poorer (Demery and Squire, 1996).

Reconstruction and development in Africa necessitates structural adjustment. That some economic and social dislocation may occur, in the short-term, is an inevitable outcome, as well as a part of the process of adjustment through which an economy must evolve if such an economy were to reap the long-term benefits of policy reform.

As usual, putting together a book such as this requires considerable cooperation and assistance. In that regard, I would like to thank the contributors for their prompt responses to my many queries. I also owe a special debt of gratitude to the Honourable Themba N. Masuku, Minister for Economic Planning and Development in the Government of Swaziland, whose opening statement set the tone for a lively and successful conference, and, as well, to Dr L.K.J. Mwansa, President of the Southern African Universities Social Science Conference and the other members of the SAUSSC Executive Committee for their support in seeing this book through to publication. Likewise, appreciation is expressed to Professor John Mukum Mbaku, General Editor of the Contemporary Perspectives on Developing Societies Series, for his enthusiasm and encouragement in seeing the project completed.

Kempe Ronald Hope, Sr.
Gaborone, Botswana

Introduction

The Honourable Themba N. Masuku

I have been asked to speak on a subject that is not only controversial but so wide that it is not possible to exhaust it within the limited time available. Be that as it may, I will try to flag some of the essential issues relevant to the subject.

I will begin by first outlining how the structural adjustment programmes (SAPs) of the Bretton Woods institutions came into being and how they have been designed and implemented in sub-Saharan Africa. Secondly, I will discuss the major weaknesses of SAPs. Finally, I will briefly talk about Swaziland's economic problems and what Swaziland needs to do to avoid involuntary structural adjustment.

Why structural adjustment?

When we look at structural adjustment we find that the major macroeconomic and financial imbalances leading to structural adjustment can be grouped under four broad categories. The first is low or stagnant GDP growth accompanied by a rapidly increasing population; the second category is unsustainable balance of payments deficits characterized by imports growing faster than exports and an inability to service external debt; the third category is budget deficits characterized by public expenditures growing faster than fiscal revenues; and the fourth category is weak monetary policies characterized by rampant inflation and negative real interest rates. When these imbalances occur the typical government responses may include the introduction of exchange control regulations, price controls, and imposed negative interest rates. While these actions have short-term political benefits they actually worsen the longer-term economic situation by preventing the operation of the price mechanism. The result is a discouragement of investment (both domestic and foreign) and the perpetuation of a vicious cycle of economic stagnation and declines in standards of living.

The first SAPs were initiated by the IMF and World Bank in the 1980s in response to the serious implications of the world debt crisis as it affected many developing countries. The sharp deterioration in the terms of trade, particularly for oil-importing countries, and inappropriate domestic policies in those countries were the direct causes of their economic problems. It became increasingly difficult for debtor countries to service their loans and for the affected developing countries to sustain the level of imports they had grown accustomed to. The situation of these countries was further aggravated by the lacklustre economic performance of the industrialized market economies. The 1979-1982 world recession was then followed by a long period (1983-1987) of slow recovery.

These factors had a disastrous impact on import-dependent and primary export-oriented African economies. With the exception of oil, the real prices of many primary products were at their lowest level for 50 years which meant that the import purchasing power per unit of export plummeted. The response of the international community, through the IMF and the World Bank, was to design structural adjustment programmes.

The structural adjustment package

What does the structural adjustment package entail? A typical structural adjustment programme designed by the IMF/World Bank to restore economic growth might consist of the following policy actions:

1 Currency devaluation to eliminate any biases against exports resulting from currency overvaluation and thus render exports more competitive on the world market as well as alleviate balance of payments problems arising from currency overvaluation;

2 Domestic demand management whose primary purpose is to eliminate fiscal deficits through adjustments in government expenditure, notably in the non-productive sectors and in the reduction of subsidies which absorb a large share of fiscal resources. Attempts to control government expenditures are often targeted at confining government to those activities which cannot easily be provided by the private sector so that privatization programmes have become part and parcel of structural adjustment;

3 Control of domestic inflation as part of sound monetary policy. This involves controlling the growth in the domestic money supply through limits on the growth of domestic credit and the introduction of market-determined interest rates. These measures, together with domestic demand management, are intended to encourage domestic and foreign investment by providing an enabling environment;

4 Domestic price liberalization in order to remove distortions resulting from price controls in the domestic product and factor markets. This would enable local demand and supply conditions to determine the prices of all goods and services in the economy, including labour, without government interference. Liberalization of prices is expected to result in an efficient and optimal allocation and use of scarce resources within an economy and allow investors to identify opportunities to make profits and;

5 Trade liberalization to encourage the development of local industry according to a country's comparative advantage. This will contribute to the efficient utilization of resources and encourage international trade thus ensuring a much needed flow of foreign exchange.

What are the shortcomings of SAPs?

While the basic principles of SAPs may be sound, they have been substantially criticized in Africa. African governments attempted to rapidly reduce fiscal deficits by cutting expenditure on capital and maintenance and thus contributing to the decline of social services. There has also been a failure to adequately identify and plan for potential negative socio-economic impacts of SAPs as well as inadequate consideration was given to the political dynamics of adjustment. Even if SAPs have been successful in improving key economic aggregates, some adjusting countries have experienced so severe a deterioration in human and social conditions such that their entire SAPs were jeopardized.

The World Bank's structural adjustment loans (SALs) were subsequently introduced to ameliorate the social problems arising from adjustment as well as to provide quick disbursing balance of payments financing intended to facilitate adjustment. In linking lending to policy and institutional changes in these countries, the Bretton Woods Institutions made the adoption and complete implementation of SAPs a pre-condition for receipt of loans and other financial support. The expectation was that the adjustment programme would succeed in putting the country's economy back on track and enable it to meet past and new debt obligations. However, this was not the case. In spite of the SALs, the SAPs were still largely unsuccessful. The failure of SAPs to achieve recovery and sustainable development in the expected time-frame has led the World Bank and other institutions to pose a number of reflective questions. They include among them:

1 Does Africa face special structural problems that have not been properly understood?

2 Has the institutional dimension been neglected?

3 Has the design of recent reform programmes been inappropriate?

4 Can adjustment and democratization be carried out successfully when they are attempted simultaneously?

The continued failure of some SAPs in Africa is attributable to an inability to implement adjustment policies and to sustain their implementation. Nevertheless, the success of the transformation of some economies in East Asia has led economists to conclude that there may be a fundamental problem related to the sequencing of the reforms entailed in SAPs. For example, it is now accepted that trade liberalization, particularly liberalization of the capital account, should not precede the liberalization of domestic factor and goods markets.

These observations point out the fact that the IMF/World Bank SAPs failed to correct the existing economic imbalances and to restore economic growth and promote sustainable development in sub-Saharan Africa. They do not, however, imply that sub-Saharan Africa countries do not need to restructure their economies. Indeed, it has to be appreciated that fundamental structural change is needed to transform African economies and enable them to survive in an increasingly competitive world.

A number of alternatives to the World Bank/IMF SAPs have been developed for African economies. These include the Lagos Plan of Action and Final Act of Lagos; the African Alternative Framework to Structural Adjustment for Socio-Economic Recovery and Transformation by the Economic Commission for Africa; Structural Adjustment with a Human Face by UNICEF; and the Programme of Action for African Economic Recovery and Development, 1986-1990.

The case of Swaziland

Swaziland is presently experiencing some of the macroeconomic imbalances which could lead to structural adjustment. There are however two characteristics which set Swaziland apart from the rest of the sub-Saharan African countries that underwent World Bank/IMF structural adjustment programmes:

1 Swaziland is starting from a relatively strong base because the country does not have a significant external debt burden and;

2 Swaziland's structural adjustment is confined to fiscal management. Swaziland's membership in the Common Monetary Area has meant that the economy has escaped many of the imbalances resulting from inappropriate monetary policy. However, this remains an advantage only as long as South Africa continues to implement a prudent monetary policy.

Having said this, I wish to point out that though there is no need to panic as yet, there is a real need to take action to avoid any imposed structural adjustment which would be an indication of our having reached a situation of economic crisis. It is the country's wish to avoid the necessity for an imposed structural adjustment programme by attempting to institute an internal adjustment programme. Furthermore, it is questionable whether or not Swaziland will be able to benefit from the potential gains from recent developments within the region such as the newly found peace which has resulted in an upsurge in tourism and rekindled investor interest and confidence. These developments will, however, aid the process of reconstruction and development in Swaziland and the Southern African region as a whole but these developments cannot be a substitute for internal adjustment in the individual countries in the region.

Since the budgetary turnaround from surplus to deficits, beginning in 1991-92, there has been increasing awareness within government that emerging trends were unfavourable. Our response was to commence the design of two complementary initiatives. These are the National Development Strategy (NDS) and the Public Sector Management Programme (PSMP). The NDS was formally adopted by cabinet in 1993 and is intended to represent a national consensus on Swaziland's objectives, strategies, and policies for long-term development. The NDS will constitute the basis for detailed medium-term planning.

The PSMP was formally approved in May 1995. This programme is intended to review current government resource allocations, expenditure trends, organizational structures, and policies and procedures in each ministry. It will assist in the development of performance indicators for all government activities. Some efforts have been made since 1991-92 to reign in fiscal expenditures, but it was only in the 1995-96 budgetary estimates that a systematic approach was adopted in terms of specific proposals and mechanisms to address the unfavourable fiscal position.

Conclusion

It was a great honour for me to have been invited to speak at this conference on such a very important subject. It is also very timely for Swaziland and I hope that in your discussions you will be able to consider not only the main features of structural adjustment but also their application to the unique set of circumstances facing Swaziland. We would very much welcome suggestions for ways to improve our internal adjustment process.

We recognize that the success of our internal adjustment programme depends on the need for consensus among all the key players in the economy. The government therefore hopes to have the full cooperation of the staff associations and all other affected groups to ensure the successful implementation of this necessary initiative.

Part One
THE ECONOMIC CRISIS, STRUCTURAL ADJUSTMENT AND DEVELOPMENT POLICY

1 The economic crisis in Africa: An analytical perspective on its origins and nature

Kempe Ronald Hope, Sr. and Gladson Kayira

The majority of African countries are experiencing a serious economic crisis. That economic crisis, though showing signs of moderation in some countries, has resulted in elusive development in most of the others with far-reaching negative consequences on their populaces. When there is no development, there is hopelessness; and where there is hopelessness, there is no effort to work toward development. The circle becomes complete and reinforcing.

Unfortunately, in most of Africa, the economic crisis has resulted in life being an endless series of vicious circles spreading economic suffering in a now concentrated fashion. The economic crisis in Africa represents a historical tragedy and the historical evidence now suggests that such a crisis need not have occurred and, despite some views to the contrary, the overwhelming point of view is that this economic crisis is the inevitable outcome primarily of the failure of post-independence development policy formulation and implementation in the majority of African countries.

In most of Africa, post-independence development policy was formulated through a statist ideological framework which was then implemented by experimentation. Moreover, some, if not all, of the countries had to contend with an adverse international economic environment. That combination produced disastrous results. Among other things, poverty and socio-economic inequalities increased, the external debt burden became heavier, the brain drain intensified, capital flight deepened, the balance of payments weakened, the physical infrastructure deteriorated, unemployment and crime escalated, famine and malnutrition became more pronounced, budget deficits soared, agricultural productivity declined, urbanization burgeoned, environmental degradation expanded, political and civil strife worsened, and corruption became more rampant.

These disastrous development results were, in turn, the catalyst behind the deepening economic crisis in Africa, and they, consequently, provided the imperative for policy reform in those countries. Policy reform can be defined as changes in government policy, institutional structure, or administrative procedures that are designed to alter economic activity and improve performance (Roemer and Radelet, 1991). Put more succinctly, it is policy change, across the board, to effect sustained economic progress that will lead to a more desirable economic outcome than current practice permits.

The policy reform which emerged in the 1980s, as a response to the ensuing economic crisis in Africa, was dominated by donor-sponsored (primarily the World Bank and the International Monetary Fund) structural adjustment programmes (SAPs). The SAPs have triggered a fierce debate as to their effectiveness as an antidote to the economic crisis in Africa and a significant body of literature has emerged which is very critical of SAPs. However, most of the critics of SAPs, although making a convincing case in some of their criticisms, have failed, on the other hand, to provide convincing and implementable alternatives for economic recovery in the African countries.

This chapter, which is structured as a comparative analytical review, examines the origins and nature of the economic crisis in Africa and the policy framework giving rise to it, drawing on Southern African country examples to illuminate and illustrate the analytical perspective.

The origins and nature of the economic crisis in Africa

The economic crisis in Africa emerged in the 1970s following on the achievement of independence in most of the countries in the 1960s. During the 1980s the crisis worsened. Basically, after an initial period of growth immediately after independence, most of the African economies began to decline. In the 1980s, the decline became more rapid and had reached crisis proportions before donor-supported policy reforms were implemented.

The primary factor precipitating the economic crisis in Africa was the implementation of development policy through a statist ideological framework. In this framework, state planning became paramount and markets and choices were deliberately undermined. To maintain this system the patrimonial state emerged through a pervasive patrimonialization of power and authority structures by the political leadership. For most African leaders, of all ideological and policy persuasions, there evolved a preoccupation with the need for greater authority over their populaces and territories (Callaghy, 1994).

The emergence of the African patrimonial state revealed a system of patronage, clientelism, and personal rule (Hope, 1996b). Patrimonial leaders rewarded political and personal loyalty more than merit. They used the state's financial and other resources to reward themselves and their supporters (Dia, 1996). This situation was in sharp contrast to the prevailing situation in the 1960s and early 1970s when the quality of leadership was a major ingredient in Africa's economic progress and a key determinant in the improvements in socio-economic conditions (Sirleaf, 1996).

The deterioration in the quality of African leadership, which began in the early

1970s, resulted in the replacement of long-term objectives and strategies with myopic and short-term policies exemplified by large public sector deficits to support politically determined projects; overvaluation of currencies; inefficient regulation of domestic and foreign trade; and the proliferation of parasitic public enterprises, for example. In other words, development policy was executed under the rubric of a statist framework which was amply supported by strong patrimonial leadership. Consequently, when asked about Africa's problems, most African leaders do not discuss the shortcomings of the continent's leadership. Instead, they tend to blame "colonialism, American imperialism, the pernicious effects of slavery, the unjust international economic system, and exploitation by multinational corporations" (Ayittey, 1992). In some instances, they even blame the international development agencies and donor community from whom they are receiving and/or seeking assistance.

There is little doubt that the magnitude of the economic crisis in Africa has brought considerable agony to the citizens of those countries and, perhaps, the best indicator of that is the rates of poverty. Although the data series are incomplete for some of the countries, based on the available data, only in Botswana and Zimbabwe the percentage of the population below the absolute poverty line is less than 50 percent. There are more poor people now than there were in 1985 in most of the African countries (World Bank, 1994a). Poverty in Africa, is exacerbated by high rates of population growth. At current rates of growth, most of the African countries will double their population within the first two decades of the 21st century (UNDP, 1995).

Contributing to poverty, in relationship to population growth, is the dismal economic performance of most of the African countries when measured in terms of national income accounts. In most of the countries, the annual growth rate of gross national product (GNP) per capita declined between the periods 1965-80 and 1980-93. During the period 1980-93, only two of the Southern African countries (Botswana with 6.2 percent and Swaziland with 3 percent) had statistically significant positive growth rates in GNP per capita while during the period 1965-80 only one country (Zambia with -1.2 percent) had a negative growth rate.

Declining growth rates in per capita income would also suggest an association with income inequality. Income inequality can be measured by the Gini index which is estimated from the Lorenz curve describing the income or expenditure distribution for a given population. The movement in the Gini closely follows the movement in poverty. Where there is an increase in poverty levels, as measured by the head count, there is usually a parallel increase in the level of inequality, and vice versa (World Bank, 1994a). Currently, there are estimates of the Gini index for several countries for varying periods ranging from 1981-82 to 1993-94. In the majority of countries the Gini index is very high ranging from 43.5 percent in Zambia to 59.2 percent in Tanzania and thereby indicating considerable income inequality (World Bank, 1994a).

In Africa, the poor are mostly rural. There are more poor rural households than poor urban households and the incidence of rural and urban poverty among countries provides some stark contrasts. The data for 1991, for example, indicate that Malawi has the largest disparity in rural and urban poverty with 85 percent of the population in the rural areas below the absolute poverty line compared to 8 percent in the urban areas while Zambia has the smallest disparity with 42 percent of the rural population being poor compared to 31 percent of the urban population (World Bank, 1995a).

However, despite the fact that most of the poor in Africa live in the rural areas, urban poverty has been increasing as urbanization has become much more rapid. With the exception of South Africa, all of the Southern African countries had urban population growth rates that exceeded 3.5 percent during the period 1980-93 with Mozambique having the highest rate with 8.4 percent (World Bank, 1995b). This rapid urbanization in Africa can be attributed primarily to rural-urban migration. Migration to urban areas is a rational economic decision for those in search of economic betterment. It is therefore a survival strategy for the rural poor. In Tanzania, for example, the percentage share of net migration in urban growth was 85 percent for the period 1975-90 (Findley, 1993).

However, when coupled with the other elements of the economic crisis in Africa, rapid urbanization has some very serious consequences. Most of those consequences are related to insufficient labour absorption capacity in the urban areas, thus resulting in increasing rates of urban unemployment, and the lack of government capacity to provide the requisite social services (Hope, 1995a).

With respect to labour absorptive capacity, with the exception of Lesotho (1.96 percent) and Mozambique (1.79 percent), all of the Southern African countries had annual average labour force growth rates that exceeded 2 percent during 1965-95 and it is projected that the majority of the countries would have labour force growth rates exceeding 2.5 percent, with some countries surpassing the 3 percent mark, during 1995-2025 (World Bank, 1995b).

However, this growth in the labour supply has not been matched by a similar growth in formal sector employment. As a matter of fact, in most of the countries, formal sector employment has been declining since the 1980s (World Bank, 1995c). In Zambia, for example, formal sector employment as a proportion of the labour force has been declining so rapidly that it is now the primary contributor to urban poverty and income inequality in the country (Seshamani, 1992). In addition, real wages in the formal sector have also been declining (Vandemoortele, 1991).

Much of the decline in formal sector employment can be attributed to the decline in manufacturing employment. In South Africa, for example, the growth rate of manufacturing employment declined from 2.9 percent in 1970-80 to 0.9 percent in 1980-90, while in Zimbabwe the decline was less dramatic for the same two periods moving from 3.48 percent to 3.14 percent (Khan, 1994). In terms of formal sector wage rates, not only has the ratio of non-agricultural to agricultural wage rates been declining but also the ratio of non-agricultural wages to per capita income.

Since 1980, real wages have declined more rapidly than per capita income. This suggests that the wage earners have borne a heavy burden of the economic crisis (Vandemoortele, 1991). In Tanzania, for example, employees in the non-agricultural sector earned about seven times the country's per capita income in 1975 compared to only two and one-half times in 1986 while, in Zambia, similar employees earned approximately five times the country's per capita income in 1975 compared to a little more than one and one-half times in 1984 (Vandemoortele, 1991).

With the decline in formal sector employment, there has been an increase in subterranean (informal) sector employment and activities. The expansion of subterranean sector employment in Africa, as well as the rest of Africa, is, ironically, one of the few positive things to have emerged from the ensuing economic crisis in the region (Hope, 1996b). The phenomenal expansion of the subterranean sector has been documented in numerous studies and reports in recent years. The great majority of that documentation suggests that the evolution of the subterranean sector has taken place because of the failure of the developing countries to formally make the kind of economic progress that would have allowed for, among other benefits, low urban unemployment rates, a reduction in national poverty rates, wages and salaries that kept pace with inflation, the ready availability of basic goods and services, a functioning infrastructure, and a relatively honest and efficient bureaucracy (Hope, 1993a; Hope, 1993b; Hope, 1996c). Fundamentally, the growth of the subterranean sector embodies the response of the populaces to the incapacity of the African state to provide the basic framework of material welfare. It also reflects the fact that the mismanaged formal sectors of Africa are thoroughly debilitated by a severe and all encompassing economic crisis (Sandbrook, 1993).

The subterranean sector now absorbs the majority of labour force entrants in Africa and government attitudes in the region have changed in favour of its role as a labour sponge and center of self-reliance and private initiative. In Botswana, for example, the government has given prominence to the subterranean sector for its increasingly important role in providing income-earning opportunities and meeting demands for goods and services particularly for the low-income population (Republic of Botswana, 1991); and in Namibia, the government recognizes and acknowledges the important contribution of the subterranean sector in reducing unemployment (Norval and Namoya, 1992). In Zambia, the subterranean sector now absorbs nearly 80 percent of urban workers (Kashambuzi, 1995), while in Tanzania it accounts for 51 percent (Endale, 1995). In South Africa, more than 16 percent of the economically active population is employed in the subterranean sector (*Sunday Times*, 1996a).

Based on the available evidence, women seem to be overrepresented in the subterranean sector in Africa. In Zambia, women now account for two-thirds of subterranean sector production of services and, in the urban areas of Botswana in 1984-85, nearly half of employed women - but only 10 percent of employed men -

were working in the subterranean sector (UNDP, 1995). In Tanzania, in 1988, 95 percent of women workers and 84 percent of male workers were concentrated in the subterranean sector (World Bank, 1995b). In Katutura, Namibia, the majority of the subterranean sector workers (60 percent) are women (Frohlich and Frayne, 1991). The involvement of women in the subterranean sector has grown as the economic crisis has reduced job opportunities in the formal sector and increased the need for an additional source of family income. In Zambia, for example, women's earnings from the subterranean sector increased considerably as a share of total household earnings in the 1980s (UNDP, 1995).

Apart from contributing positively to employment and domestic product, the subterranean sector also constitutes an important component in the rural financial markets in Africa. It is a dominant source of credit in the rural sector in Africa where the institutional lenders are absent or ineffective, and access to formal credit is extremely limited. The numerous types of money-lenders and credit suppliers in the subterranean sector include friends, relatives, landlords, storekeepers, traders, and employers of agricultural and domestic labour. In Zambia, for example, it is estimated that the percentage of total loans in the rural areas accounted for by the subterranean sector was 43 percent for the period 1981-82 (Mrak, 1989).

At the national level, the subterranean sector also accounts for most of the financial services provided to small-scale savers, producers, and enterprises. Informal deposit services are provided through group savings associations and temporary loans can be arranged. Perhaps the most popular form of subterranean sector finance is the rotating savings and credit association (ROSCA). The ROSCA has different names in the various African countries. For example, it is known as *motshelo* in Botswana; in Malawi it is called *chiperegani* or *chilimba*; in Mozambique it is *upato* or *xitique*; in South Africa and Swaziland it is *stokvel*; in Tanzania it is *upato*; in Zambia it is referred to as *chilemba* or *upato*; and in Zimbabwe it is *stockfair* or *chilemba* (Hope, 1996b).

In ROSCAs, members ranging from six to forty, pool their money into a fund. The fund is held by a group leader, informally selected from among the members of the group, who is responsible for periodically collecting a fixed share from each member. The money collected is then given in a rotation as a lump-sum payment to each member of the group thus allowing some members to finance expenditures much sooner than if they had relied on their own other savings efforts. The basic principle by which resources are shared is balanced reciprocity. Each ROSCA member draws out of the pool or fund as much as he or she puts into it.

ROSCAs represent a very important form of savings among the low-and middle-income groups in Africa. For example, in a survey of seven regions in Tanzania, 45 percent of the households were found to rely heavily on informal credit to finance their basic needs, small business ventures, and other sources of livelihood (Hyuha, Ndanshau, and Kipokola, 1993). In Zambia, it was determined that 80 to 90 percent of the urban population participate in ROSCAs (Mrak, 1989). In South Africa, it is estimated that *stokvels* currently have more than 3.5 million members who save more than US$25 million per month (Smith, 1996).

Turning to social services, although access to these services has been increasing over the years, the budgetary constraints of the governments have resulted in a situation where there are still too many people without access to health care, safe water, sanitation facilities, and adequate housing, particularly in the rural areas. In some countries, such as Zambia, for example, only 28 percent of the rural population, compared to 70 percent of the urban population, had access to safe water during 1988-93 (UNDP, 1995). In other countries, such as Lesotho, only 23 percent of the rural population and 14 percent of the urban population had access to sanitation facilities during the same period (UNDP, 1995).

One major area of concern, in terms of access to services, relates to housing. While some countries, such as Botswana, seem to have an oversupply of urban housing, there are several others where the housing situation has become environmentally hazardous as a result of overcrowding and the increasing concentration of squatter settlements. In Johannesburg, South Africa, for example, squatter housing was estimated to have reached 22 percent of the total housing stock by 1990 while in Dar es Salaam, Tanzania, squatter housing by 1990 was 51 percent of the total housing stock (*The Economist*, 1995). This represents a serious situation regarding lack of access to adequate shelter and a potential source of societal conflict.

Of all of the indicators reflecting the seriousness of the economic crisis in Africa, two of the most significant are the persistent budget deficits and the aggregate net resource flows. With the exception of Botswana since 1983 and Swaziland (for some years), all of the countries recorded budget deficits throughout the 1980s. The budget deficit/surplus (excluding grants) is a measure of the ability of a government to finance its activities from its own resources. For most of the countries, the deficit as a share of GDP had reached unsustainable levels by the beginning of the 1980s. In both Malawi and Zambia, for example, the deficit was equivalent to approximately one-fifth of GDP by 1980. Such budget deficits suggest that the governments were consistently spending much more than they were capable of raising as revenues from domestic activities despite their high levels of taxation (Tanzi, 1992). In Zambia and Zimbabwe, for example, total expenditure as a percentage of GDP exceeded 35 percent during the period 1981-86, while total revenue as a percentage of GDP during the same period was 30 percent in Zimbabwe and 23 percent in Zambia (World Bank, 1994b).

Contributing significantly to these budget deficits has been the very poor performance of the public enterprises which, in turn, resulted in the need for governments to inject substantial sums of money into those enterprises to keep them afloat. Basically, public enterprises in Africa have failed to internally generate a sufficient amount of working capital. Consequently, "they have demonstrated a limited ability to finance new or replacement investments or to maintain existing ones" (Nellis, 1994). These public enterprises are not only a burden on the national treasury but also a major burden on the domestic banking system and capital markets. For example, the public enterprises share of domestic credit during the period 1986-90 averaged 55 percent in Mozambique and 27 percent in Zimbabwe (World Bank, 1995a). The budget deficit situation, in turn, led to a heavy reliance on foreign financing primarily in the form of external borrowing and official grants. During the 1970s and 1980s, the external debt of all the countries increased and some countries also relied heavily on official grants. In Tanzania, for example, during 1974-80, the nominal value of foreign aid per capita increased nearly fourfold and more than doubled in real terms (Hyden and Karlstrom, 1993), while in Mozambique, foreign aid as a percentage of GNP reached 59.2 percent in 1989 (Kyle, 1994). Also, with the exception of Malawi, by 1993 the total external debt burden per capita in all of the countries exceeded US$250. In Zambia, the total external debt burden per capita was US$849 by 1986, the highest in the developing world, while its GNP per capita was only US$260 (World Bank, 1995a; Fardi, 1991). Clearly such a state of affairs would be unsustainable.

Further evidence on the harsh realities of the debt problem as a major contributor to the economic crisis in Africa can be gleaned from an examination of the debt service ratios. From the available data for Southern Africa, with the exception of Botswana, Swaziland, and Lesotho, all of the countries had double-digit (exceeding 15 percent) debt service ratios (debt service as a percentage of exports) by 1993 with both Zambia and Zimbabwe exceeding 30 percent. Furthermore, and again with the exception of Botswana, Lesotho, and Swaziland, all of the countries had external debt that exceeded 40 percent of GNP by 1993. In some countries, such as Mozambique, Zambia, and Tanzania, the net present value of external debt as a proportion of GNP had exceeded 100 percent by 1988 with Mozambique at the top with 376 percent (World Bank, 1995b; World Bank, 1990).

The economic crisis in Africa is also reflected in the inflation rates and the foreign reserves situation. The fiscal deficits and the resultant heavy borrowing have fuelled inflation. During the period 1980-93, the average annual rate of inflation exceeded 10 percent in most of the countries. In some countries, such as Tanzania and Zambia, the inflation rate exceeded 25 percent during 1981-86 (World Bank, 1994b). For Zimbabwe, it was also determined that the deficit was very responsive to changes in the rate of inflation with a one percentage point change in domestic inflation increasing the deficit by 0.31 percentage points of GDP in the 1980s (Morandé and Schmidt-Hebbel, 1994).

Due to poor balance of payments performance, as a result of deteriorating terms of trade, among other things, the import coverage ratio of reserves declined in all of the countries during the 1980s except for Botswana. In Botswana, the balance of payments has been in surplus since 1982 primarily as a result of the outstanding export performance of the diamond industry (Hope, 1996a). By the end of the 1980s, Botswana's import coverage ratio of 18 months was eighteen times that of Lesotho, South Africa, and Zambia; nine times that of Malawi, Mozambique, and Zimbabwe; and six times that of Swaziland. In contrast, by the end of the 1980s, Tanzania, for example, did not have enough foreign reserves to cover a full month of its imports and, in this regard, the country was worse off than it was in the 1960s (Sarris and Van den Brink, 1994).

The final aspect of the economic crisis to be considered relates to savings and investment. It has been shown elsewhere that the presence of high and variable inflation lowers both investment and domestic savings, while large debt ratios tend to crowd out savings and investment (Hadjimichael et al, 1995). In the Southern African region, with the exception of Botswana, gross domestic savings as a proportion of GDP declined during most of the 1980s. The worst performer was Lesotho whose dependence on the South African economy cast it in the role of an exporter of labour and dependent on remittances and on receipts from the Southern African Customs Union (Petersson, 1993). Lesotho had negative gross domestic savings during the 1980s, reaching a high of -93.7 percent of GDP in 1984 and declining to -46.4 percent of GDP by 1989 (World Bank, 1995a).

Savings determine the rate at which productive capacity, and therefore income, can grow. On average, the more rapidly growing countries, such as Botswana, have had higher rates of savings than the slower growing countries such as Tanzania. In addition, savings indicate the flow of real resources that are not consumed and therefore available for possible investment. Investment in Africa was uneven in the 1980s and was too low to support both a sustainable expansion in output and greater economic diversification.

During the 1980s, Angola had the lowest rate of gross domestic investment, measured as a proportion of GDP, in Southern Africa. By 1989, Angola's gross domestic investment was only 12 percent of GDP. On the other hand, Lesotho's gross domestic investment in the latter half of the 1980s was the highest in Southern Africa averaging more than 50 percent of GDP during 1985-89 compared to 28 percent during 1975-79 and 24 percent during 1980-85 (World Bank, 1995a). The average annual growth of gross domestic investment in Lesotho was 15.9 percent in 1985-95 compared to -1.7 percent in 1980-85 (World Bank, 1994c). This performance was achieved primarily through improved rates of private investment.

Conclusions

The economic crisis in the majority of the African countries is rooted in the post-independence policy framework which put considerable faith in the role of government to plan and allocate resources for economic development. Although such external factors as fluctuations in the terms of trade did also have some influence on the resultant economic crisis, it is the internal policy framework that played the much more crucial role in the birth and growth of the economic crisis in Africa.

The majority of the African countries embarked on development policies in the 1960s and 1970s that, among other things, distorted their price structures and removed their comparative advantage. Development planning and other forms of state interventions in the economic process resulted in the diversion of resources from their socially most productive uses (Rimmer, 1995). As a result, economic growth and development became elusive and the majority of the African countries accelerated into a deep economic crisis.

The impact of that economic crisis has been so devastating that the 1980s are now correctly referred to in the literature as 'Africa's Lost Decade' (Ndegwa and Green, 1994). Some authors, such as Landell-Mills (1992), have gone even further by arguing that "the first three decades of African independence have been an economic, political and social disaster". This economic deterioration at the national level, and the ensuing economic deprivation at the human level, provided the imperative for policy reform which emerged most dominantly in the form of structural adjustment programmes.

However, although this chapter is not concerned with the policy response to the economic crisis in Africa, suffice to say here that the SAPs have met with varying degrees of success. Nonetheless, to date, there have been no real alternative policy frameworks, to the SAPs, that have been adopted and implemented by the African governments. Consequently, the SAPs retain their dominance as the preferred policy response to the economic crisis in Africa.

This chapter has provided one analytical perspective on the economic crisis in Africa. It does not claim to be exhaustive. Nevertheless, it provides considerable detail on the economic decline and human setbacks which have gripped most of the African countries and which now present a considerable development challenge for those countries as they approach the 21st century. More particularly so for the poorer countries such as Malawi, Sierra Leone, Ethiopia, Mozambique, Tanzania, and Zambia, all of whom have GNP per capita below US$300 and a large percentage of their population below the poverty line.

On the other hand, two of the countries - Botswana and South Africa - are well poised to maintain and/or improve their economic performance. Botswana has been a model of economic success with its sound development management and good governance (Hope, 1995b). However, the country needs to diversify its economy beyond dependence on diamond exports to come to grips with its problems of unemployment and income inequality (Hope, 1996a). With respect to South Africa, the transition to majority rule in 1994 created an internal environment for increased domestic and foreign private investment and a receptive external environment for increased exports. Given its already substantial industrial base, South Africa has the potential to become a major economic power in the world economy and the current economic conditions for investment and growth in the country are regarded as the best they have ever been (*Sunday Times*, 1996b). Such a potential must be prudently tapped to, among other things, particularly mitigate the estimated 30 to 40 percent unemployment rate among the Black population (Lundahl and Moritz, 1993), and accumulate resources for reconstruction and development projects.

2 Structural adjustment policies: Some lessons for development momentum in Africa

S.N-A. Mensah

For many countries in Africa the structural adjustment programmes (SAPs) experiment has lasted for more than a decade. The IMF/World Bank hypothesis in connection with SAPs is that their package of economic restructuring policies would, after some time, help to create the environment in which market-led and self-sustained economic growth would take place in stagnating economies. The package was also expected to induce the entrepreneurial spirit that thrives in and drives market-led economies. The long-term results would include, among other things, healthier balance of payments, internal balance, lower rates of inflation, higher real rates of growth, and lower rates of unemployment. A decade of practice is long enough for some of these results to be realized if the SAPs hypotheses are to be accepted as valid bases for economic recovery and sustained growth in Third World countries (TWCs).

The problems that SAPs are meant to address relate to the balance of payments, external debt, budget deficits, inflation, unemployment, capacity under-utilization in industry, and so on. These problems were either unknown or existed only as minor ailments at the time of political independence (Khan, 1987). But not too long thereafter they grew into such serious problems that the smooth functioning of some economies, especially in Africa, was badly impeded. The situation has been blamed on a multitude of factors including poor Keynesian-type planning from the centre; active state participation in business; unsustainable welfarism (low tax rates, subsidies on food items and education and health, and so on); nepotism; and corruption in government, for example.

From a purely economic stance, various competing theories provide suggestions on the types of macroeconomic management that would promote development and thereby address the kinds of problems that have slowed down development in many African countries. The SAPs packages are based on one of these theories. This chapter reviews the theoretical basis of SAPs, examines how SAPs have been implemented in Africa, and discusses their results in the light of the expectations based on theory. Lessons would then be drawn for macroeconomic management and policy in Africa.

The theoretical basis of structural adjustment programmes

SAPs recommend reliance on the free interplay of market forces for allocation of resources and distribution of income (goods and services). Countries that have, prior to SAPs, planned their economies on the basis of fixed interest and exchange rates that were adjusted periodically, were urged to abandon this practice. Exchange rates would be determined in the foreign exchange market that would not be restricted to the banks. This explains the proliferation of the foreign exchange bureau in countries implementing SAPs. Interest rates would be determined by surplus and deficit units in the economy through financial intermediation and without interference by government. Prices of commodities would be determined by demand and supply and no price, not even of essential commodities consumed mainly by the lower income groups, may be subsidized or subjected to controls. Trade would be liberalized, with all restrictions on imports and exports removed. Free markets, it is recommended, would improve efficiency in production and consumption (Khan, 1987).

The labour market, however, presents a problem to this deregulation policy. Because of the significance of institutions on both the supply side (labour unions) and the demand side (private employers' associations and governments as the major employers) wages tend to be dependent more on negotiation than on market forces. There is, however, the belief that labour incomes are on the high side, especially in government employment, and should therefore be made to glide downwards, at least in real terms.

SAPs packages also seem to subscribe to the position that "the business of government is not business" and so recommends the withdrawal of government from economic activities. Enterprises that are owned by government but could be more profitably run by private companies are recommended for privatization. These may include trading companies, manufacturing industries, and even airlines. Those government-owned enterprises that, by their nature, are essential or strategic should be commercialized. Thus, eventually, every enterprise would be run as a private enterprise or like a private enterprise.

SAPs also focus on the government sector itself and urges elimination of budget deficits as a means of dealing with inflation. While increased tax rates and an expanded tax base are recommended, the main focus seems to be on reducing government spending and eliminating subsidies. This means that services provided by government, especially in the education, health, and housing sectors, must be paid for at market price - a virtual end to welfarism. Also directed toward the problem of inflation is the requirement that the growth of the money supply should be restricted and the caution that discretionary monetary and fiscal policies may be destabilizing.

The IMF and World Bank prescribe these policy recommendations to countries in need of assistance in the hope that their economies would start functioning properly, output and incomes would grow and, in turn, these economies would be able to repay their loans from their external earnings. The basic issue underlying these recommendations, therefore, is income determination. That is, the identification of the variables that explain why a country's output is at a certain level and why it increases more rapidly in some years than in others, and the identification of the forces that affect these variables and how those forces could be controlled to ensure that a country's economy functions as desired.

The orthodoxy in economic theorizing on income determination in the mid-1940s became Keynesian. Keynes argued the following contrary to the general neoclassical position:

1. Falling prices, in a recession, will not reduce aggregate supply, increase aggregate demand, and restore equilibrium at full employment. Rather, it would reduce the revenue of proprietors, reduce incomes of employers and employees, and thus reduce aggregate demand which will make aggregate supply fall even more and unemployment will worsen;

2. Falling interest rates, when savings exceed investment, will not reduce savings and increase investment until equilibrium is re-established at full employment; during the down-swing when deficient aggregate demand makes the profit position bleak, capitalists will not invest in new plant and equipment no matter how low interest rates fall and so even if interest rates should fall, investment will not rise to the level of savings and full employment will not automatically be restored; and

3. Falling wage rates in the whole economy will not increase demand for labour and reduce the supply, thus restoring full employment. Rather, falling wage rates will reduce aggregate income and spending and unemployment will worsen.

Because of this obvious inability of markets, even when they function properly, to restore equilibrium at full employment - and sometimes monopoly powers in product and factor markets do not make them function properly - Keynes recommended the interventionist state to take care of under-consumption and over-production to ensure full-employment. When the second World War transformed the situation in most Western countries from severe unemployment to acute shortage of labour, the Keynesian position was upheld and even the United States government for the first time acknowledged responsibility for employment (Hunt and Sherman, 1990: 161-162). But the triumph of Keynesian economics did not go unchallenged for long and that challenge took the form of a revival of traditional neoclassical theory.

Because of the connection between money and the general price level, via the quantity theory of money, the Keynesian revolution was also taken as a demolition of neoclassical monetary theory. The essence of the Keynesian revolution was to shift the subject-matter of monetary theory, from concern with determination of price levels and with economic fluctuations, placing the emphasis on the level of employment (Johnson, 1973: 226-227). Keynesian monetary theory initially showed how, through the interest rate and investment and output, the money supply could affect the level of employment.

Thus, Keynesians recognized the importance of money. However, they argued that there are limits to the effectiveness of money in dealing with unemployment and inflation. If banks have extra reserves over and above the maximum required reserve ratio, if corporations use internal funds for further investment instead of borrowing from banks, and if expected profit rates are rising faster than interest rates when the money supply is contracting, then monetary policy will have little success in curbing inflation and unemployment. In fact, if profit expectations are bleak, business people will not increase investment no matter how low interest rates are. For these reasons, when dealing with unemployment, Keynesians in the 1950s and 1960s down played the importance of monetary theory and monetary policy, while putting their faith in government spending and tax cuts (Hunt and Sherman, 1990: 497-499). Also, the Keynesian emphasis on the role of government is more consistent with fiscal policy than with monetary policy.

Meanwhile, economists at the University of Chicago had refused to let-go of the quantity theory of money. They continued to teach and develop a more subtle and relevant version, one in which the quantity theory was connected and integrated with general price theory and became a flexible and sensitive tool for interpreting movements in aggregate economic activity and for developing relevant policy prescriptions (Friedman, 1973). Milton Friedman championed the cause of this new way of looking at things and through a series of articles he developed it into what is now mainstream monetarism. The main aspects of which include:

1 Free markets are efficient and will bring about an equitable distribution of goods, will promote growth, and will generally solve their own problems. When serious economic disturbances occur, these could be traced to random shocks and misguided government economic policy. One implication of this position is that prices and wages are flexible.

2 The money supply is the principal determinant of the levels of output and employment in the short run and of the price level in the long run. This view is based on the monetarist's position that the velocity of circulation of money is regular and predictable.

3 There are lags between changes in money supply and their impact upon aggregate demand and these lags are variable and unknown. So

governments that try to use discretionary monetary policy (to correct short-run problems) will tend to either over-react or under-react and thereby create further distortions. So, instead of discretionary monetary policy, monetarists recommend allowing the money supply to expand at a fixed rate - 3 to 5 percent per year. This is their monetary rule. Also, discretionary fiscal policy (unless it is accompanied by monetary policy) may not solve the problems of inflation, unemployment or sluggish growth, since the associated changes in government spending may be dependent on changes in taxes or in government debt which would cancel each other out. The implied crowding out may leave aggregate demand virtually unchanged and so any impact would be negligible.

The schism between the Keynesians and monetarists is obvious. Monetarists believe that the economy has a tendency to adjust to full employment and so stabilization is unnecessary. In fact, they argue that discretionary monetary and fiscal policy may be destabilizing. Keynesians however argue that equilibrium could occur below or above full employment and so the market economy needs to be stabilized by discretionary monetary and fiscal policy (Modigliani, 1977). Not even Samuelson's grand neoclassical synthesis filled the gap completely. He had expected a synthesis in which the Keynesian theory would keep the economy at full employment and the more traditional neoclassical monetarist thought would support the market in allocating resources within the Keynesian framework. Though the two schools have moved closer over the years with respect to the role of money and monetary policy, the gap with respect to stabilization policy has remained as wide as ever (Edgmand, 1983: 223).

Government policy in the industrialized countries have, therefore, been guided by one theoretical construct or the other. For example, from 1946 to the early 1960s, government policy in the United States was based on Keynesian economics. Though there were mild recessions, there was no serious depression during that period, and government, through its spending, tried to keep the economy at full employment. However, during the late 1960s and early 1970s, the American economy experienced high unemployment rates and high inflation rates simultaneously. Keynesian theory had no answer to simultaneous unemployment and inflation because the government cannot both stimulate demand and reduce demand at the same time (Hunt and Sherman, 1990: 528-529). Policy makers in the United States concluded that Keynesian economics had failed, and so turned to monetarism in the late 1970s (Samuelson and Nordhaus, 1992: 645).

The attack that was launched against inflation in the United States in the 1970s was called a "monetarist experiment". The government stopped "smoothing interest rates and instead focused on keeping bank reserves and the money supply on predetermined growth paths" (Samuelson and Nordhaus, 1992: 645). Interest rates rose sharply, the economy slowed down, unemployment increased, and the growth of wages and prices took a down-turn. The monetarist experiment had succeeded in holding inflation in check. The monetarists' preoccupation with inflation stems from the thinking that inflation affects the balance of payments, the level of unemployment, and the rate of growth. They claim that increases in the money supply result in claims by workers and other income groups for higher wages and salaries. This reduces profits and the incentive to invest. Production and growth rates would then fall and unemployment would increase (Kiguel and O'Connell, 1995; Ahamed, 1986).

Of great theoretical and policy importance was the fact that the monetarist experiment also revealed that the money velocity could be quite unstable - it changed more in 1982 than it had in several decades because of the heavy reliance placed upon monetary policy (Samuelson and Nordhaus, 1992: 646). This relative success of monetarism in the United States may have inspired the IMF and World Bank to conduct the monetarist experiment in TWCs plagued with inflation and other related ailments. This view is supported by the fact that SAPs are basically monetarist and SAPs experiments in TWCs started in the early 1980s.

This raises a number of concerns about the likelihood of the success of SAPs in Africa. For example, SAPs advocate reliance on markets - product markets, factor markets, foreign exchange markets, financial markets, and so on. Are markets in Africa, for example, developed enough to fit the monetarists' view of the world? Historically, markets did not just spring up but developed in response to the need to distribute goods that had been produced. In other words, the focus must be on production structures that improve productivity and output and then markets will develop concomitantly. This was the truth in Say's law. In fact, it was only after the roots of industrial capitalism had been significantly laid that the invisible hand (implying deregulation) was recognized and emphasized. Also, how could markets be relied on when large concentrations of rural dwellers are subsistence producers who operate virtually outside the market economy? The modern sectors in most African economies have many large monopoly or oligopoly producers and labour unions. These monopoly powers distort the markets in which they operate (Wellisz and Findlay, 1988). And so resources may not be allocated efficiently and incomes may not be distributed equitably by the unaided market. In the absence of the anti-trust laws which operate to moderate the excesses of monopoly power in the American economy, would monetarism be successful in halting inflation?

Also, monetarism is built on the assumption that the velocity of money is stable. The American monetarist experiment, however, showed that money velocity could be highly unstable when reliance is placed upon monetary policy. How will an unstable money velocity affect the operation of SAPs in those African countries that are not members of a monetary union and so could independently implement monetary policy? Could such unanswered questions explain the problems with SAPs in many African countries?

Then there is the question of lags between changes in the money supply and their impact on aggregate demand. Monetarists use the existence of these lags to argue against discretionary monetary policy and to recommend their monetary rule.

Would these lags not affect the impact of money supply expansions or contractions even when this is done at a fixed rate per year? To what extent would the problems of underdeveloped markets and unstable money velocity affect these lags? Implementing SAPs in Africa without first addressing these gaping questions could bring about disastrous consequences. And this is what may have happened in many African countries currently implementing SAPs.

The implementation and results of SAPs

The nature of SAPs is such that time is required for all its policy prescriptions to be implemented. Also, all countries have not followed the same steps in implementation. There have even been differences in the degree of implementation. This may be because the theoretical framework does not specify any sequence of implementation. All of these factors make a rigid comparison of implementation and results on the basis of how long a programme had been running quite difficult. Even then, time, extent, and degree should affect how much of the expected benefits are realized and so such differences should not be the basis of success or failure.

Our consideration of the implementation of and results from SAPs will focus on two country experiences - Uganda and Zambia - one a success, the other not so successful. In summing up what Zambia has done in implementing SAPs, Mwase (1995) mentions currency devaluation, the adoption of market-determined prices, privatization of state enterprises, staff retrenchment and the abolition of subsidies. For Uganda, Oyowe (1993) lists the liberalization of internal and external trade, the liberalization of the foreign exchange market, the relaxation of import and export regimes, the privatization of state enterprises, the reduction of the size of the civil service, among others, and adds that Uganda has rigorously applied the measures.

Two observations should be made about the two sets of lists. First, the programmes implemented in the two countries are basically the same and, in both cases, privatization was off to a slow start before the process began to accelerate. In Zambia, 95 percent of the 160 parastatals (representing 80 percent of GDP and 140,000 jobs) were earmarked for privatization. In Uganda, a Public Enterprises and Divestiture Statute was enacted in 1993 to confirm the government's three-tiered approach of liquidation, reform, and divestiture. The statute contains a classification of public enterprises under which the government will (1) retain 100 percent shareholding in 10 enterprises; (2) retain a majority shareholding in 17 enterprises; (3) retain minority shareholding in 20 enterprises; (4) fully privatize 43 enterprises; and (5) liquidate 17 enterprises (Sharer, De Zoysa, and McDonald, 1995).

The massive depreciation of the currencies of countries implementing SAPs has adversely affected fixed incomes, wages, pensions, and so on, and has led to sharp increases in prices of both local and imported commodities and inputs. Monetarist approaches to this problem of inflation created by SAPs have pushed interest rates very high. In Zambia, for example, when the interest rate reached 150 percent in July 1993, "about 100 urban-based factories and more than 200 large and medium-scale farms... collapsed," with serious implications for unemployment and poverty (Mwase, 1995). The percentage of urban dwellers who live below the poverty datum line has increased from 4 percent in 1975 to 50 percent in 1993 and to 55 percent in 1995, and SAPs are an important contributory factor. Also, life expectancy declined from 52 years in 1985 to 45 years in 1992 while the infant mortality rate rose from 84 to 113 per thousand during the same period (Mwase, 1995). SAPs must produce significant social benefits to justify such social costs, otherwise the people will eventually resist it (Haggard and Webb, 1993).

Reduction of the fiscal deficit also involved measures that have added their toll to the social cost. This is not at all obvious in the case of Uganda where the massive inflow of foreign resources has been the backbone of the recovery programme. Between 1986 and 1993 a total of US$1,500 million came in as loans and grants. Because of this massive inflow of foreign resources, inflation was brought down from 200 percent in 1986 to 3 percent in April 1993 without the accompanying hike in interest rate affecting the investment needed for reconstruction. The investment in roads rehabilitation also helped the recovery of the agricultural sector and food exports to neighbouring countries, through the World Food Programme, has brought in revenue that has helped to reduce the fiscal deficit. Improved revenue collection through the newly created Ugandan Revenue Authority has also helped.

The situation in Zambia, however, has been different. The pressure to bring down the fiscal deficit has led to a reduction of government expenditure and the withdrawal of subsidies. Spending on social services fell from 7.4 percent of GDP in 1991 to 0.4 percent in 1993; per capita expenditure on education declined from US$25.60 in 1982 to US$8.20 in 1992; and real health expenditure fell by 20 percent between 1991 and 1992. Even the subsidy on maize flour, the local staple, which has been a thorny issue since 1986, eventually had to go despite protests and strikes.

For Zambians, especially the lower income groups, SAPs have meant sharp declines in real wages and salaries; rising costs of food, health services, and education; and a general decrease in the standard of living. This is more of a worsening of the crisis to them than a path to recovery. On the other hand, for Ugandans the SAPs experience, for an identical period, has produced the opposite effect on the population, including the lower income groups. In 1986 when the National Resistance Movement government came into power and decided to seriously implement SAPs, which had not had a chance since 1980 because of the war, Uganda was an economic wasteland with inflation over 200 percent; the health infrastructure in ruins; most roads not motorable; farm and factory output falling; exports declining; and the treasury was nearly empty (Oyowe, 1993). In such a situation welfare was a meaningless word. The important thing was survival. The commitment to SAPs was a requirement for foreign funding for reconstruction. Over the years of SAPs implementation, key factories have resumed production; agriculture has been revived; inflation has dropped from three digits to a single digit; the tax base is expanding; and government revenue has increased rapidly since 1992, for example. Though export earnings have declined despite the increasing export volume, the inflow of foreign aid has ensured that there is no shortage of foreign exchange for reconstruction. For Uganda, SAPs also brought social benefits and many lessons could be learnt from these Afican experiences with SAPs.

Lessons for restructuring policy in Africa

It is not every country in Africa that has implemented SAPs, but the lure of SAPs is very strong. It promises increased resource inflows in the short- to medium-term and so could give governments considerable breathing space when their economies are resource-starved. The discussion in the two previous sections provide insights that could guide policy makers in deciding for or against SAPs; and if they should decide for SAPs, the conditions that must be taken into consideration and the manner in which SAPs could be implemented beneficially.

One fact that stands out is that not all countries that have adopted SAPs have realized the objectives of low rates of inflation and unemployment, healthier balance of payments, improved capacity utilization in industry, and so on (Khan, 1987). However, some countries, like Uganda, have come close to realizing most of these objectives. Because of the dynamics of SAPs, healthier balance of payments and better capacity utilization in industry are often illusory. It was observed in the case of Uganda that "while coffee production remains high and export volume is as high as it was before 1986, earnings declined dramatically from US$400 million to US$117 million in 1992" (Oyowe, 1993). This is because of the low elasticity of demand for primary produce which makes expansion in production, given demand, benefit the importer and not the exporter. Often, falling export prices do not translate into cheaper imports of manufactured goods and so difficulties with balance of payments can only be addressed by drastic reductions in imports. Thus, expanding the production of agricultural produce for export has become a way of transferring surpluses from TWCs to the industrialized nations. African countries that have adopted SAPs should therefore keep the production and export of agricultural produce in line with price movements.

The role of markets in SAPs has been discussed. The Ugandan success story shows that where markets are undeveloped SAPs could still be implemented. The Ugandan government had "a three-year Rehabilitation and Development Plan in 1987 which was streamlined the following year to incorporate most of the structural changes demanded by the Bretton Wood institutions" (Oyowe, 1993). Even foreign investors were allowed to go only into areas that were consistent "with the government's overall strategy of developing enterprises which allow greater use of local resources and promote intersectoral linkages and export diversification" (Oyowe, 1993). This type of policy also ensures that the stimulus provided by foreign investment activates not only the target sector, but also those sectors that are linked to it. This improves domestic value-added and increases the rate of growth. The lesson here is that countries adopting SAPs should not feel obliged to comply completely with the structural changes demanded by the IMF and World Bank. Countries should first work out their own strategy of development and then incorporate those IMF/World Bank conditionalities that are consistent with their strategy.

It was also pointed out that, historically, markets developed concomitantly with the development of production structures. The focus of African countries should therefore be on improving the production system in the region by diversifying on the basis of resource endowment instead of by producing and exporting raw materials to industrialized countries. As the production structures improve, so would the markets and so would regional trade, and then market-oriented policies would have better chances of success. The Southern African Development Community (SADC), for example, provides one institutional framework within which efforts at improving the production structures in the Southern African region could be coordinated.

Monetarists seem to suggest that workers should share the blame with governments for the economic crisis. They argue that the inflation that results from excessive monetary expansion makes workers and other income groups demand higher wages which reduce profit levels and the incentive to invest. Production then drops and employment levels fall. The implication of this argument is that workers become the conduit through which excessive monetary expansion translates into an economic crisis. SAPs have therefore been quite harsh on workers, especially those in the lower income group. The Zambian case brings this out quite clearly. The assertion that high wages in Africa was a contributory factor to the crisis that made SAPs necessary, has been challenged (Lindauer, Meesook, and Suebaseng, 1988). The Ugandan experience does not provide much assistance in addressing the issue of workers suffering under SAPs because of the level to which the welfare of Ugandans had dropped before SAPs. What could be gleaned from that experience, however, is that if governments implement SAPs within a national development strategy that takes a certain minimum living standard of workers as given, then the social cost of SAPs could be considerably reduced. In other words, governments could complement the implementation of SAPs with a compensatory mechanism (Haggard and Webb, 1993).

No school of thought is absolutely right in predicting how the real world is or will be, and the real world is not the same every place. The situation in Zambia and Uganda in the 1980s, for example, when both countries started implementing SAPs, was not the same. This would suggest that the eclectic approach may be more pragmatic in restructuring economies in Africa. This approach is based on the view that different forces move the economy at different periods and so a wide variety of policies should be employed in influencing aggregate demand (Samuelson and Nordhaus, 1992: 459). So, instead of taking sides in the four-decade old controversy between Keynesians and Monetarists, African governments should choose between recommendations on the basis of the relevance of the underlying assumptions at a given point in time. After all, the debate between Keynesians and monetarists have ideological implications which may have contributed to a polarizing of the two groups. Keynesian policies favour workers while monetarists policies favour employers. African governments should favour the development of their countries and their peoples.

Because of the human cost of restructuring, the most important lesson from this analysis is that governments in Africa should desist from policies and measures that distort the structure of their economies including, among other things, disproportionately large expenditures on the military; unreasonable welfarism meant to entrench political positions; wasteful spending on state functions and propaganda; unnecessary meddling by politicians in state enterprises; and the common practice of putting square pegs in round holes as a reward for political support.

3 Structural adjustment and the new conditionalities: Towards development in Africa

Ben C. Chikulo

As Africa approached her fourth decade of independence, there is a growing concern among African scholars and observers that the independence and credibility of the African polity could be seriously endangered due to the protracted socio-economic crisis facing the continent. The continuing crisis of the African state - which has been beset by socio-economic decline since the late 1970s, and as a result has been unable to meet popular aspirations and expectations, - has been labelled the "African condition" (Adedeji and Shaw, 1985) or as Africa's "lost decade" (Chazan et al, 1992). The gravest development crisis is in sub-Saharan Africa which, after reasonable growth rates in the 1960s and 1970s, experienced considerable economic deterioration.

The concern with how to address and arrest the low standard of living, poverty, and high levels of indebtedness led to two developments. First, alarmed at the worsening socio-economic crisis in sub-Saharan Africa in particular, and the emerging global crisis, the World Bank published *Accelerated Development in Sub-Saharan Africa: An Agenda for Action* (often referred to as the Berg Report) in 1981 and suggested appropriate measures to overcome the crisis. The end result was the adoption of the structural adjustment programmes (SAPs) as a policy instrument with which to resuscitate African economies. Secondly, the crisis sparked-off a debate on the democratization of the continent. The one-party system, which had been the dominant form of political organization on the continent was criticized and followed by calls for more democratic polities (Anyang Nyong'o, 1988). Former Tanzanian President Julius Nyerere's (1986) recantation of his earlier advocacy of one-party democracy, which he had deemed central to Africa's development path, not only reinforced the debate on democratization but also gave new momentum to the forces struggling for democracy in African countries.

The pressure for political reform in Africa during the 1980s renewed the debate about the relationship between democracy and development. There are two documents which stand out on this debate because of their thought-provoking analysis of Africa. The United Nations Economic Commission for Africa (UNECA,

1989) report, *African Alternative Framework*, which linked economic progress to political accountability and popular participation, and the World Bank's (1989a) *Sub-Saharan Africa: From Crisis to Sustainable Growth* which directly linked successful economic rehabilitation to political liberalization. The latter document identified a crisis of governance behind Africa's development problems. Thus, Africa's-socio-economic problems came to be seen as political in character. Consequently, political reform was held to be a basic condition not only for arresting Africa's decline but also for stimulating and sustaining development.

The new conditionalities

Since Africa's problems were increasingly perceived to be of a political nature, political reform was elevated to the top of the reform agenda. The World Bank's (1989a) report which directly linked political liberalization to successful economic rehabilitation should therefore be seen as the precursor of the new conditionality. In the early 1990s, Western governments and donors began to tie economic aid and technical assistance to the issue of multi-party democracy. Since then political reform has become a package deal linked to the structural adjustment programmes.

Political conditionality

Generally, since the turn of this decade, Western donors have insisted that political reform was a necessary condition for foreign aid to Africa. Consequently, political conditionality has since become an instrument of foreign policy for most of the Western countries. The centrality of political conditionality was reinforced and highlighted at two very important forums: the Harare Commonwealth Heads of Government Meeting in October 1991, and the European Community (EC) in November 1991. At the latter, the EC signed a charter which linked future aid disbursements to the implementation of democracy in recipient states. Thus, in the eyes of Western governments and donors, the intended development benefits from SAPs had not been achieved due to inherent problems in the political structure of the recipient states.

The political conditionality entailed the insistence on "good governance" and the institutionalization of the following in recipient African states:

1 Political pluralism;

2 Constitutional government;

3 Accountability, efficiency, and transparency by those in public office;

4 Free elections;

5 Freedom of expression including a free press; and

6 Greater respect for human rights and the rule of law.

Structural adjustment programmes (SAPs)

The orthodox stabilization and structural adjustment programmes (SAPs) are well known in Africa and include the following:

1 Removal of all subsidies;

2 Reduction of public expenditure on social services;

3 Devaluation of national currencies, coupled with foreign-exchange auctions;

4 Reliance on market forces;

5 Privatization of parastatals;

6 Liberalization of inputs; and

7 Reduction of public sector workforce.

The above conditionalities have been viewed as the safest and fastest routes to Africa's socio-economic recovery and prosperity. Since the early 1990s Western donor countries have been insisting that international economic assistance should be conditional on political pluralism and economic liberalization. What this has entailed in practice is that foreign aid to individual African countries has been linked to their perceived progress towards political and economic liberalization. As a response to these (and other) pressures, political reform has swept across the African continent. These reforms, which have been dubbed as "Africa's second coming" or "second liberation" (Onimode, 1992), have been predicated on political pluralism and an open market-based economy.

The reforms

Sub-Saharan Africa, because of the extent of the socio-economic crisis, which we have already noted, has increasingly been subjected to extreme pressure to institute radical policy reforms. In order to comply with the new conditionalities and attempt to overcome the socio-economic crisis, African political leaders have initiated two major reforms. These are economic liberalization and political liberalization.

Economic liberalization

With a few exceptions, most African governments have been forced to adopt a free market economic system. In the initial years of the 1970s and early 1980s the most direct pressure for African countries to liberalize their economies came from the IMF. Thus by, 1990, about 32 African countries had implemented SAPs and drawn on the IMF standby facility to support their reform programmes. Since then, the pressure to liberalize has come from a variety of other sources. Initially, a-short-term horizon was envisaged for SAPs. It was anticipated that a country's programme could take between three to five years to restore the economy to good health. Subsequently, the World Bank realized that the process would take much longer and accordingly adopted a long-term perspective.

There has, therefore, been a general move away from statist development strategies with the guiding principle being that of encouraging private initiative and creating an environment that rewards such initiative. Diamond (1988:27) has argued that the move away from statist policies has been "the most significant boost to the democratic prospects in Africa". In short, private enterprise has come to be viewed as the main dynamic for economic growth and development. Under this new dispensation, African governments have moved away from excessive governmental regulation, over involvement in the economy, and the ownership of business enterprises. Thus, the governments are supposed to concern themselves essentially with the task of creating an enabling and hospitable environment for private capital initiative.

Political liberalization : Towards multi-party democracy

Concomitant with the liberalization of the economy have been moves to open up the political system by the adoption of reforms to permit greater pluralism, political competition, and good governance within the polity. From the end of 1989 up to the end of October 1995, the movement towards pluralism in Africa had made significant advances (*Africa Confidential*, 1995; Africa Institute, 1992; Bratton and van de Walle, 1992; Austin, 1993). It was assumed that pluralism would make African governments more responsive and hence better managers of their economies. Furthermore, the link between democratization and market economies, entailed by SAPs, was intended to fully integrate the markets of African countries into the international capitalist economy.

The political and socio-economic impact of the reforms

About 15 years have elapsed since the advent of orthodox SAPs and almost six years since the new conditionality surfaced. How has the economic liberalization and political democratization process faired? To what extent have they succeeded in realizing the goals set for them? With respect to the economic reforms, evidence provided by the IMF and World Bank tends to paint a rosy picture by arguing that structural adjustment has worked in those countries where they have been implemented and thus presented the most viable route to recovery. Ghana, Tanzania, Zambia, Burkina Faso, Nigeria and Zimbabwe were judged to be the best reformers because on average they had achieved the fastest annual growth rates. The World Bank (1994b: xi) proclaims the success of structural adjustment policies by stating that: "There are rewards to adjustment, however, as countries that have come the furthest in implementing good policies — particularly good macroeconomic policies — have enjoyed a resurgence of growth".

However, some critics have argued that economic reforms have not worked in any country, where they have been pursued vigorously (Riley, 1992; UNICEF, 1992; Hellinger and Hammond, 1994). Indeed, it has been pointed out that in the sub-Saharan region adjustment programmes were not associated with improvement in economic performance (Mosley and Weeks, 1994). It has also been pointed out that while the reforms may have marginally improved the external account, their impact on economic growth, have been insignificant. First, the economic reforms have resulted in declining export prices and net financial outflows to service debts — including payments to the IMF and World Bank — without reducing the size of the debt burden. The reforms have also been associated with a drop in living standards and blatant inequalities. SAPs have thus generated adverse social effects and weakened the state and its internal structures (Mosley, Subasat, and Weeks, 1995; Noula, 1995).

The negative impact of these reforms on the economies of African countries have been highlighted in case studies on Tanzania, Sudan, Somalia, Zambia, and Nigeria where it was shown that SAPs had in fact aggravated the economic crisis in these countries (Onimode, 1989). Indeed, although World Bank officials claimed Ghana to be their most successful story, the case study undertaken by others revealed the extent of the negative impact of the reforms including sharp reductions in real incomes, rising external debt, increasing inequalities, and the desperate plight of the poor (Onimode, 1989). Also, it has been pointed out that the statistical data is neither convincing nor internally consistent (Mosley, Subasat, and Weeks, 1995). Schatz (1994: 691) even goes further and points out that not only is the statistical data suspect but the implementation of structural adjustment "has actually impeded economic growth in Africa".

Ironically, although the World Bank (1994b) paints a rosy picture and optimistically predicts a general recovery, the Bank has admitted elsewhere that its reform programmes have largely been unsuccessful in sub-Saharan Africa (World Bank, 1992a: 27). In view of this, the World Bank's (1994b) report should not be taken seriously but be viewed in its proper context as a public relations exercise by the embattled Bank to justify its operations on the African continent.

The conclusion which comes out of all these studies is that SAPs have not stimulated recovery in Africa. As Shaw (1992: 1187) aptly pointed out:

"Adjustment is unfortunate as well as unworkable ...". In fact, this is the reason for the continuing debate on adjustment. An overview of the African socio-economic situation presents a gloomy picture. Africa's socio-economic condition began to deteriorate in the 1970s and worsened in the 1980s. On the whole, whatever socio-economic indicator is used, the picture that emerges is a rather depressing one.

Economic growth

The rate of economic growth, the *sine qua non* of development is very low. However, the litany of statistics from development reports (UNICEF, 1992; World Bank, 1992a; World Bank, 1994e) only reveal part of the story. Yet, the Bretton Woods institutions still insist that their economic policies are working and they forecast a general improvement in the economies of sub-Saharan Africa in the next decade, albeit with many riders such as stable commodity prices, more political stability and, of course, effective implementation of the new conditionalities.

However, the majority of African observers, scholars, NGOs and even some UN agencies (particularly UNICEF) hold out little hope for any meaningful improvement in Africa's economic condition, without a radical shift in the direction of economic reforms and the pattern of development assistance. Furthermore, even the World Bank's projected growth range of 2.4 percent to 3.9 per cent in African economies, is below the average annual growth rate of 5 percent achieved in the period 1966-73. In addition, Africa's GNP in 1992 was US$450 less than it was in 1972. More recent data to the mid-1990s reveals that the average growth in the period 1990-94 was a meagre 1.2 percent compared to almost 2 percent for the 1985-89 period (Mosley, Subasat, and Weeks, 1995: 1459). In short, Africa is struggling to get back to where it was in the 1960s and early 1970s.

Africa, as has been previously pointed out, is the only continent where standards of living have declined continuously. As noted by OAU Secretary-General Salim (1992: 15) "The economic crisis threatens to undo entirely the social gains made in the 1960s and 1970s when Africa achieved appreciable growth".

Thus, the sad fact is that most African countries are worst off today than they were two decades ago. The UNICEF report (1992: 51) paints the following depressing picture:

> For the first time in the modern era, a sub-continent is sliding back into poverty. The number of families in sub-Saharan Africa who are unable to meet their basic needs has doubled in a decade. Average incomes have fallen by a third. The proportion of children who are malnourished has risen ....

Debt crisis

One of the biggest obstacles to the democratization and development process is the debt burden. This burden threatens the economic and political stability of most African countries and the major root causes of the crippling debt crisis are the economic reform policies entailed by SAPs. As pointed out by Samboma (1995: 23), "The only thing Africa can show for its religious adherence to the economic dictates of the West, is its monumental debt burden".

We have noted the magnitude of Africa's indebtedness. What we have not highlighted is the extent of the vicious circle of indebtedness afflicting the continent. For instance, Africa's projected external service payments in the 1990s are over US$20 billion per annum (UNICEF, 1992: 52). Such an outflow of much needed capital is incompatible with Africa's economic recovery. The promises that the level of democratization would determine the extent of development assistance, seem to have amounted to very little (Obasango, 1991: 44).

Indeed, unless drastic debt relief measures — such as the total cancellation of debt of the least developed African countries — are undertaken not much progress can be made. Thus, unless the debt issue is resolved, the prospects for the survival of the democratization process in Africa are bleak. Unfortunately, so far the results have not been very promising and there are no indications that the industrialized nations will come to Africa's rescue in a big way. The demise of the Soviet Union and the emergence of a new Eastern Europe has led to the marginalization of Africa. As *The Economist* of 2nd February 1991 put it:

> With cold-war interests gone, it is tempting to forget Africa. East Europe and still-useful clients such as Egypt, are also clamouring for aid; recession in the rich world makes generosity harder. Besides, aid to Black Africa has a depressing record. In the 1980s the region swallowed more than US$100 billion of it and defiantly got poorer. Perhaps money for Eastern Europe would be money better spent.

The marginalization of Africa has also been reflected at recent Bretton Woods institutions meetings where, for the most part, discussions have centred almost exclusively around Eastern Europe and how to underpin the democratization process in those countries. These Bretton Woods institutions, who frown at suggestions to make drastic cuts in the African debt because it "would constitute a moral hazard by rewarding those who do not pay their debts" (UNICEF, 1992: 52), did not hesitate to implement the cancellation of Poland's official debt. Similarly, following the Gulf War, it was not difficult for the Western Allies to find ways to halve Egypt's US$40 billion debt. As Obasango (1991: 44) lamented:

> In so far as it [debt] continues to hang on our neck like an albatross, we will remain impaired and incapacitated in our efforts to face challenges

> confronting us. I cannot conceive as fair and equitable a situation in which generous debt reduction and forgiveness is accorded to middle-income countries like Egypt and Poland and much poorer countries in Africa are denied similar relief.

Such action raises serious doubts about the commitment of the West to the democratization and development process in Africa. Recently, the World Bank proposed a debt relief plan for some of the world's poorest countries (*Business Day*, 1995). According to this proposal, the Bank envisaged establishing a facility to pay off debt of about US$11 billion owed to multi-lateral institutions such as the World Bank itself and the IMF. Unfortunately, due to resistance from the IMF, the plan had to be withdrawn (*Sunday Times*, 1995).

The issue of sovereignty

The implementation of the new conditionality actually erodes the legitimacy of the African state. Democratization implies consent, legitimacy of the government, and accountability to the electorate. Yet, the insistence on the new political conditionality by the Bretton Woods institutions and donors is placing severe strains on the political base of the new African régimes. In fact, resistance to the reforms in some countries, such as Egypt, Morocco, and Zambia, resulted in the so-called food riots. It is ironic that it is now assumed that democracy may facilitate the implementation of orthodox SAPs.

We have to bear in mind that most of the African régimes have inherited huge pent-up demands set against empty state coffers. The dilemma facing these régimes is that if they pay less attention to their domestic constituencies, they would not meet the stringent demands of their external constituencies — the Bretton Woods institutions and donors. In other words, the régimes have to delicately balance the conditionalities of the West against the pressing needs of their newly enfranchised citizens.

There is, therefore, a strong possibility that in some instances strong public pressure could lead to a strong temptation to abandon austerity programmes and also to the emergence of anti-IMF political parties. The pertinent question to pose at this juncture is how would Western governments react if a populist political party, strongly opposed to Western conditionalities won in a free and fair election? Beckman's (1992: 87) axiom seems very appropriate here: the "political crisis of the African state is also the crisis of SAPs".

Through the process of "informal governance" (Mkandawire, 1991: 40) the Bretton Woods institutions have usurped the sovereignty of African states. The implementation of SAPs entails the monitoring and in some cases, the actual control of key ministries (Please, 1992: 292) thereby placing them beyond the pale of domestic politics. As Mkandawire (1991: 40) observes:

> Processes of structural adjustment are eminently political and the attempt to depoliticize are not only self-deceptive but also reflective of the apprehension of international financial institutions about democratic management of economic affairs. Their ideal remains that of a Ministry of Finance that is insulated from the democratic process and conducts 'policy dialogues' with the outside world unencumbered by domestic politics.

To sum up, the policies of the IMF and World Bank, particularly SAPs are considered by many to be anti-democratic and anti-people.

Democratization of society

From 1989 to date, significant reform measures to permit greater pluralism, competition, and good governance within African politics have been implemented. The opening up of politics has brought a plethora of political parties into the arena. However, although the democratic process was put in motion by the introduction of pluralism, the promised democratic governance, which was supposed to provide the enabling environment for economic development, has yet to be institutionalized. The concern, for the most part, has been with attempts to establish formal multi-party democracies rather than with the substantive issues of democracy.

Pluralism was expected to promote good governance, peace, and political stability. However, it has become apparent that in most countries the result has been the exact opposite:

Political stability and peace Civil unrest in Togo in late 1991, in the Congo in 1992, and in Kenya in 1993, demonstrated that the move to pluralism has not brought about stability, peace, and national accord. Several countries continue to be plagued by military indiscipline and civil unrest (Riley, 1992).

Human rights Pluralism has not brought about expected improvements in human rights. In fact, in most countries, the advent of civil rights such as freedom of expression, association, and free flow of information are still as remote as they were under one-party régimes (Aidoo, 1993; Kelso, 1994; Tungwarara, 1995).

Good governance Similarly, the expectation that pluralism would usher in a new political order of transparency in the conduct of public affairs, and accountability, with high standards of probity and efficiency, have yet to materialize.

Despite the multiplicity of political parties, most of them lack effective organization; do not have distinctive policies; and only seek a chance to vie for political power. Indeed, in some countries such as Zambia, there are signs of popular scepticism of the new breed of politicians, as manifested by low electoral turnouts (Chikulo, 1993). *Africa Confidential* (1992) had predicted that the establishment of the multi-party system would simply entail the re-circulation of the élites "with the existing political élite in a new set of relationships. It will do little to alleviate corruption or stimulate the economy." In a feature article French (1995) laments the fact that:

> All across a continent that was swept dramatically by the winds of multi-party politics at the turn of the decade, incumbents have been rewriting the rules of the games, bullying opponents and restricting the press so as to be able to hold on to power regardless of the popularity or the success of their programmes.

In short, nothing has really changed. Furthermore, the West now seems to have reduced pressure on African countries to fully implement the widely recognized minimum standards of democracy, as required by the new political conditionality. There is thus a visible waning of the West's commitment to democracy. In addition, the "good governance" conditionality has been inconsistently applied, a development which has left donors open to the charge of double-dealing. To sum up, there has been little genuine transition to democracy in African countries.

New directions

The African experience with orthodox SAPs has shown that IMF/World Bank policies cannot bring about the self-sustaining development expected by neo-liberal theorists in the Bretton Woods institutions and elsewhere. However, donors have steadfastly stuck to the view that Africa's socio-economic crisis is mainly attributable to internal political factors. As a result of such a perception in the West, Africa has witnessed a proliferation of assistance programmes aimed at promoting and strengthening democracy. The most prominent, for example, being the US Agency for International Development (USAID) "governance programme" and the British government's "public sector reform programme". These programmes entail the building or the reinforcing of the capacity of political and public institutions, independent judiciaries, and the training of political activists. With specific regard to USAID, Diamond (1994: 52) has noted a significant increase of resources, from US$5.3 million in 1990 to US$19.3 million in 1994, to support its democratic governance programmes in Africa. These include elections assistance; constitution drafting; regulatory reform; strengthening legislatures and judiciary; and fostering local participation and empowerment.

The aim is to strengthen the capacity of the political system and broaden political participation. In recent years, the World Bank too has increased its attention to the governance agenda (World Bank, 1991; 1992b; 1994d). However, unlike other bilateral donors whose concern is with civil and political rights and democracy, the

World Bank's explicit concern is with the economic and social dimensions of governance (Stevens and Gnanaselvam, 1995). Thus, the Bank's explicit concerns are about efficiency and accountability of public institutions with a strong orientation toward improving the climate for the free market. To sum up, as far as the donors are concerned, economic reforms in Africa have not been effective due to inherent problems in the political structure of the recipient states.

Finally, some scholars question the wisdom of imposing the conditionality of Western-style liberal democracy, which Africa may not be ready for. While we agree that Africa is in dire need of better styles of governance, of greater political accountability and that the political reform process offers new solutions to some old problems, the West's insistence on setting the standards for democracy is irritating, especially in view of the West's record of propping up dictatorial régimes in the Third World. At best, it smacks of ethnocentrism. The new conditionality means that Africa will be heavily biased towards Western values. Leftwich (1993: 65) calls this new trend the "new orthodoxy". These conditionalities are, therefore, tantamount to the re-colonization of Africa (Arnold, 1992). In response to this overtly Western aggressiveness, some eminent African personalities have pleaded that the promotion of democracy in Africa should be the responsibility of Africans themselves (Obasango, 1991: 42). However, the fundamental question which has been brought to the fore by the current crisis is which political system would really be appropriate for Africa?

Conclusions

The new conditionalities have been seen as the *sine qua non* of socio-economic development in Africa. About six years have elapsed since the political liberalization process was set in motion. Yet, the economic situation, according to available data, has in fact deteriorated. In almost all sub-Saharan African countries, the austerity measures entailed by SAPs have proved to be both politically and socially unsustainable and are likely to endanger the stability of these states. It is evident that the economic and political conditionalities that have been imposed on African countries have, in the final analysis, inhibited the genuine self-sustaining development of the continent.

What is urgently needed, if Africa is to climb out of its current quagmire, is a cut of its debt and an extension of sufficient external support so that the continent could be given a new lease on life to carry on with the essential internal reforms needed for a successful re-generation of the momentum for sustained socio-economic development. Without such critical efforts the hopes which have been placed in the magic wand of pluralism and economic liberalization will be dashed. To put it differently, unless the socio-economic crisis is resolved, the prospects for the survival of the democratization process in Africa are very bleak.

4 Structural adjustment policies in Africa: Designing chaos or chaos in implementation

G.S. Maipose

Structural economic and political reforms, such as those being implemented by many African countries, have two main objectives. First, they are aimed at arresting many years of economic decline while attempting to achieve sustained growth. Second, they are expected to enhance prospects of institutionalizing the new proclaimed vision of open democratic systems of government. But the impact of the reforms has been mixed. Progress economically has been a great deal slower than was originally envisaged and largely disappointing (Oxfam, 1991; Harvey, 1996). The extent to which the new wave of democratization facilitates economic reforms and development has yet to be empirically established in Africa. While the number of democratic states has tremendously increased, and still on the increase under the new wave of change, it is also true that there has already been slippage or democratic reversal in some countries such as Algeria, Nigeria, Burundi, and Gambia. Furthermore, what was originally designed as a swift and separable exercise of macro-economic stabilization has gradually become a persistent and diversified reform process which is hardly any longer distinguishable from development policy itself (Toye, 1996: 120). These observations raise questions and mixed interpretations about the impact of the reforms and the role of the state in development.

Taking a retrospective approach, with references elsewhere, the Zambian case will be examined in this chapter as illustrative of the underlying problems and prospects in the state's capacity to deliver economic and political reforms. In Zambia, the design of economic reforms seem to have concentrated on expenditure reduction policies or stabilization measures. However, a balanced implementation of expenditure switching policies to stimulate growth and diversify the economy became increasingly difficult as the country was also expected to adjust to too many other conflicting policy measures and reforms in an inappropriate sequence. The reforms seem to have interacted with each other counter-productively, while at the same time overloading the weak institutional capacity of the state.

The analytical framework and some underlying questions

The model which is used to analyze the impact of structural adjustment programmes (SAPs) in Zambia is basically an elaboration of the growth model in which the classical economists argued that the rate of economic growth depended on the proportion of an economy's activities that were productive and the rate of surplus earned for reinvestment. The theory is applied taking into account some modern restatements such as Hicks (1965) and Bacon and Eltis (1975) and as currently articulated by the IMF and World Bank. Associated with this is the recognition that the main objective - attainment of socio-economic development - is itself a long-term task and a composite theme which must take place in a conducive socio-political environment. A number of over-lapping questions have been posed over the years. Amongst the central ones are the following: Is there a relationship between a given political system and sustained socio-economic development? What must be the role of the state in development?

In view of the above observations, this chapter is guided by two main propositions or hypotheses. The first central proposition is that part of the economy - the tradable/market sector - produces a surplus that makes it possible for the remainder of the economy to function. If the surplus producing sector grows rapidly, as was the case during the first decade of independence in Zambia, the economy grows rapidly. If it declines, as has been the case for the past two decades, the economy collapses. Thus, the market/tradable sector fulfils the vital surplus-producing role, leading to a realization that everyone who produces anything "marketable", that is anything sold at home or abroad, produces a potential surplus which can be reinvested for further development. If the tradable/market sector produces too little, it means private consumption or exports or investment or revenue to finance public service or all four are bound to suffer (Bacon and Eltis, 1975: 92-118). The second central proposition is that the role of the state is crucial for modern socio-economic development as no country has achieved economic growth without some targeted state intervention (Shapiro and Taylor, 1990). For this to happen effectively, a developmental political system is necessary to ensure compliance and to facilitate public accountability and good governance (Leftwich, 1996). Hence, all development models place a high premium on the effectiveness and capacity of public institutions, leading to the justifications for political reforms - currently democratic reforms. The phrase developmental democracy, as used here, implies an end-means relationship (Sklar, 1996: 25). In this exposition, democracy is considered to be a means to (or a viable context for) development.

The immediate questions to address concern the functional relationship between the two waves of changes - economic and political reforms - and, most importantly, how to assess or evaluate the impact of the reforms. According to Toye (1992) and Berlage and Stoke (1992: 5), the success of a plan or policy measures can be assessed by comparing such plan or policy achievements with envisaged targets or a hypothetical scenario of what would have happened in the absence of such plan or policy interventions. Unfortunately, the evaluation of structural reforms tend to face difficulties because their objectives are directed at changing the policy environment rather than at simply increasing key variables such as investment, output, employment, exports, number and strength of political parties. In this discussion, we are confronted with the Zambian experience where the economy is still as dependent on the mining sector and traditional exports as it was thirty-one years ago at independence, despite many years of economic reform and complementary political reforms. In this exposition, both economic and political reforms are considered to be means, while development signifies an end or the realization of valued outcomes to any degree (Sklar, 1996).

The main objectives of the economic reforms have been macro-economic stability and economic diversification which were aimed at increasing the domestic production of traded goods and services. On the economic side of the reforms it is, therefore, imperative to analyze the economic performance of the country in terms of its effort towards economic diversification and domestic output of tradables. This criterion is actually regarded as one of the major objectives of development and its explanation is obvious. "A diversified industrial structure, which is capable of supplying a significant proportion of its own requirements, is seen by many as a prerequisite of a self-sustaining programme for long run growth" (Weiss, 1988: 9; Oxfam, 1991: 11-12). In addition, diversification becomes especially important in adjustment to changes in the external environment because it makes the economy less vulnerable to future shocks (Streeten, 1987: 1470). SAPs should therefore be designed to encourage this development and should be as broad-based as possible in order to have a significant impact on employment opportunities and poverty alleviation. Diversification, as a yardstick, is used in broad terms to cover a general increase in the domestic output of tradables, being import substitutes and non-traditional exports.

In their quest to help borrowing countries to "get prices right", adjustment policies advocated by the IMF and World Bank focus on massive currency devaluations; fiscal retrenchment, especially reducing public spending; trade liberalization, including liberalization of agricultural markets; financial reforms that increase nominal interest rates to get real interest rates; and privatization of public enterprises. Given the extensive agenda of adjustment policies, appropriate sequencing of the reforms and reform ownership are essential for successful implementation (Lipumba, 1994: 3). Relatedly, it would be a mistake to view each reform measure as an independent package without any inherent interdependence.

The logic of political reforms entailed having either, as in the past, an authoritarian government with both the will and the power to put through reforms or, as is the trend now, a democratic government with unimpeachable electoral legitimacy and structures for ensuring accountability of those in power. Reforms, political or economic, do not operate in a vacuum, devoid of their economic or political function, and the universal political motivation of the politicians in power is to maximize their chances for winning elections in democracies or do what they can to remain in power in authoritative régimes. This is one of the underlying lessons of public choice theory. Thus, the issue to explore on the political side of the reforms is the extent to which a given or envisaged political system facilitates socio-economic development (Leftwich, 1996).

Until quite recently, the logic of this argument led some scholars to believe that authoritarian governments were better positioned than democratic governments to promote economic development (Huntington, 1968). Taking an end-means functional relationship, it was believed that authoritarian governments would be able to resist popular pressures and vested interests opposed to reforms. This partly explains why authoritarian political systems, such as communist, military, and one-party régimes, were common until quite recently. The dominance of this view was well reflected in the pessimistic future that Schumpeter (1942) saw for capitalism in his classic book *Capitalism, Socialism, and Democracy*. Indeed communist China, and Chile under a military dictator, managed to introduce substantial economic reforms and have been rewarded with enviable rates of economic growth. Given this experience, there are some who still believe that it would even now make a great deal of sense for economic liberalization to precede democratization because opening up the political system is likely to complicate economic reforms in certain circumstances.

In other circumstances economic liberalization may require a democratic government and the current world-wide shifts from authoritarian to democratic political systems is seen as a victory of the latter over the former. The concept of developmental democracy, as used by Sklar (1996), implies an end-means, rather than an end. Democracy signifies a form or method of social control which gives power to the people over leaders and office-holders. Under these circumstances political élites and office-holders are held accountable from time to time, if not at regular intervals, and poor performers are voted out of power. It follows from this observation that a theory of developmental democracy would demonstrate the efficacy, as well as the probable limitations, of liberalization methods in pursuit of development.

According to Huntington (1994), the underlying problem in effecting structural political and economic changes, at least in theory, is that both political democratization and economic liberalization limit governmental authority and the power of the state. The paradox at the level of practical efforts (in getting things done) is that it has been easier to adopt political reforms, to organize elections, and to announce economic reforms than to increase administrative or institutional capacity and organize markets. The weak legacy of public institutions or the relative administrative incapacity would matter less if a country is able to rely on an extensive indigenous private sector or foreign investment to develop its economy, and if public accountability would be forthcoming with a well established civil society (Tordoff, 1993: 266). But foreign investment may not be readily available while indigenous entrepreneurial activity could be generally limited, both in terms of capital owning and managerial capacity, and a civil society may have yet to be enlightened and strengthened. It follows from these observations that problems and prospects of the major economic and political reforms need to be re-examined along the lines of the capacity of both the state and economic institutional structures.

In the World Bank (1994b) report assessing the results of structural adjustment in Africa, it is concluded that adjustment policies are working. In that analysis, African countries that improved their policies achieved better economic performance. Where does Zambia, which has been getting IMF and World Bank financial support and reform prescription since 1978, fall? Our review of the Zambia case is done in the context of salient global issues in political economy and the significance of the current simultaneous waves of economic liberalization and political democratization. We now relate the analytical framework to the Zambian experience.

Rapid growth with distorted structural changes, 1964-72

On the attainment of political independence in 1964 the then existing racial and narrow democratic system of government was opened up to accommodate the newly empowered black population along the Westminster model (Tordoff, 1974: 24). On the economics side, Zambia inherited an economy which was relatively strong and was one of the most prosperous among the independent African countries with the forecast for rapid growth and development (Baldwin, 1966; Fry, 1980). But the inherited economy was structurally lopsided in three fundamental ways. First, the economy was extremely dependent on the copper mining industry which accounted for about 40 per cent of GNP, 92 per cent of total export earnings, 71 per cent of government revenue, and about one-third of the employment in the directly productive sectors (Elliot, 1971: 5). The second weakness was the lack of internal sectoral linkages. The mining sector had been developed with minimal backward or forward linkages to the rest of the economy. For example, the industrial-manufacturing and agricultural sectors were largely underdeveloped, accounting for 6 per cent and 11 per cent, respectively, of GNP. Thirdly, the economy manifested regional and racial dualism by having a wide imbalance between relatively developed urban areas and backward rural areas; and racial inequality, in which the economy and good jobs were monopolized by settlers and expatriates on the basis of an institutionalized colour-bar or reservation schemes of one sort or another in economic, education, and employment opportunities (Dresang, 1994).

Against the background of the relatively strong (but structurally lopsided inherited) economy, the development policy agenda before the nationalist government was patently clear and the main objectives were:

1. To diversify the economy along agricultural and industrial lines, primarily as a means of both reducing dependency on copper exports and enhancing

sectoral linkages;

2 To reduce the rural-urban gap by accelerating the pace of rural development and the latter was accorded top priority in policy declarations;

3 To promote indigenous control over the economy (in the form of state and Zambians' participation) and to redress racial inequalities in access to economic and employment opportunities, education and social amenities; and

4 To build social and economic infrastructure to facilitate socio-economic development (Republic of Zambia, 1964).

Given the inherited dominant role of the copper industry, the main thrust of the early development strategy was to expand the productive capacity of the then booming copper industry in order to serve as an engine of national development by providing a dependable source of foreign exchange earnings and government revenue to support the economy during the transitional period. The government, beginning in 1967, justified and legitimized its intention to effect the above policy objectives along the socialist-oriented philosophy of Zambian Humanism (Kaunda, 1968; Fortman, 1969; Molteno, 1973).

With regard to state capacity to meet popular demands and to fulfill the development goals, the immediate post-independence government had a mixed record. Despite a lack of most of the preconditions for liberal democratic success, as outlined by Sandbrook (1988: 25), and the inherited chronic shortage of qualified manpower, the record of performance was relatively impressive in many respects, including sustained GDP growth rates, economic diversification to cover the manufacturing sector along the import-substitution strategy, and expanding socio-economic infrastructure. This is partly supported by good development indicators and by the fact that the country was ranked as one of sub-Saharan Africa's middle-income economies (Elliot, 1971).

Similarly, the impact of the policies designed to achieve equity and distribute social services were relatively successful. Health and education facilities, previously narrow and élitist, were expanded and provided freely to all classes. These achievements owed something to the geological good fortune of extensive copper deposits and sheer luck in the sense that political independence coincided with a rising trend in copper prices for almost a decade. This was also complemented by deliberate and selective state interventions to speed-up the process of socio-economic development.

Notwithstanding the early good performance, there were fundamental negative developments to the national income accounts and this offers a starting point for our analysis of Zambia's economic problems. First, the sectoral sources of Zambia's

GNP growth changed in three aspects: the share of the public sector in GNP; the ratio of the tradable/market sector in the economy; and thirdly, the role of private foreign investment in the economy. Since the national income accounts offer the most comprehensive frame of reference in which to review an economy (Musgrave and Musgrave, 1989: 17), it is helpful to understand both the role of the government and the functional interdependence of the public and private sectors in these accounts.

First, following the series of economic reforms initiated in April 1968 and completed by 1972, the government asserted its control over the economy through the policy of nationalization and increased equity participation (Martin, 1972; Fortman, 1969). The main effect of these reforms was to enlarge state participation in the economy, both at the capital-owning and managerial levels. In fact, the state itself became the main agent of development and the economy began to be dominated by the huge parastatal sector (Johns, 1980). Second, and relatedly, the reforms undermined and threatened the role of the private sector with long-term direct and indirect negative consequences on national development. These were reflected in a number of ways. One of these was the diminishing inflows of private foreign investment and this was also accompanied by large-scale flight of capital from the country (World Bank, 1984; Maipose, 1989: 23). Further, the record of performance of many statutory boards and state-owned companies proved disappointing (Simwinga, 1980; Turok, 1979).

The third and probably the most important change was the movement in the ratio of the tradable/market sector in the economy. Analytically, the effects of booming revenues, in this case originating from a favourable terms of trade effect (made possible by a rising trend in copper prices) can be divided into a resource movement and a spending effect. The impact of the policy of diversifying the economy was relatively successful in the manufacturing sector, based on the import-substitution strategy, but rather disappointing in agricultural development. The fast growth in the manufacturing sector and the outcomes in the agricultural sector were changes of special interest. From 1965 to 1974, manufacturing output grew by 11 per cent per annum in real terms and, although the economy's performance did deteriorate thereafter, the contribution of manufacturing output to GNP doubled from 6.1 per cent in 1964 to 12.3 per cent in 1974 (Elliot, 1971; Harvey, 1991).

However, the policy of import-substitution had some inherent weaknesses and certain negative consequences. The main policy weaknesses were (1) the concentration of industrial development in urban areas; (2) high capital intensity and import dependency for raw materials; and (3) lack of internal linkages especially with the agricultural sector where performance was rather disappointing. Negative consequences were felt in accelerating rural-urban migration and rising urban unemployment because very few jobs were created out of the huge sums that were invested (Mwanza, 1979). Unfortunately, and this is important to note, the impressive growth in manufacturing did almost nothing to increase or diversify the sector's share in total exports. The manufacturing sector produced final consumer goods for domestic consumption. Moreover, the sector was allowed to grow under a protective wall of tariffs and subsidies, leading to inherent inefficiency and an inability to compete on the world market.

The other disappointing record of policy performance was in the promotion of agricultural and rural development which, paradoxically, was accorded priority in policy development. The sectoral contribution of agriculture to GNP had actually fallen from 11.5 per cent at independence in 1964 to 8.3 percent in 1968 and did not go beyond 12 per cent when the First Republic ended in 1972. Food subsidies and controlled producer prices tended to favour the urban population at the expense of the farmers and rural areas. According to the ILO (1981: 78), the state agricultural credit facilities, pricing, policy, marketing, and distribution arrangements varied between chaotic and poor. It must be added that the dismal performance in the agricultural sector together with the subsequent rural-urban migration were among the ways through which resources were shifted from the potentially productive agricultural sector to the industrial/urban sector where many people remained unemployed.

What conclusions can one derive? First, what actually emerged was a remarkable paradox. According to Elliot (1971: 3), "the rate of economic development in Zambia was exceptionally rapid, not only in comparison with earlier periods in Zambia but also in comparison with growth rates achieved in many other countries". This was due to the active role of the state and the impact of the copper industry. An important result of the dominant position occupied by the copper industry was that the level of copper production was sufficient to earn foreign exchange and generate tax revenues on a scale that was not far short of, and was until 1970 well in excess of, the absorptive capacity of the economy as a whole (Elliot, 1971: 4). Thus, rapid growth occurred partly by the opportunities and ambitious plans of the government after independence and in large part augmented by the mounting levels of foreign exchange and government revenue made available from the high value of copper export, royalties, and taxation.

But, it may be argued that the growth which Zambia achieved during the first decade of independence, though rapid, was not as rapid as it would have been if (1) skilled manpower and state experience to govern had been in optimal balance with other resources instead of in relative scarcity (Jolly, 1971: 45); and (2) if a number of state policy interventions had not undermined the growth potential (Hall, 1969). The thrust of our observations seem to suggest that the Zambian economy was not sufficiently prepared for sustainable development. The overall development can be seen or explained in terms of the effects of booming mineral revenue, the resource movement effect (of labour and capital) in the direction of the non-tradables sector as a result of the spending effect, and public policy interventions. These can be analyzed from economic and political perspectives.

On the economic front, four inter-related factors can be identified. First, the spending effect of rising government mineral revenues was mainly channelled through the public sector. Government final consumption expenditure, as a percentage of GDP, increased from an average of 12 percent in the late 1960s to 35 per cent in the 1970s (Fry, 1980). Second, a series of far-reaching economic reforms which the government undertook, between 1968 and 1970, to diminish foreign and minority economic dominance and to increase state control of the country's economic structure, were counter-productive to a significant degree. In addition to shifting resources from the private to the public sector, enlarging the poorly managed parastatal sector, the reforms led to large-scale flight of capital from Zambia; and the financial resources used to buy shares in existing companies could have been used for other development projects. Third, the limited resources that went into agriculture and rural development and the subsequent rural-urban migration meant the shifting of resources, especially labour, from tradable activities in agriculture to the urban areas where many migrants increasingly became unemployed.

Fourth, the existence of widespread subsidies together with a tariff structure to protect final consumer goods in the import-substituting manufacturing sector and the general domestic wage-price increases led to the distorted growth of import-substitution industry, and the fixed exchange rate became increasingly overvalued, except with regard to the balance of payments position. The tendency associated with an appreciation of the real exchange rate during the period under review in Zambia can also be analyzed from the view that the country did not change the nominal exchange rate until 1973 when Zambia got the first standby financial assistance from the IMF. Thus, the Zambian Kwacha became increasingly overvalued from 1964 onwards, and therefore the international competitiveness of non-traditional exports declined and diversification away from copper was discouraged. Consequently, non-traditional exports remained insignificant in relationship to mineral exports.

On the political front, two waves of change had significant adverse effects on the country's socio-economic development. First, Zambia was one of the leading campaigners for and joined the rest of the world to impose economic sanctions against Southern Rhodesia (now Zimbabwe), following the latter's unilateral declaration of independence in 1966, and, subsequently, against the apartheid régime in South Africa. This development should be understood in the context of the fact that Zambia had close economic ties with and depended very heavily on these two Southern African states for the main routes to the sea and supplies for domestic consumption. These political decisions, together with Zambia's commitment to support the liberation wars in Southern Africa, entailed costly re-orientations as reflected in new routing networks, such as the building of the Zambia-Tanzania railway and roads; direct public investment in new industries; and expansion of the defence force and increasing its real expenditure. The implications of all these and the price Zambia paid are well documented by Hall (1969).

The second major political development was the introduction of the one-party system in 1972. The main economic effect of this change was to enlarge yet again the public sector. In Zambia, and unlike the situation in some countries like Malawi, for example, the party machinery was made pervasive with its structure running from the centre to the village and it was also given an additional role - a full-time instrument for policy direction and mass mobilization for development. The party and its central committee operated side by side with the civil service and both were politically led by the cabinet. Both structures were also sustained by the public budget.

In a nutshell, the effects of the early domestic policy choices, including the way the economy was managed, were long-term and entailed resources shifting in favour of the unproductive public sector in a manner that discouraged economic diversification and reduced the internal competitiveness of the tradables sector. Clearly, a major transformation was taking place which increasingly shifted resources from the tradables to the non-tradables sector, from the productive to the non-productive sector, and enlarging the public sector, all with adverse consequences for future dynamic growth. From the macro-economic perspective, the public sector, defined to include the government, the ruling party, and the parastatal sector, was allowed to grow rapidly and became too huge for the economy to sustain. The full weight and problems of restructuring began to be felt during the Second Republic (the one-party régime) which coincided with an unprecedented economic decline triggered off by the fall in copper prices in 1974. It is now necessary to reflect on the salient aspects of the economic reforms during this one-party régime.

Demand/conflict management and postponement of structural adjustment, 1974-83

One-party politics was introduced in 1972 and a few years later, in 1974, copper prices fell and remained depressed for most of the next ten years. The thrust of the development policies in place during this period may be described as demand/conflict management and postponement of structural adjustment. Conflict and demand management may be discerned from the political side by the way the one-party system was introduced and made to function and, on the economic side, by the manner in which the government reacted to the fall in copper prices and the subsequent deterioration in the terms of trade.

On the side of economic policy those who sought to manage the Zambian economy or advised on its management (following the drastic fall in copper prices starting in 1974) were regarded as tinkerers or stabilizers and not as fundamental structuralists. They believed that a country's economic ills could be cured by adjusting demand through monetary and fiscal policies, and if necessary, exchange rate adjustment complemented by short-term external borrowing, and by persuading workers to accept periods of wage restraints. A big bang approach in terms of structural adjustment was avoided for two reasons. First, according to the economic logic of the time, the drastic fall in copper prices was a temporary set-back; and second, the deterioration in the terms of trade (with the real copper price declining by almost 46 per cent) was so huge that it was considered that the government would not be able to stabilize let alone swiftly restructure its economy under those circumstances (Colclough, 1988). In response, a two-part demand-related adjustment was adopted. This was a strategy that concentrated on polices to reduce expenditure and the mobilization of external short-term credit complemented by minor devaluations to discourage imports and to improve the profitability of the mining sector.

Whether Zambia's initial response was wrong or not might have been debatable then. But we try to show in what follows below that the policy, which was relatively well implemented, was misdirected. It is argued that the design of the policy overlooked the fact that the structure of the Zambian economy during the boom period had not been well prepared for the fall in copper prices. Furthermore, one may wonder why the policy was maintained until 1983. It was basically a policy to improve the current account and not primarily aimed at changing the structure of the economy in the long-run. According to the IMF (1987: 6), on whose advice Zambia partly relied, "it is generally easier to reduce absorption than to increase production and for this reason policies affecting absorption are often first put in place when a rapid decline in a current account deficit is mandatory". Accordingly, Zambia concluded standby arrangements with the IMF in 1973, 1978, 1981, and 1983. The country also qualified for many other sources of short-term credit. Even though conditional on minor devaluations of 10 to 20 per cent, to discourage imports and improve the profitability of the mining companies, all four of the arrangements with the IMF emphasized the need to reduce spending, especially by the government, without any attempt to restructure the economy.

But it is important to recognize that what was originally designed as a quick fix, aimed at correcting structural deficits in the balance of payments, was allowed to become a persistent and undiversified reform process sustained by foreign loans, and became the thrust of a policy régime without attempting to restructure the economy. Given the status of the country and the creditworthiness the country then enjoyed, the profile of Zambia's loans were largely commercial, short-term, and non-concessional. Consequently, Zambia's external debt grew rapidly and soon became a brake on the country's economic growth.

Our main argument, to illuminate the policy deficiency, is that while there seemed to be no available policy options that would have given a short-term solution to Zambia's problems, the chosen option of demand-related adjustments was over-extended and became the thrust of the policy régime for almost 10 years. This was done without trying to change the economic structure either through resource reallocation, institutional reform, or the liberalization of markets. The option proved costly in the medium- and long-terms. It entailed postponement of structural adjustment reforms. Foreign debt, almost negligible during the first decade of independence, rose dramatically; and those who provided credit/loans and advised on that option, appeared to have taken no risk as the country was obliged to service the loans even when its creditworthiness changed and it was re-classified as one of the poorest countries in the world. While there was a significant decline of about 31 per cent in import volume and a reduction in budget deficits, especially in 1976 and again in 1979 (UNCTAD, 1987), the adverse effects, as reflected in zero or negative growth, capacity under-utilization, unemployment, rising inflation, lack of diversification in exports, and debt burden became increasingly dominant.

On the political side, it suffices to say that the transition from the multi-party to a one-party system of government was fast, relatively peaceful, and elections were orderly. This occurred despite the fact that the one-party system was actually imposed by legislating it into existence with some leaders of the opposition detained and some co-opted (Scott, 1980; Molteno, 1972). The change was mooted in December 1971 and a *de jure* one-party state legislated into existence in December 1972 and general elections were held in August 1973. President Kaunda justified the decision to introduce the one-party state on the ground that it would enhance his vision of "one-party participatory democracy" and that it would enable national energies to be focused on development instead of being dissipated into factional conflicts (Tordoff, 1974: 390-400). One can add that Kaunda's vision was partly inspired by the ideas of then Tanzania President, Julius Nyerere, on how to make a one-party system democratic. Kaunda's vision was also to some extent in line with the argument of some leading modernization scholars of the time who believed that authoritarian rule might, for the purpose of rapid socio-economic change, be preferable to democratic government in some situations (Huntington, 1968; Molteno, 1972).

It must be admitted that Zambia's one-party system had some elements of intra-party democratic provisions, especially for parliamentary elections, and the system enhanced state capacity for conflict management (Chikulo, 1979). The political leadership allowed open primary elections within the party and allowed up to three candidates to run for each parliamentary seat, and the turnover rate among incumbent members of parliament (MPs) and government ministers was relatively high. The country also appeared to have enjoyed unprecedented internal peace and stability. But, like all one-party régimes, the system was largely authoritative and progressively autocratic (Wina, 1990). The elections did not allow voters to change the direction of government policy, let alone unseat the government itself.

At the institutional level, the one-party system entailed fundamental changes in the organization of state power and institutional relationships. In addition to retaining the hybrid system of government, partly parliamentary and predominantly presidential, the main effect of the one-party system constitution, as already alluded to, was to create a dual system of administrative structure. The government and the party machineries ran side by side, all on the public budget. If one adds the huge parastatal sector, headed by the Zambia Industrial and Mining Corporation (ZIMCO), there were actually three main structures. The constitution enshrined the principle of party supremacy, giving directives issued by the ruling party's central committee precedence over any parliamentary or government decisions.

It is also important to note that under the one-party régime, decision-making on key issues was increasingly centralized in the president's office and the leadership came to display authoritarian tendencies which resulted in a less than critical assessment of questionable presidential initiatives in a number of policies ranging from rural development to structural adjustment reforms. Moreover, the governing party élite manipulated the electoral rules in order to consolidate their control over the recruitment and rise of political leaders. A certain degree of free expression, which was previously tolerated by the private ownership of some media networks, was suppressed by the policies which led the state to own and take control of the print and broadcast media, including the country's only two daily newspapers at the time.

One of the unfortunate results of the one-party régime was that it was the period of the worst economic performance in the history of Zambia. Yet, the one-party system was introduced at a time of sustained socio-economic development and, as already noted, it was preferred to, or perceived to be better positioned than, the multi-party system to promote development and put through reforms. The country, which had one of the most prosperous economies in Africa, ended up in a prolonged state of economic decline starting from 1975. As a result of many years of economic decline, Zambia was also re-classified from being among the middle-income countries to one of the impoverished low-income countries.

Thus, taking the economic and political reforms together, it is clear that the period under review was underlined by a continuation of the structural process of shifting economic resources from the private sector to the public sector, and from productive to unproductive sectors, all signifying a structural bias for producing non-traded goods and services as against tradable production and marketed output for domestic consumption and exports. This situation seemed to had been aggravated by the political environment. This, in our view, is how Zambia went, and continued to go, wrong and this is an important background for understanding why both expenditure reduction and patchy expenditure switching policies were unable to arrest many years of socio-economic decline and stimulate growth. Fortunately, structural rigidity and the possibility of copper prices not recovering in the short- to medium-term were recognized by the government and its creditors at the beginning of the 1980s, albeit probably too late. Moreover, economic structural adjustment and, subsequently, political reforms became unavoidable.

Conflicts in design and implementation of structural reforms, 1983-94

Between 1983 and 1994 the thrust of economic policy was characterized by a combination of expenditure reduction measures to attain macro-economic stabilization and expenditure switching policies for more efficient resource allocation, and the promotion of exports mainly through exchange rate adjustments. The period under review can be demarcated into three distinct policy reform phases. The first was the World Bank/IMF supported stabilization and drastic expenditure switching policies from 1983 to 1987. This was followed by the home-made stabilization and state intervention and control phase, known as the New Economic Recovery Programme (NERP), which was put in place when Zambia broke away from the IMF Programme from 1987 to 1989. The last phase is the progressive and diversified economic and political reforms, gradually from 1990 and as continued by the new government which came to power in 1991. These phases represent shifts in policy and the degree of commitment at the level of implementation. While the two main macro-economic policy approaches to bring about the desired transformation can be mutually re-enforcing, they did not seem to have been well applied. One can see clear cases of conflicts in policy design or improper sequencing of the reform measures.

The first structural adjustment programme

The big bang approach, supported by the IMF and World Bank, was attempted between 1983 and 1987. The agenda of policy reforms gradually changed from a package of quick fix measures for macro-economic stabilization through expenditure reduction to include structural adjustment proper. The latter included resource reallocation within the public sector, the liberalization of a wide range of markets, and devaluations which after 1985 became the dominant policy instrument through the weekly foreign exchange auction. The exchange rate was liberalized simultaneously with trade, interest rates, and other prices (Ncube, Sakala, and Ndulo, 1987). In addition, the programme included measures to allow exporting companies to retain 50 per cent of their exchange earnings; to increase agricultural producer prices; to reduce and eventually abolish subsidies; and for various forms of retrenchment in the public sector. But foreign financial support, especially IMF/World Bank loans in support of policy changes was conditional on a number of criteria - most notably a commitment to implement the reforms, the reduction of debt payment arrears, and timely debt service (Meijer, 1990: 673).

Theoretically, the policy régime in this period should have been beneficial for the production of tradables because the package of reform measures emphasized the need for expenditure switching and the production of tradables. But the outcome was largely disappointing in achieving the main policy objectives of macro-economic stabilization, economic diversification, and an increase of non-traditional exports. In practice, the combination of drastic devaluation and expenditure reduction policies together with the imposed obligation to service debt and delays in releases of pledged foreign financial support made severe demands on the design of the adjustment programme to prevent the adverse effects (contraction, unemployment, inflation, and so on) from becoming dominant (Meijer, 1990: 669-682). Many problems encountered at the implementation level could have been foreseen and avoided. Conflicts in policy design and implementation undermined the expected transformation.

The main weakness was that the reforms focused mainly on policy-induced distortions that discouraged efficiency in the use of resources ignoring a number of factors in the design. First, the design ignored the physical bottlenecks that required investment expenditure. Second, it seemed that the programme lacked a chronological sequence of adjustment measures to ensure that they interacted with each other in a beneficial rather than a counter-productive manner. Third, there were no measures to reduce Zambia's external debt burden but only to ensure timely debt repayment and mobilization of conditional foreign aid. Above all and relatedly, the programme lacked coherent linkages between the short-term objectives of attaining balance of payments equilibrium and improving allocative efficiency and the long-term objective of sustainable development.

It is important to note that the area of conflict in design and implementation of structural adjustment arose from inappropriate sequencing of reforms. Macroeconomic stability requires that countries establish and maintain realistic exchange rates, keep budget deficits and inflation low, and increase public sector savings. This could not have been expected in Zambia. The expenditure reduction policy, which was continued from the previous policy régime, conflicted with the policy of expenditure switching through massive devaluation which was intensified by the weekly foreign exchange auctioning, and this mechanism led to macro-economic instability in the absence of effective measures to either ensure the inflow of foreign aid or to deal with the budget deficit. To put it differently, austerity in the government budget (expenditure side) could not have been checked due to rising prices associated with the continuous extensive devaluations, while import liberalization, without adequate depreciation of the real interest rate, appeared to have increased the balance of payments deficit, promoted de-industrialization, and discouraged exports.

Apart from a purely economic analysis, the failure of the structural adjustment programme during the period under review can also be approached from the political side. First, it seemed that the political viability of the programme was not adequately analyzed or taken into account. The programme did not include compensation measures to protect the most vulnerable groups. This oversight in reform design appeared to have led to mass frustration and labour militancy. Severe economic penalties on many people (as prices rose, wages fell, and subsidies were reduced) provoked widespread discontent with the government. Further, the way the reforms were implemented did not only undermine government authority, it was also the subject of a continuous dispute between Zambia and its donors, especially the IMF, to the extent of provoking the withdrawal of foreign support.

With regard to the "management/administrative factor", the programme had no objective and did not include measures for building effective institutional capacity to design and implement development policies. The dominant opinion among the population was that the reforms were designed by the IMF/World Bank and imposed on Zambia for implementation. The result was that the policies were neither understood nor supported by most of the people who were expected to implement them (ERG, 1989). The government leaders also increasingly felt that the donors had a "hidden agenda" to have them over-thrown (Republic of Zambia, 1987). In May 1987, the government abandoned the donor supported structural economic reforms and developed its own programme with the theme of growth from our own resources.

The new economic recovery programme (NERP)

The NERP was adopted following a break with the IMF-inspired reforms and was implemented between 1987 and 1990. The programme entailed abandonment of structural adjustment and the agenda of policy reform contained a wide range of measures as follows: (1) revaluation of the exchange rate from US$1 = K25 to K8 in May 1987 followed by devaluation to K10 in 1988 and again to K16 in June 1989; (2) down-ward adjustment in the interest rate from 35 per cent to 17 per cent followed by increases to 25 per cent in 1989; (3) guided trade liberalization focusing on removing the restrictions on imports of intermediate capital goods and raw materials and the controlling of imports of consumer goods that were also domestically produced; (4) the imposition of price control on 12 basic goods and the monitoring of general price increases based on producers or importers recommendations; (5) imposition of a wage freeze; (6) reduction of government expenditure and deficit financing; (7) selective and targeted food subsidy through the use of coupons; (8) a debt service moratorium by imposing a 10 per cent ceiling on debt servicing after deducting the needs of the key economic lifelines - the mining company, Zambia Airways obligations, and imports of oil and fertilizer; (9) debt-equity swaps and debt withdrawals for local reinvestment at a discount; (10) the foreign exchange retention for non-traditional exporters was increased from 50 to 100 per cent with the option of selling unused portions of their export retention to holders of debt claims at a discount; (11) a return to the administrative allocation of foreign exchange taking into account priority economic sectors for growth; and (12) retrenchment and redeployment in the public sector.

The emphasis of the measures were on economic stabilization by controlling inflation and selective state intervention to stimulate recovery (Republic of Zambia, 1987). It can be seen that while there were no differences regarding the main objectives (such as economic diversification, promoting exports, and reducing budget deficits and inflation), the framework of the NERP was in sharp contrast to the IMF/World Bank inspired structural adjustment programme. There were fundamental differences in their major instruments for attaining the stated objectives. In fact, it must be emphasized that some of the new instruments were diametrically different to those preferred by the IMF and the World Bank. The NERP measures entailed revaluation instead of devaluations, downward instead of upward adjustment in interest rates, guided trade and domestic price controls instead of open-ended liberalization, and a partial debt service moratorium instead of timely debt service. Similarly, there were differences in how to achieve a reduction in the budget deficit and overall public expenditure. Under the NERP, revaluation was not good for exporters. The concession was made to increase, from 50 to 100 per cent, the foreign exchange retention for the non-traditional exporters and allowing them access to discount rates used in the debt-equity swap scheme. This arrangement entailed, in the final analysis and practice, multiple exchange rates.

The impact of the Zambian go-it-alone strategy was mixed. On the positive side the break with the IMF brought some relief. The period coincided with a rising trend in copper prices and the downward trend in mineral output was arrested. Agricultural output increased tremendously, mainly as a result of good rainfall, and capacity utilization increased. The economy grew at 4 and 2.5 per cent, respectively, in 1988 and 1989. The decision to impose a 10 per cent ceiling on debt servicing reduced the budgetary share of this item from 31 to 7 per cent and this in combination with other measures, especially the targeted food subsidy, reduced the budget deficit (ERG, 1989: 6). The overall budget deficit fell from 14 per cent of GDP in 1987 to 9.3 per cent in 1988. The measures also brought some stabilization to the economy in the sense that the uncertainty associated with the auction system ended. Furthermore, government attempts to reduce dependence on imports were reinforced and companies were encouraged or even forced to look for local resources for their production process.

But the policy performance was largely disappointing in many crucial respects. By revaluing the exchange rate drastically, the local currency became increasingly overvalued and prevented further diversification in the economy. While the reduction in the budget deficit was a positive development, its impact on the economy had little to celebrate. Following the break with the IMF-supported programme, the international community withdrew their financial support. This meant that the larger part of the reduced deficit had to be financed through domestic sources. This again led to unbalanced growth in the money supply and fuelled inflation. This period also revealed the revival of parallel markets for essential goods and foreign exchange. The moratorium on debt service moderated the adverse impact of foreign debt on the government budget, but it did not reduce the debt burden and ended up aggravating the arrears which put the country into deep confrontation with its creditors who then took steps to isolate Zambia and undermine its reform efforts.

Again the design of the reform package was more to blame than implementation and the problems encountered were complicated by the withdrawal of donor support. The need for donor support brought Zambia back to negotiations with the IMF and a new policy framework paper was approved in September 1989. This development coincided with the agitation for the restoration of multi-party politics and led to the next phase of simultaneous economic liberalization and democratization and the birth of the Third Republic.

This phase in Zambia started as part of a worldwide wave of change or snowballing phenomenon following the collapse of the Eastern European dictatorships, and the wave had already started cutting across Africa. When agitation for change started in 1989, Frederick Chiluba, the then Chairman of the Labour Movement asked: "If the owners of socialism have withdrawn from the one-party system, who are the Africans to continue with it?" (*Times of Zambia*, 1989). Widespread support for democratization in Zambia had, to a large extent, its roots in Zambia's economic problems and the authoritarian one-party rule. The tidal wave of change was triggered off by unprecedented political unrest. There were food riots in 1989 against the decision by the government to reduce maize meal subsidies under the economic reforms supported by the IMF and World Bank. The climax of this political unrest was an attempted *coup d'état* in 1990 which took thousands of Zambians to the streets in celebration of the overthrow of the government.

The shift from a one-party régime to a democratic political system of government occurred quickly and even relatively painlessly. The constitutional changes to facilitate the right to organize political groups were made in July 1990, and in December 1990 the constitution was amended introducing the multi-party system of government, followed by elections at the end of October 1991. A new government was sworn in at the beginning of November 1991. According to the observer groups, Zambia had set a standard for free, fair, and peaceful transition to democracy with a swift and orderly transfer of government (Andreassen, Geister, and Jostensen, 1992: 1; Commonwealth Observer Group, 1992: 21). In this regard it can be concluded that the political transition in Zambia was successful. According to Huntington (1994: 5) "the rudimentary elements of democratization are achieved if reasonably fair, open and inclusive elections are held in which parties and candidates compete relatively equally, the votes are counted honestly and the winners form a government". The process of democratization in Zambia cannot be questioned on any of these issues. But the transition to democracy was not an end in itself. The new democratic system of government had to be sustained and institutionalized; and it was re-established in the belief that it was going to lead to good governance and economic development.

The political philosophy underlying the new government was an open democratic system and a market economy. This was a vision based on liberal democracy and capitalism. They advocated pursuing policies of selective state interventionism in which the government would restrict itself to rehabilitate and build socio-economic infrastructure with a small public sector in the midst of a basically private enterprise economy. The agenda of policy reforms, as reflected in their policy framework paper and the budget in 1992, typically involved the usual IMF prescriptions, though the reforms were claimed to be Zambia's own initiative. The new programme included measures for macro-economic stabilization and structural adjustment measures, which entailed liberalization of foreign exchange, trade, interest rates, prices, and agricultural marketing. Institutional reforms were marked by retrenchment in the public sector; privatization of public enterprises; and the restructuring of public expenditure including the removal of subsidies. Some of the reforms which were subsequently added included the introduction of "cash budgets" to control budget over-runs and the use of treasury bills as an instrument of monetary policy and not for the short-term financing of government expenditure.

The new Zambian government did not only adopt and consistently implement needed economic reforms, it also displayed tremendous capacity to implement them with a determined stance. Within one year of being in power the government implemented the most crucial reforms. These were market determined exchange and interest rates; price decontrol covering all commodities; and removal of the food subsidies including maize marketing and fertilizer subsidies. The budget deficit was reduced significantly, financed in a non-inflationary manner with donor support. Since 1993 the government has attempted to bring the budget into balance. Tax administration and tax compliance have also been improved especially following the introduction of the Zambia Revenue Authority in 1994. Compared with the previous government, significant progress has been made in many reform measures, including the controversial public sector retrenchment, and the party machinery is no longer part of the public service budget. A number of parastatal companies have been privatized, and some have been restructured to facilitate their privatization. A number of other parastatals have been abolished and some parastatals which relied heavily on state subsidies, such as Zambia Airways and the United Bus Company of Zambia, have been forced to liquidate. Nearly all forms of foreign exchange controls had been abolished by the end of 1994.

Major efforts have also been made both to service Zambia's external debt and to reduce the magnitude of the debt burden through some write-offs and debt buy-back operations. According to the 1995 Budget Speech, Zambia's external debt stock at that time was US$7.7 billion or about $800 in per capita terms and falling among the highest in the world. Of that amount US$3.5 billion was in arrears. By February 1996, all arrears had been eliminated, 67 per cent of the US$2.7 billion bilateral debt owed to the Paris club creditors was written off with debt service obligation falling from US$139 million to US$37 million a year, and the completion of the Rights Accumulation Programme (RAP) with the IMF enabled Zambia to convert US$1.3 billion in arrears to a soft loan under the Enhanced Structural Adjustment Facility (ESAF).

According to the Economic Intelligence Unit (1994: 8) and the opinion of the business community, there were many causes for celebration and economic prospects were brighter than ever before. Seen against the background of almost two decades of economic recession under the former government, the numerous positive changes signalled an economic turnaround. Moreover, foreign exchange was no longer rationed; the normal day to day affairs of business were conducted free of government intervention; basic consumer and investment goods were no longer in short supply; and physical infrastructure was being repaired. Another positive development is that Zambia's overall balance of payments deficits have been narrowing since 1992 and the country is likely to begin registering small surpluses if the current rate of aid inflow continues.

However with regard to macro-economic stability, one has to be cautious of the achievements so far because these have been on an *ad hoc* basis. In fact, all the indicators of macro-economic stability - inflation rate, interest rate, exchange rate, and the rate of money supply - have not been stable for any considerable period of time. Noticeable achievements in macro-economic stability appear to have depended more on the external inflows of aid than on internal market resilience. It must also be added that the extent to which some monetary, fiscal, and trade policies were sequenced at the level of implementation was rather disruptive to creating conditions for sustained economic development.

The across-the-board reforms, leading to the lack of appropriate sequencing, appear to have contributed to poor or unsatisfactory economic performance. A number of illustrative examples can be taken. Liberalization of imports had been undertaken before adequate adjustment of the exchange rate and before removal of policy restrictions that discouraged exports. Interest rates were significantly increased prior to both fiscal discipline by the government and the commercializing of public enterprises (the main borrowers from banks) and before introducing measures to reduce fiscal deficits. This led to an inflation-devaluation spiral with harmful impacts on the adjustment process. To complicate the situation, commercial banking was opened up before strengthening the supervisory capacity of the central bank. Parastatals for sale were listed before capital markets were improved. Import liberalization without adequate depreciation of the real exchange rate, increased and/or failed to moderate the balance of payments deficits, promoted de-industrialization, and discouraged exports.

Some issues can also be raised by analyzing the impact of the adjustment programme from the political side. Given the intensity and the number of the reform programmes and the speed at which they have been implemented, one gets the impression that both the managerial and the political viability of the programmes, like during the era of the previous government, were not adequately analyzed. The development crisis in Zambia seems to be, first and foremost, a crisis of the Zambian state with low capability to design and implement workable policies and the government appears to have surrendered this crucial responsibility to donors, especially the World Bank and the IMF. Many Zambians are not happy with this situation. The role of donors is widely acknowledged, but it would be appreciated most if their assistance is directed at increasing the ability of the government to determine its own policy agenda.

Fortunately, the dominant public attitude towards the two main waves of transformation Zambia is undergoing - democratization and economic liberalization - have so far been favourable to the new government. But for how long!! The government appears to have got away with many economic reform measures including the removal of the food subsidies, decontrol of prices, increases in education and medical fees, redundancies in the public sector, and chaos in food marketing (especially maize) without the riots which occurred during the previous régime. There is no easy explanation for this. It would seem that the government has so far taken advantage of both the initial euphoria, extensive public support, weak opposition, and unimpeachable electoral legitimacy to forge ahead with the across-the-board reforms.

With regard to democratization, the sequence of dominant public attitudes can be described as first euphoria, then disillusionment, and finally resignation and acceptance. People were excited about the political reform and the subsequent change in government. They became disappointed when their saviour - the new government - failed to deliver what it promised to do, but many could not turn to the opposition, because they were widely held responsible for the country's problems in the first place. Given the weak opposition, the government has continued to press ahead with the reforms.

Conclusions

A number of observations can be made. First, taken individually, many of the elements of adjustment programmes are necessary conditions for promoting recovery, and the need for reforms and their continuation are not in question. But the adjustment programmes, as they have been designed and implemented in Zambia since 1974, seem to have lacked coherent linkages between the short-term objectives of attaining balance of payments equilibrium or macro-economic stability and improving allocative efficiency and the long-term objectives of sustainable development. Neither of the objectives appear to have been achieved. The reforms have not adequately tackled the objectives of stabilization and economic diversification. Macro-economic conditions have continued to be unsatisfactory and the vulnerability of the economy, especially its dependence on copper, has hardly changed during the thirty-one years of Zambia's independence.

To stress the importance of having coherent and workable policy reforms and appropriate sequencing of the measures, as suggested in this chapter, is not to deny the relevance of the reforms. Rather, the thrust of our argument is to question the way reform measures have been designed and applied or sequenced. There is, for example, an overwhelming case for movement towards selective trade liberalization and realistic currency alignment. The sequencing and magnitude of that movement is crucial and it is in this area that World Bank and IMF policies seem to be at their most flawed and inconsistent combination. It has been suggested that stabilization measures have been over-extended and the package of the reform measures had neither been designed nor implemented in a proper sequence to ensure that they interacted with each other in a beneficial rather than in a counter-productive manner.

Further, there seems to be a case for suggesting that the combination of democratization and economic liberalization reforms seem to have overloaded the inherited weak institutional system, making it even more difficult to implement economic reforms and casting doubts on programme sustainability. Political democratization and economic liberalization complement each other in that they both have been striving to limit governmental authority and the power of the state. The paradox of structural adjustment reforms, as Whitaker (1991: 345) observed, "is that it envisages a stronger society and a weaker central state yet, to implement the policy reforms, a vastly stronger state than currently exists is required". The experience in Zambia has been complicated by the lack of policy ownership and the overwhelming dependency on foreign assistance or the low capability of the Zambian government to design and implement workable development policies.

Assistance by donors would be appreciated in improving state capacity and confidence to deal with development problems. At the moment, the donors seem to be in charge of designing development policies and imposing a wide range of conditions with the result that policies are neither properly understood nor supported by most of the people who are expected to implement or benefit from them. The other interpretation is that the rate of donors' interventions in the policy agenda appears to have overloaded the weak institutional system in Zambia with too many reforms either in an inappropriate sequence or without clear priorities. Under these circumstances, it is not easy to determine whether the chaos is in the design or in the implementation of structural economic and political reforms.

Part Two
ASSESSING THE IMPACT OF STRUCTURAL ADJUSTMENT PROGRAMMES: THE ECONOMIC EFFECTS

5 Structural adjustment policies: An assessment of the economic impact in Southern Africa

Gladson Kayira and Kempe Ronald Hope, Sr.

The deepening of the development crisis in Southern Africa, which began in the 1970s and intensified in the 1980s, presented a difficult challenge to the political leadership, policy advisers, and the development community. It required policy measures to reverse the declining trends and place those economies on a path of sustainable growth and development. There was need to, among other things, arrest the deepening of poverty, reduce the socio-economic inequalities, lighten the external debt burden, reverse the brain drain, create new employment opportunities, improve the efficiency of the physical infrastructure, narrow down the fiscal deficits, and improve the balance of payments. To avert famine and malnutrition, there was also a critical need to increase productivity. In the early 1980s, the policy response to this crisis emerged in the form of structural adjustment programmes (SAPs). SAPs were formulated by and with the support of the International Monetary Fund (IMF) and the World Bank. However, their efficacy has been the subject of considerable debate. This chapter reviews the nature and objectives of SAPs and analyzes their economic impact on the economies of the Southern African countries.

The nature and objectives of structural adjustment programmes

There is no universally accepted definition of SAPs. SAPs are a combination of two types of policy responses--stabilization policies which are the domain of the IMF, and structural adjustment policies which are the province of the World Bank. Stabilization policies aim at returning an economy to an equilibrium path that was followed prior to a shock. They tend to be short-term in perspective and they rely more on demand management (Demery, 1994). Structural adjustment policies are designed to address the long-term growth issues through better supply responses to market liberalization and efficient macroeconomic management. In their institutional form, SAPs are comprised of three major components (Demery, 1994). These are:

(1) the importance of macroeconomic stability; (2) the need for prices to reflect relative scarcities; and (3) a reduction in the role of the state in economic affairs.

Generally, as a precondition for a country to enter into a structural adjustment programme, agreement must be reached on a set of stabilization measures with the IMF. Similarly, bilateral donors and commercial banks insist on the borrowing country reaching an agreement with the IMF and the World Bank as a precondition for rendering economic support. The primary objectives of SAPs are: (1) the restoration of long-term growth; (2) improvement of the balance of payments position; (3) a reduction of domestic financial imbalances, including government fiscal deficits; (4) the promotion of trade liberalization; (5) increased domestic savings in the private and public sectors; (6) the elimination of price distortions in various sectors of the economy; and (7) the mobilization of additional external resources (Tarp, 1993).

However, in recent years, there has been a shift in emphasis with higher development objectives assuming equal importance as growth-oriented adjustment. For example, it is now common to conceptualize and formulate adjustment "with a human face" or to evaluate the social dimensions of adjustment. Moreover, the objectives of structural adjustment now include reducing its impact on the poor and other vulnerable groups; avoiding sharp declines in personal consumption; and providing for the delivery of basic social services, which, if neglected, could result in the decay in the fabric of society. More recently, concern has gone beyond the social cost of structural adjustment to consideration of its environmental impact also (World Bank, 1994b).

To achieve the objectives of SAPs, the primary policy instruments employed are: (1) exchange rate adjustment, primarily devaluation; (2) control of the money supply and credit ceilings; (3) interest rate policy, allowing interest rates to respond freely to market forces; (4) debt rescheduling; (5) fiscal policy, including measures to reduce public expenditure and mobilize resources; (6) deregulation of prices of goods, services and factor inputs; (7) liberalization of trade and payments arrangements; and (8) the reform of institutions with an emphasis on building capacity for policy analysis, for implementing public investments, and privatization of public assets (Balassa, 1989; Tarp, 1993). These instruments are interdependent, and in some cases they are mutually reinforcing.

Usually, these instruments are combined in complex packages, which define the criteria, or in the parlance of the IMF and the World Bank, the conditionalities against which the country's economic performance would be evaluated. It is through these conditionalities that successes or failures of SAPs are judged. For the IMF programmes, conditionalities are a norm for a country intending to borrow more than 25 percent of its IMF quota. However, for the World Bank the imposition of conditionality is a recent phenomenon. Nonetheless, increasingly, there is a tendency towards convergence in approaches between the IMF and the World Bank, and the separate identity of these two institutions seems to be disappearing (Mosley, Subasat, and Weeks, 1995). Recently, the IMF stated that "the objective of the IMF policy advice to member countries is to contribute to the promotion and maintenance of high levels of employment and real incomes and to the development of their productive resources" (IMF, 1995). In addition, the IMF now recognizes that its role in alleviating poverty "is to provide support for adjustment programmes that make economic growth sustainable and to mitigate the adverse effects that essential adjustment measures may have on the poor in the short-run" (Bernstein and Boughton, 1993). However, in the past, it was primarily the sister organization of the IMF--the World Bank--which was concerned with poverty and development issues.

In the Southern African countries, the need for adjustment is no longer a matter of debate. Many policy-makers in the Southern African countries, as well as other parts of Africa, have openly recognized the mistakes they made in the past and they are now attempting to address the problems which arose out of those past policies. However, some controversy exists with respect to the distributional aspects of adjustment. That is, the extent of some of the hardships experienced under adjustment and the pace of recovery in economic growth. Initially, it was thought that the period of adjustment would be about five years from the start of implementation of the programmes but it is now widely recognized that adjustment requires a long-term perspective (World Bank, 1989a; World Bank, 1994b). This is so principally because the supply-side responses have been somewhat weak and have tended to take much longer periods to emerge.

Another controversy relates to the relative balance in the role of market forces and that of the government in the economy. In its advocacy of market-friendly policies, the World Bank states that "Sustained growth requires more than a high rate of investment. It requires unleashing the market forces so that competition can improve allocation of economic resources. It also requires getting price signals right and creating a climate that allows businesses to respond to those signals in ways that increase returns to investments... But trade, agricultural, and other regulatory reforms ... are essential complements to reducing the government interventions that distort prices and tie up markets" (World Bank, 1994b). The premise of the World Bank approach is that government allocation of resources is inefficient, while the markets are essentially efficient. However, market failures could have similar adverse impacts on economies as do government failures. Arguably, to create a dynamic set of competitive industries in economies with traditions of weak industrial entrepreneurship and low levels of technological capabilities, selective government interventions may be appropriate (Lall, 1995). Moreover, reducing public sector investment expenditure could have an adverse impact on growth prospects (Mosley, Subasat, and Weeks, 1995).

The term "structural adjustment" came into popular use in the early 1980s. It is associated with the policy-based lending of the IMF and the World Bank which were designed to reverse economic decline and stimulate growth. While the IMF and the World Bank sought to demonstrate that countries that had implemented SAPs achieved faster economic growth (Balassa, 1989; World Bank, 1989a; World

Bank, 1994b), some critics provided evidence that questioned the effectiveness of SAPs in terms of generating growth (Mosley and Weeks, 1993; Mosley, Subasat, and Weeks, 1995). The controversy on the impact of SAPs is largely attributable to the fact that results achieved to date seemed to have remained below the expectations of dramatic increases in economic performance. However, it must be borne in mind that it is now recognized that structural adjustment policies seek to stimulate productive capacity and to achieve sustainable economic growth over a longer term than had been originally conceived (Killick, 1995).

The impact of structural adjustment programmes

As a reflection of the diversity and nature of the economies in the Southern African group of countries, the experiences with and the impact of SAPs have been somewhat dissimilar. Some countries have experienced stable macroeconomic environments, while others have suffered severe shocks. Some countries have sustained policy reforms for some time, while others have experienced reversals in policy. In this section, the focus of the analysis is on two categories of countries: (1) a country which has implemented SAPs under civil war conditions--Mozambique; and (2) those countries which have implemented comprehensive SAPs in non-war or relatively peaceful conditions--Lesotho, Malawi, Tanzania, Zambia, and Zimbabwe. Angola, Botswana, Mauritius, Namibia, South Africa, and Swaziland are excluded from the analysis since they have not had SAPs with the IMF/World Bank.

Adjustment under war conditions

Mozambique started implementing SAPs under the siege of a devastating civil war. That fact differentiates the Mozambican experience from that of the rest of the Southern African countries which had adjustment programmes with the IMF and World Bank. In 1987, Mozambique abandoned its central planning system and began to implement SAPs while the civil war still intensified. That war made much of the countryside an exceedingly risky area for agricultural production and it also resulted in the massive destruction of much of the country's physical and social infrastructure. Moreover, the sudden change from the central planning system to a market-oriented economic system required radical institutional reforms. To rebuild the economy, priority was given to reviving the productive sectors of the economy, primarily agriculture; correcting macroeconomic imbalances, particularly reducing inflation; and strengthening the role of the private sector in the economy. That SAPs could have positive impacts on an economy under such difficult circumstances is remarkable. However, by all measures, the Mozambican economy is in much better shape today than during the era of central planning (de Abreu and Baltazar, 1994).

In response to the policy changes, economic performance in Mozambique improved significantly during 1987-89. Over this period, GDP grew at an average annual rate of 10 percent, in sharp contrast to the declining economic activity in all sectors of the economy in the previous five years (Kyle, 1994). However, after this initial momentum, the economy contracted during 1990-92. In 1993, there was a robust recovery in the economy with a growth rate recorded at 19 percent and an increase in the share of gross domestic investment in GDP from 26 percent in 1987 to 42 percent in 1993 (World Bank, 1995a). In addition, price distortions were corrected and the rate of inflation declined from 91 percent in 1987 to 45 percent in 1992 (IMF, 1994a). However, because of the civil war, heavy government military expenditures contributed to large fiscal deficits, averaging around 25 percent of GDP during the adjustment period.

The liberalization of the Mozambican economy has been the most important element in the success of its SAPs. Not only has the volume of exports increased but in parallel, the composition of exports has diversified as the proportion of new products in total exports increased. Merchandise exports grew at an average annual rate of 9 percent during 1986-1993, compared to a steep decline of 25 percent during 1980-85. Through a series of devaluations, to establish more realistic exchange rates, the ratio of the parallel market rate to the official exchange rate fell sharply from 42 in 1986 to 1 in 1992, and thus leading to the virtual elimination of the parallel market premium.

Marking an ideological departure from the central planning system, the state also reduced its intervention in the economy. For example, its monopoly on foreign trade was eliminated. The agricultural pricing and marketing systems were liberalized, resulting in a substantial increase in production. Also, to allow for more private sector participation in the economy, more than 200 small scale public enterprises were privatized (de Abreu and Baltazar, 1994).

The Mozambican experience with SAPs clearly demonstrates that, even under exceedingly adverse conditions, appropriate policy reforms could have favourable impacts on the macro-economy (Kyle, 1994). Now that the civil war has ended, the challenge currently facing Mozambique is that of maintaining and capitalizing on the gains made to date for sustainable growth and development in the future.

Comprehensive adjustment programmes

Lesotho, Malawi, Tanzania, and Zambia implemented comprehensive SAPs from the mid-1980s, while Zimbabwe started its SAPs in 1991. By 1991 there was some improvement in economic performance with all of the countries except Zambia recording positive GDP growth rates. In 1992, the Southern African region experienced considerable drought which, combined with the world recession, resulted in marginal or negative growth rates in some of the countries. Malawi and Zimbabwe recorded the steepest declines of around 8 percent, while Zambia's decrease in economic performance was moderate at approximately 3 percent. In

1993, there was a marked improvement in performance with Lesotho, Malawi and Zambia all achieving growth rates of more than 6 percent while for Zimbabwe it was 2 percent.

Large fiscal deficits indicate the extent of government failures to achieve fiscal balance. In all five of the countries there has been progressive improvements in their fiscal situation compared to the pre-adjustment period. Between the mid-1980s and 1993, Lesotho, Tanzania, and Zambia showed major improvements in their fiscal performance. Lesotho's fiscal deficit declined from 30 percent of GDP in 1987 to almost a balanced budget by 1993. Equally remarkable, Zambia's fiscal deficits as a percentage of GDP fell from 23 percent in 1986 to 1.2 percent in 1993 while in Malawi and Zimbabwe fiscal performance during the adjustment period has been less spectacular.

The impact of SAPs on fiscal deficits is determined through a set of conditions, including the reduction of government spending. It has also been increasingly recognized that unless the role of government is limited to those activities where market failures predominate, growth of the private sector could be crowded out and stifled. In almost all of the five countries the share of government expenditure in GDP has continued to decline. Zambia has had the most dramatic decline from 46 percent of GDP in 1986 to 18 percent of GDP in 1993. Similarly, in Malawi, during the adjustment period, government expenditure as a share of GDP declined from 33 percent in 1987 to 25 percent in 1993. Public sector wage bills account for a large proportion of total government expenditures. Typically, in these adjusting countries, the public sector wage bill accounts for more than 20 percent of total government spending.

Apart from reductions in government expenditures, maintaining a healthy fiscal balance also necessitates measures to increase revenues. Unfortunately, for some of these countries (Malawi, Zambia, and Zimbabwe) government revenues declined during the adjustment period and this, in turn, increased their dependence on external financing. Only Lesotho and Tanzania have experienced modest increases in revenues during the adjustment period. All of the countries have weak and narrow tax bases. In addition, for Zambia, the decline in revenues has also been caused by the erosion in the real value of tax revenues associated with very high rates of inflation (World Bank, 1994b).

Under SAPs, there have been serious attempts to reduce the rates of inflation. However, the degree of success has varied. In Zambia, for example, inflation accelerated from approximately 10 percent in 1980 to almost 200 percent by 1992 while in Lesotho and Tanzania there has been some modest success in reducing the rate of inflation during the same period. However, none of the countries have yet achieved single digit rates of inflation, which are considered desirable for macroeconomic stability. Moreover, inflationary pressures due to seigniorage--average long-term monetary financing which is calculated as the nominal change in the money base divided by the consumer price index--have been a common phenomenon. In Zimbabwe, for example, to collect additional seigniorage of one percentage point of GDP, during 1965-89, required a 10 percent increase in inflation (Easterly and Schmidt-Hebbel, 1994).

Increasing investment in the productive capacity of any country is considered central to long term economic transformation and sustainable growth. During the adjustment period, there has been a sharp contrast among the countries in terms of investment performance. Lesotho had the highest share of gross domestic investment in GDP, which had risen from approximately 49 percent in 1988 to approximately 76 percent by 1993. This has been attributed to massive investments in the Lesotho Highland Water Project (Petersson, 1993). Tanzania has also maintained high investment levels, averaging around 37 percent of GDP in the 1988-93 period. In contrast, the data on Malawi and Zambia indicate that there were continuous declines in investment rates. For Malawi, the proportion of gross domestic investment in GDP has declined from approximately 25 percent in 1980 to approximately 13 percent in 1993. Similarly, in Zambia it has fallen from 24 percent in 1987 to approximately 11 percent in 1993. This primarily reflects cuts in public sector capital expenditure during the adjustment process. However, this declining trend in investment also suggests the need for the pursuit of complementary policies to stimulate private investment. Reversing these declining trends in investment is critical to sustained economic recovery.

The Southern African countries have been adjusting under a difficult international economic environment. That environment has been characterized by deteriorating commodity terms of trade; a heavy burden of servicing of debts; and a recession in the industrial countries (Kirkpatrick and Weiss, 1995). In Lesotho, Malawi, and Tanzania, for instance, the terms of trade started to deteriorate around the mid-eighties and continued through to the early nineties. The international prices of the major crops, coffee and cotton, declined by 70 percent and 28 percent, respectively, between 1980 and 1990. One consequence of this state of affairs was that total debt service as percentage of exports rose from 25.3 percent in 1980 to 32.8 percent in 1993 for Zambia, and similarly, over the same period from 3.8 percent to 31.1 percent for Zimbabwe. Malawi and Tanzania have made modest improvements in their debt performance, but still their debt service burden has remained large at around 20 percent in 1993.

Promoting growth and diversifying exports have been central to SAPs. All five countries experienced rapid growth in the value of their exports. For Malawi and Zambia, for instance, growth in exports almost doubled between 1987 and 1993 (IMF, 1994b). Correspondingly, there has been an increase in the export of manufactures, predominantly from the light industries such as textiles and clothing. Furthermore, there has also been export diversification. For instance, in Malawi three major exports--sugar, tea, and tobacco--accounted for 81 percent of the total value of exports in 1987, and that increased to 88 percent in 1991. Since exports have a large impact on growth, all countries should strive to remove policies which impede their export competitiveness (Jones and Kiguel, 1994).

There has also been major strides toward the liberalization of imports. In the pre-adjustment period, most of these countries had overvalued exchange rates and they rationed their foreign exchange through administrative measures. However, domestic currency depreciations, combined with appropriate macroeconomic policies have now eliminated foreign exchange rationing and reduced the import scarcity premiums which tended to be reflected in the prices in the parallel markets. For instance, Tanzania and Zambia experienced severe distortions in their foreign exchange markets. The ratio of the parallel market rate to that of the official exchange rate decreased from 4.9 in 1986 to 1.4 in 1992 in Tanzania, while in Zambia, the ratio increased from 1.3 in 1986 to a peak of 7.8 in 1989 before the black market for foreign exchange was wiped out in 1991 (World Bank, 1994b).

Further evidence of import liberalization has been the progressive elimination of non-tariff barriers (NTBs). Barriers to imports were pervasive in the 1980s. To have access to foreign exchange, for example, required a valid import licence. In some sense, licensing had become a mechanism for rationing foreign exchange. Import licenses were also used to protect inefficient domestic production from foreign competition.

Progress has also been made on reducing the number of goods requiring approval for import. In Malawi, Tanzania, Zambia, and Zimbabwe, before the implementation of SAPs, all imports were subjected to NTBs, including quantitative restrictions and special licensing requirements other than for health and safety reasons. In late 1992, Tanzania still had about 100 import items subjected to NTBs, while Malawi and Zimbabwe had only a few items. In contrast, Zambia had made greater strides with no items facing NTBs by late 1992 (World Bank, 1994b). In addition, the introduction of the open general license (OGL) scheme in all of these countries has contributed to import liberalization. Under the OGL scheme, goods are placed on the list automatically approved for imports and for allocation of foreign exchange. While this falls short of complete import liberalization, the OGL scheme has been an important transitionary mechanism.

Reforming trade policies has been a central feature of the World Bank's structural adjustment loans. All of the adjusting countries in Southern Africa have embarked on trade liberalization. This has contributed to improved trade performance, measured in terms of export growth and diversification, particularly shifts towards manufacturing, as noted earlier. Increases in imports has been the immediate impact of trade liberalization. The proportion of imports in GDP has increased considerably during the adjustment period. Zimbabwe's imports as a share of GDP increased from 29 percent in 1990 to 40 percent in 1993. Over the same period, Malawi's import share rose modestly from 24 percent to 27 percent.

For macroeconomic policy reforms to succeed, they should be implemented with corresponding changes in the social and political institutions. Even if the reforms, purely in economic terms, may initially be sustainable, if economic liberalization is politically unacceptable, then policy reversals would be inevitable. As Bates and Collier (1995) observe, for example, the government of Zambia, in 1985, shifted to a policy of liberalization and, in 1987, it re-imposed controls on the markets for commodities, credit, and foreign exchange. Consequently, the donors, following the lead from the IMF and World Bank, suspended their lines of credit. Two years later, the government reversed its position and shifted back to market-based economic policies. These oscillations in economic policy reflected the vacillations in the political arena. The role of politics as a major determinant of sustainability of economic policy reforms has also been demonstrated in Malawi (Killick, 1995).

Unless there is political will, implementing public sector reforms will continue to be intractable. And yet, improving public sector management has been deemed essential for the success of policy reforms. For example, an effective civil service is central to ensuring that a sound macroeconomic framework can be implemented. However, in recent years considerable progress has been made toward the restructuring of the public sector. For instance, in Zimbabwe, between 1991 and 1993, more than 20,000 public sector employees were retrenched (Mhone, 1995). To a lesser extent, other countries, such as Malawi and Tanzania, have also reduced the size of their civil services.

In addition, reforms have also been directed at improving civil service pay and restructuring of grade levels. In many of the countries, the erosion of average salaries was the major issue to be addressed by pay reform. This took the form of attempts to decompress the wage structure so as to be able to recruit and retain higher-level staff whose salaries had sunk to very low multiples of the lowest ranked employees. In Mozambique, for example, the ratio of the highest-paid echelon to the lowest-paid widened from 2:1 in 1985 to 9:1 by 1991 (World Bank, 1994b; Robinson, 1990). Likewise, Tanzania adopted a package of pay and employment reforms which decompressed public sector salary scales to a ratio of 12:1 by 1994 (Stevens, 1994).

Further to the attempts at public sector reform in the Southern African countries, there has also been some progress in the reduction of state ownership of enterprises. These public enterprises are generally inefficient and are in various stages of dilapidation. Moreover, they absorb large amounts of funds that could be better spent on basic social services. In Tanzania, for example, central government subsidies to public enterprises equal 72 percent of central government spending on education and 150 percent of central government spending on health (World Bank, 1995d). The data currently available indicate that Zambia, for instance, has privatized 86 of its 152 public enterprises (Phiri, 1995). The Government of Zambia has also created a Privatization Trust Fund which will facilitate the acquisition of minority stakes reserved for Zambian citizens (Bell, 1995).

Perhaps, the most controversial aspect of the debate on SAPs has been their impact on the poor. In the Southern African countries, the majority of the poor live in the rural areas. As producers of agricultural commodities they have benefited from policy reforms in agricultural marketing and also from foreign exchange and trade liberalization. Prices paid to the rural farmers have increased and the delivery of agricultural commodities has improved. However, rising food and other prices as well as declining opportunities for employment in the formal sector have tended to have an adverse impact on both the urban and rural poor (Mlambo, 1995; Kayizzi-Mugerwa and Levin, 1994). Consequently, some of the countries now have social impact programmes as a part of their SAPs. For example, in 1991, Zimbabwe initiated the Social Dimensions of Adjustment (SDA) programme to mitigate the social costs of adjustment.

Conclusions

This chapter has provided a comparative analytical review of the objectives and impact of structural adjustment programmes as the policy response to the development crisis in the Southern African countries. It was determined that the impact of SAPs in the Southern African countries has been somewhat mixed and that the full adjustment process was likely to take a good deal longer than had been initially expected.

Nonetheless, there are currently no credible alternatives to SAPs as the policy response to the development crisis in the Southern African countries and the rest of Africa as well. As a matter of fact, much of the recent literature on structural adjustment, including those authored by the critics of SAPs, recognize that adjustment is a necessary condition for an effective long-term attempt at economic recovery and development. Consequently, the issue is not whether adjustment is necessary but rather what the adjustment package should contain (Mosley, Subasat, and Weeks, 1995; Mwanza, 1992; Killick, 1995; Ndegwa and Green, 1994).

In that regard, much attention must be given to the problem of the counterfactual over which there seems to be considerable conceptual confusion. The extreme form of this conceptual confusion is to conflate structural adjustment and the development crisis which then leads to negative generalizations about the actual impact of SAPs on African economies (van de Walle, 1994). However, the impact assessment approach needs to be one of trying to determine what would have happened in the absence of SAPs. For example, do SAPs result in a worse poverty situation than would have obtained without them? Killick (1995), for example, argues that the critics of SAPs have exaggerated the adverse impact of adjustment on the poor since "adjustment measures are not, for the most part, addressed to variables which are the prime causes of poverty in many developing countries". As a matter of fact, "African governments were never particularly effective in "reaching the poor" with social services or poverty alleviation policies before the era of structural adjustment" (van de Walle, 1994). Moreover, many SAPs now contain social impact provisions.

Whatever the limitations of SAPs, as implemented in the Southern African countries, they contain many of the elements which comprise the list of the necessary conditions for dealing with the development crisis. Consequently, to blame SAPs solely for the continuing development crisis in those countries or in Africa, in general, may be politically appealing in the short-run but it would not be credible nor helpful in the pursuit of economic recovery in those countries (Ndegwa and Green, 1994). Moreover, some of the empirical research now forthcoming on SAPs indicate that intense adjusting countries have a superior growth performance in economic welfare than non-adjusting and other adjusting countries (Kakwani, 1995).

Basically, what is required in the Southern African countries, and the rest of Africa as well, is not an abandonment of SAPs, since there currently exists nothing better as a replacement to mitigate the development crisis in those countries, but a structured approach at indigenous policy-making to complement the SAPs. Such a structured approach would require national governments to engage in economic behaviour that promotes self-reliance and reduces external dependence, particularly in the post-SAPs era, if the economic crisis is not to be a recurring or permanent one.

A policy of self-reliance remains the only means through which the poor, for example, would be able to improve their circumstances. The poor would benefit most from self-reliant activities which allow them to work their way out of poverty. All African governments must therefore develop and implement policy to empower the poor. Without government collaboration, the lot of the poor cannot be significantly improved (Hope, 1996c; Friedmann, 1992).

Self-reliance is taken here to mean autonomy of decision-making and full mobilization of a society's own resources under its own initiative and direction. It also means rejection of the principle of exploitative appropriation of the resources of others (Hope, 1984). A strategy of development emphasizing self-reliance also focuses on increasing cooperative relations in and among African nations and reducing their individual and collective dependence on the industrial countries (Ndegwa and Green, 1994).

The operational framework of self-reliance focuses on four elements (Hope, 1984). The first element pertains to basic human needs, which means attacking poverty directly and not through the trickle-down process. In other words, it means giving priority to the provision of food, shelter, housing, education, health care, and jobs, at the least. The second element relates to maximization of the use of local resources and values through the educational system as appropriate to the needs, resources, and values of the populace. It entails, therefore, the development of individuals as well as nations. Education should be used to meet the basic needs of individuals to receive a foundation of knowledge, attitudes, values, and skills on which to build a better life for the benefit of themselves and society.

The third element in the framework of self-reliance deals with participation of the poor in the development process (Hope, 1983). Participation by intended beneficiaries is a fundamental ingredient for successful development performance. The final element here pertains to the issue of interdependence or collective self-reliance. That is, active economic and political cooperation among African nations for their individual as well as collective development. Such cooperation is aimed at generating or adapting the knowledge and resources needed for endogenous self-sustained development.

Perhaps the most important element of the operational aspect of this self-reliance framework is the need to improve the incomes of the poor through employment. In that regard, one often overlooked solution is the promotion of growth in the subterranean (informal) sector. The subterranean sector currently contributes significantly to GDP and employment in Africa. It is the major source of employment for the urban poor and particularly so for women. All restrictions on this sector should therefore be eliminated so that it can flourish as a means of promoting growth and reducing unemployment and hunger in the region.

6 Industrial development in sub-Saharan Africa: The impact of structural adjustment

Ben Kaluwa

Cross-section studies indicate that the level of economic development among countries depends on the structural transformation that takes place in the form of changes in the composition demand, trade, production, and factor use. The most pronounced accompanying changes tend to be the relative shares of primary production and manufacturing in total output. The former tend to fall steeply and the latter tend to rise substantially as per capita GNP rises. This is why structural transformation has been closely associated with industrial development and both with economy-wide development.

The role of industry in African development

In developing countries, there is characteristic segmentation in the factor markets (typically labour and finance capital) as, for example, between the primary and secondary sectors, and between the informal and formal sectors. This segmentation is more pronounced in the more underdeveloped economies like those of the sub-Saharan Africa region. This means that there tends to be systematic variations in labour productivity in different uses and this is worsened by high population growth rates. Industry's role in development can be seen as providing a destination for resource reallocation because labour productivity in industry is much higher than in the rest of the economy. The following are some of the characteristics of manufacturing industries which are important for general economic development (Chenery, Robinson, and Syrquin, 1986):

1 The income elasticity of demand for manufactures (domestic or international) is relatively high which means that the demand stimulus for manufacturers will also be strong as incomes rise, the converse being also true;

2 Manufactures are highly tradeable which means that for most lines of products the market can be globalized;

3 The establishment of industries according to comparative advantage can take advantage of the gains from specialization and large scale operation;

4 Manufacturing growth is one of the main areas of high international technological interface and therefore a major source of technological change and of subsequent higher productivity gains;

5 Manufacturing provides for national economic integration through the intensification of backward and forward linkages within the sector itself and between it and others and;

6 Manufacturing, whether it is import-substituting or export-oriented, provides some measure of safety against the risks associated with unstable primary export earnings.

Although African countries have recognized the critical role of industry as exemplified by their earlier interventionist strategies, this enthusiasm has largely not been shared by the current main policy sponsors, notably the International Monetary Fund (IMF) and the World Bank. These two institutions have tended to cling to the view that the pace of industrialization should not be forced (Riddell et al, 1994). And yet, other observations suggest that there is no developed economy which has not had an interventionist stance towards industrial development (Shapiro and Taylor, 1990; Griffin, 1989; Kirkpatrick and Nixson, 1983). Even in the successful export-led policies of the newly industrializing countries of South-East Asia, the experiences have incorporated active interventionist policies albeit, subsequently, with heavy reliance on market incentives (Shapiro and Taylor, 1990; Chenery, Robinson, and Syrquin, 1986).

In sub-Saharan Africa the industrial sector is typically fragile in terms of relative size, structure, orientation, and performance. For example, in 1985, sub-Saharan Africa had a share of 9.5 percent of the world's population and 11.4 percent of the population of developing countries. The respective shares of world and developing countries GDP were only 1.3 percent and 7.0 percent and those of manufacturing value added (MVA), 0.76 percent and 3.8 percent respectively. The total African MVA was equivalent to or less than that of some individual developing countries (Riddell et al, 1994). Around 1984 the share of non-traditional industries in total MVA was 46 percent for low-income Africa and 57 percent for middle-income Africa, compared to 71 percent for low-income Asia, 58 percent for middle-income Asia, and 77 percent for the world. When it comes to export performance, in 1986 sub-Saharan Africa accounted for only 0.23 percent of the world's manufactured exports and 1.5 percent of those of developing countries, which in per capita terms translates to US$8 compared to US$57 for the developing countries and US$1,552 for the industrialized market economies. Trend-wise, the less developed countries/world exports ratio was rising and more sharply so since 1975. The Africa/world exports ratio had a declining trend and so had the Africa/less developed countries (LDCs) exports ratio. Moreover, African trade is dominated by that between Africa and the industrial countries which accounts for about 70 percent of the total value of African trade while regional trade accounts for between 10 percent and 12 percent (Hardy, 1990).

Lall (1990) blames the problems of African industry on inward-looking and interventionist trade and industrial policies that have fostered little competition, too much state ownership concentration, and protectionism. Also to blame are the low levels of skills, knowledge, and technologies which, in turn, result in low productivity, lack of competitiveness, and lack of linkages between sectors and between the large scale and the smaller scale enterprises.

It might be argued that given the vulnerability of the industrial sector up to the early 1980s, sub-Saharan Africa industries faced an exposure risk depending not only on the effects of world-wide economic turmoil but also on changed policy directions and the manner in which the economic policy reforms were implemented. The following section gives a brief outline of the context in which policy change was deemed necessary. The section after that looks at the implementation of the structural adjustment programmes (SAPs) and that is followed by a critique of the reform measures and, thereafter, by concluding remarks.

Background to SAPs

Following on the first major oil price crisis of 1973-75, the second one of 1979-82 triggered off a worst international recession for the developing countries. This resulted in a protracted period of deteriorating international terms of trade and rising international real interest rates. For many African economies, these economic ills were compounded by geopolitical instability and drought cycles related to global warming. The consequence has been serious balance of payments and debt-repayment problems, the compression of vital imports, mounting government budget deficits, the deterioration of socio-economic infrastructure, and escalating inflation, for example. General economic performance deteriorated with consequent declines in real earnings and a rising incidence of poverty.

In response to the crisis, the International Monetary Fund and the World Bank introduced policy based conditional lending which now covers over 75 developing countries that are diverse in size, politico-economic orientation, and geographical location (Krueger, 1993). By 1986, 29 sub-Saharan Africa countries had embarked on economic policy reforms under SAPs.

The implementation of SAPs

The theoretical basis

The pre-SAP status of sub-Saharan Africa's industrial strategy was based on the ideas of early development economics (1950s and 1960s) which espoused state intervention for the industrialization of relatively backward economies. The industrial strategy comprised directed public interventions at the sectoral or firm levels aimed at stimulating particular lines of economic activity using microeconomic policy targeting and complementary economy-wide policies (Shapiro and Taylor, 1990). Such a stance had to be adopted for a number of interconnected reasons including:

1 The fact that late industrializers, because they coexisted with the early industrializers, often had to start at the capital-intensive technological end and yet their economies were likely to face severe finance capital constraints with entrepreneurs who were financially weak and risk averse (Gerschenkron, 1962);

2 Economic development (as opposed to growth) could not be entrusted to the decentralized market-oriented short-run decision making since some necessary industrial projects would be large relative to the size of the economies and would generate benefits (and costs) not likely to be reflected in the private profitability calculus (Schumpter, 1934; Hirshman, 1958) and;

3 Conditions prevailing in the less developed countries were not conducive to the achievement of dynamic optimal resource allocations by the price mechanism. Incomplete or malfunctioning markets result in structural rigidities where prices do not reflect the true opportunity costs so that private costs to investors could be greater than the social opportunity cost and thereby understating industry's social rate of return (Scitovsky, 1954; Prebisch; 1950).

These reasons were deemed necessary for the preemption or the assistance of the price mechanism and private sector activity by the state. This would be done through direct state participation in economic activity, particularly in industries where investments would tend to be lumpy; state intervention in factor markets and other input markets; and state support for a particular direction in the orientation of industrialization, for example, import-substitution versus export- oriented industrialization. The former entailing public interventions to support investments through protection, cheap credits, subsidies, and so on.

SAPs have been based on the neoclassical economists' reaction to the preceding views. The neoclassical approach is basically directed at the 1950s and the 1960s development economists' faith in the state as an agent of change and its presumed superior capacity to allocate resources and undertake sectoral targeting and interventions (Shapiro and Taylor, 1990). For the neoclassical economists, the imperfect state is basically inferior to the imperfect market because the latter is capable of self-correction while the former is associated with various forms of government failure, for example, corruption or rent-seeking behaviour and its lack of capacity to achieve the efficient allocation of resources or undertake sectoral targeting. The resulting inefficiencies were considered to be worse for the economy than imperfectly functioning markets, which could be contributed by state imperfections in the first place.

The cornerstones of the economic reform agenda have therefore included monetary and fiscal reforms; the streamlining of the public and state-owned enterprise sectors; and the liberalization of the whole pricing régime in the primary and manufactured goods markets, the factor input markets (labour and finance capital), the market for foreign exchange, and the pricing of utilities (electricity, water, and posts and telecommunications). Foreign trade liberalization would naturally complement the liberalization of exchange rates and would enhance access to imported inputs and international competitiveness. Similarly, greater competition in the financial and industrial sectors would also enhance efficiency in resource allocation.

Since these measures are supposed to directly or indirectly contribute to the improvement of the incentive environment which enhances the operation of markets and private sector-led economic activity, they have been termed neutral or first-best (Mullei, 1994) and would relegate the role of the state to that of a "night watchman" (Shapiro and Taylor, 1990).

The experience

A major source of information relating to sub-Saharan Africa's implementation of the economic reform measures under SAPs is World Bank (1994b). Here it will only be necessary to point out some of the salient features for the periods 1981-86 and 1990-91:

1. Fourteen out of 26 countries did manage to reduce their fiscal deficits (before grants): the highest incidence of slippages occurred among the group of countries which initially had high deficits. The median fiscal balance to GDP ratio was -7.6 for 1981-86 and -8.0 for 1990-91;

2. Fifteen out of 23 countries for which information was available had frozen or reduced the expansion of their civil service personnel between 1985 and 1992;

3 Sixteen out of 24 countries managed to lower or maintain the government's resort to the central banks for financing (seigniorage). The median seigniorage rate was 1.1 percent in 1981-86 and 0.9 percent in 1990-91;

4 The success rate in bringing down inflation was generally good but better in countries with low seigniorage;

5 Fifteen out of 29 countries had divested over 10 percent of their public enterprises between 1986-92 and most of these countries had more than 50 public enterprises before divestiture;

6 Interest rates for deposits went up in 17 out of 21 countries. In 25 out of 29 countries some degree of liberalization had been implemented and in most cases governments were reducing their share-holdings in the capital of commercial banks;

7 The overall scores of government intervention in selected markets declined markedly by late 1992;

8 Twenty out of 27 countries achieved a narrowing of the gap between the parallel and official exchange rates and 21 of the countries achieved an increase in the real effective exchange rates which constitutes a depreciation;

9 In a more limited sample of countries, the vast majority achieved some relaxation in the control over the allocation of foreign exchange and reduction of the number of import items subject to nontariff barriers and;

10 Based on key agricultural exports, the majority of the countries had moved towards liberalized producer prices compared to the pre-reform period.

Generally, the sub-Saharan Africa SAPs can be regarded as having been broadly successful in terms of the number of countries adopting many of the prescribed measures. But because of other factors, including foreign financial inflows, it is not that simple a matter to directly relate to the SAPs whatever short-term successes have been achieved in production-related macroeconomic variables. And, in any case, the real test of success would be the achievement of the structural changes necessary for longer-term sustainable growth. Of course, there would also be the question of whether what may have been achieved with SAPs and the manner in which they have been implemented was necessarily the best.

The World Bank (1994b) indicates some improvements in manufacturing performance, in terms of growth, for the periods 1981-86 and 1987-91. But the improvements do not seem to be highly correlated with improvements in macroeconomic policies. And the report also chides the fact that improvements did not arise from structural reorientation, there having been no progress with manufactured exports even for countries like Zimbabwe which have broader-based manufacturing sectors. Steel and Webster (1992) have analyzed evidence from Ghana which indicates that small manufacturing enterprises have also been adversely affected by adjustment measures, reducing the potential for the sector to act as an agent for promoting domestic linkages.

These outcomes should come as no surprise, considering that some of the market liberalization measures were implemented with little or no attention to sequencing even though they exposed firms to economic and financial risk. All measures that involved the liberalization of input prices (including agricultural commodity prices, interest rates, utilities prices, and foreign exchange rates) were bound to raise costs and yet little had been done to remove, beforehand, the supply constraints in the respective markets. Technology in African industry is typically out-dated in a global environment where attraction of foreign investment has become extremely competitive. Trade liberalization has therefore opened the industries to competition they cannot match. This applies to most industries with the exception of supply-based ones producing inexpensive and bulky goods and which would be protected by distance. Notable casualties have been the textile industries which in a number of countries have been threatened with extinction.

A critique and prognosis

The stabilization programmes advocated by the IMF stress the control of the money supply and credit (through interest rates) as a key monetary policy instrument. Silumbu (1995) provides empirical evidence of the uncertainty of some of the macroeconomic policies of SAPs on economic performance in an African context. Based on 26 African countries his results show a diminished but positive effect of money and credit on real income during the 1980s (the early implementation years of SAPs) compared to the 1960s and 1970s (the pre SAPs years). This suggests the appropriateness of using more directly growth-oriented policies.

Vandermoortele (1994) in a study of the impact of austerity budgeting in Malawi, suggests that the manner in which fiscal restraint is undertaken can be counter-productive. Firstly, inefficiencies can be promoted in some sectors of the public service starved of working capital because of cuts in the "goods and services" element of the recurrent budget. Secondly, key investment elements of the development budget can be adversely affected. Both could be detrimental to the government activity required for human development which is a key factor in long-term industrial and general development, and is one aspect in which sub-Saharan Africa countries have been found critically wanting (Lall, 1990).

Bourguignon, Branson, and de Melo (1992) have argued that the advocated macroeconomic packages, because of their excessive demand management policies, are inimical to the removal of some of the structural bottlenecks, for example, inadequate and deteriorating economic infrastructure and supply responses. Thompson (1992) has also attacked the packages as being excessively oriented towards export-performance to ensure foreign debt payments. These tend to be high and constitute huge drains on the economies, suffocating them of much needed foreign reserves for physical and working capital. Output and employment performance in the productive sectors are also impaired while cuts in the social services have their own adverse distributional effects which negatively affect the demand for goods from key sectors such as industry.

The hope for African development lies in the exploitation of the duality and disequilibrium among sectors by promoting high productivity activities, for example, industry and exports as opposed to agriculture and the manufacture of goods for the domestic market. Needless to say, these avenues are likely to be more technology-intensive. But the benefits of large scale production (economies of scale) would also be quite significant in some cases especially where both domestic and foreign markets can be simultaneously exploited. The reduction of internal and external bottlenecks would be necessary for promoting such activities and government action, including expenditure, would feature prominently, for example, in promoting science-oriented education and improving economic infrastructure in any form, physical, human, or financial.

The proponents of SAPs have implicitly advocated quick structural adjustment by the movement of economies into sure-fire export areas which would necessarily be in, or close to, the traditional export avenues dictated by short-term comparative advantage. Yet, stable and sustainable adjustment and development would require a longer-term view of the dynamics and a somewhat more activist role for governments. Industry must be given the opportunity and time to restructure and gear itself for export orientation which requires costly inputs into reducing the infrastructural bottlenecks. For sub-Saharan Africa to feature in the non-traditional export market, it has been argued that in view of the friction of space and wide dissimilarities, for example, in technology and factor productivity, between those countries and the North, there is need for trade reorientation towards regional markets (UNIDO, 1990). This would more readily accommodate the exports which currently face high entry barriers in the North. But this will also be long-term and requires government facilitation.

Market prices reflect the economic situation as it is and not necessarily as it will be or should be. Markets can therefore coordinate current production decisions but may not help in the type of restructuring or reorientation that would be envisaged for sub-Saharan Africa. Singer (1950) and Prebisch (1959) had pointed out the need for government strategic intervention in the industrial sector. Their argument was based on the observation that static comparative advantage, as revealed by current prices, and which for Africa would favour the primary sector, could not capture secular trends. For example, differences in price and income elasticities between primary and manufactured goods would mean that the export of raw materials could not pay for manufactured imports in the long-run. Apart from being another argument for economic diversification through industrialization, it is also one for at least a strategic role for government in the industrialization process.

There is increasing consensus about the critical and strategic role of government intervention in the lessons of the successful industrializing East Asian countries (Pack and Westphal, 1986; Shapiro and Taylor, 1990; Pack, 1988; Griffin, 1989) and, more recently, for Mauritius (Bheenick and Schapiro, 1989). In fact, it has been argued that all governments engage in industrialization strategies and that no country has entered into modern economic growth without the state's targeted intervention or collaboration with large-scale private entities (Shapiro and Taylor, 1990). UNCTAD (1994) strongly endorses this view. However, the role of the state cannot be the same at all times and in all economic and political contexts. The external political and economic environment, consisting of the debt burden and IMF/World Bank conditionality, makes it difficult to apply measures that may have been successfully applied elsewhere, for example, targeted subsidies or to attract foreign investment into domestic-oriented industries through protection.

Depending on country size, Shapiro and Taylor (1990) offer a menu which can be judiciously used in an industrial strategy. The following is an extended version of their menu:

1 The creation of either a centralized or decentralized (through development banks, planning ministries, producers organizations, and so on) collection of highly able and politically backed people to guide industry through consultations among the state, producers, and export and labour organizations;

2 The provision of venture capital and long-term investment and finance at favourable interest rates through development banks which themselves should be capable to undertake project development.

3 The state can give support in the form of incentives to "thrust industries" but must be prepared to withdraw such support if firms do not meet performance criteria such as export expansion or use of best-practice techniques;

4 The incentive menu which can include, among other things, import bans, import tariffs, and cheap credit must be weighed against whether they add to or drain the treasury; whether they promote rent- seeking activities; their effects on the rest of the economy; and their administrative difficulty;

5 Performance criteria for meriting the incentives should be straightforward and transparent;

6 Gearing up the health and education sectors for supporting national and industrial technological capability;

7 The state's investment programme should be designed to raise productivity in both the public and private sectors. Consequently, the state should be ready and willing to invest in areas which will attract and facilitate private investment;

8 Minimize distortions from market signals and;

9 Improve and maintain the economic infrastructure (power, water, sanitation, roads, telecommunications, and the financial sector).

In the present context of globalized competition in manufactures, the critical role of scarce resources cannot be exaggerated. These include finance capital, technical skills, entrepreneurship, economic infrastructure, and foreign exchange. As the state facilitates the improvement of the financial sector and human capital, it can also do a lot in the short-run through strong incentives for foreign investors to infuse foreign capital and skills into export-oriented or key utility industries through joint ventures or other arrangements including tax incentives.

Infrastructural projects, which are increasingly becoming costly and burdensome for domestic budgets (UNIDO, 1990), could be one area in which the state should actively seek foreign assistance. Also, debt repayment obligations constrain domestic economic growth generally and particularly constrain the performance of heavily import-dependent industries. In order to address these problems it is in their interests for African states to canvass for debt remission and to advance industrial integration, for example, through the promotion of the domestic sourcing of inputs. The latter could be another important element of performance criteria that could be used for meriting incentives. But this would invariably involve the state taking a key role in industrial research and technology development centres.

Conclusions

The combination of macroeconomic and market reforms under SAPs have obviated the role of the state in influencing the pace and the direction of industrialization which is vital for the transformation of African economies. Most of the market reforms were expected to worsen the exposure of African industry at the firm level and yet there was little that had been done to cushion or reduce the adverse effects. Moreover, contractionary macroeconomic measures have severely limited the role the state could play in investment with a long-term strategic impact such as in all forms of infrastructure (including finance, communications, utilities, human capital, and so on. The emerging wisdom is that African states ought to resume such investments and other selective interventions and this assumes greater urgency given the fragility of their industrial sectors and the weight of competition from globalized trade. Some of these will require recourse to external funding and in this respect debt forgiveness would play an important role.

7 Some constraints of structural adjustment on the production of peasants in Malawi

Pacharo H. Simukonda

There is perhaps no other country in sub-Saharan Africa more dependent on agricultural production for economic prosperity than Malawi. But because much of Malawi's agricultural output comes from peasant activities, state policy has been directed towards supporting this sector so that it can continue to play its role of contributing not only to wider national economic and welfare goals but also to allow the peasant population to meet their consumption and economic needs. This support has included state delivery of agricultural inputs and the purchasing of all the surplus produce offered for sale. This, in turn, has necessitated the subsidizing of inputs and the institutional delivery system. It is the economic burden implied by the subsidy which Malawi's structural adjustment programmes (SAPs) have, among other things, aimed at removing or reducing, in order to improve the performance of the market delivery system, peasant production, and the national economy.

This chapter attempts to show how Malawi's SAPs may have acted to constrain, rather than stimulate, peasant production. It further examines the implications for national agricultural input and output supply, and economic progress and welfare in the context of the liberalization of agricultural marketing.

The peasant sector in Malawi's economy

Malawi attained independence in 1964 with an entirely agricultural economic base and as one of the poorest countries in the world. Although agriculture accounted for about 58 percent of GDP then and its share has since been steadily declining (to 40 percent in 1979, 36 percent in 1987 and 31 percent in 1992), it has remained the base of the economy. Almost all export earnings have been from agricultural products and domestic industry has been dominated by agro-based and import-substitution activities.

The agricultural sector itself is of a dual structure comprising private estates and the much larger peasant sub-sector. The former is confined to the high value export crops - tobacco, tea, and sugar, which together accounted for almost 87 percent of export earnings in 1990, with tobacco alone accounting for more than 70 percent (Government of Malawi, 1971; 1980; 1988; 1992). The rest of the crops include cotton, coffee, rice, and groundnuts, all of which (except coffee) are grown by the peasantry and are mostly consumed domestically.

The significance of the peasant sector

The peasant sector is much larger than the private estate sector both in terms of the amount of land held (about 86 percent) and the volume of production (about 72 percent). At the time of independence the estate sector had shrunk to about 3 percent of the land from about 16 percent at around 1900 (Pachai, 1978). The government soon after independence embarked on a policy of promoting both peasant and estate production, and with the entry by indigenous Malawians into tobacco farming, the estate sub-sector rapidly expanded. In the process, there was a reduction in the proportion of the value of peasant production. Nevertheless, the peasant sector has remained significant for a number of reasons.

In the first place, about 88 percent of Malawi's ten million population is rural based and dependent on subsistence production (Government of Malawi, 1987). Secondly, it is from the small household surpluses that this sub-sector is able to produce that the state is able to mobilize a significant proportion of the national marketed output. About 30 percent of peasant production is considered to be marketed output. In addition, this sector accounts for a much larger proportion of the agricultural labour force of approximately 89 percent (World Bank, 1989c). Lastly, it is the peasant sector which supplies most of the domestic consumption requirements in terms of food supplies and agro-industrial raw materials, as the estate sector is primarily export-oriented.

Malawi's approach to supporting peasant agriculture

The Malawi government has sought to stimulate peasant agricultural production within the framework of rural development projects (RDPs) and schemes. These are of an area-bound and multi-sector type (Chambers, 1974; Lele, 1975), and are considered to provide the best possible basis for organizing and controlling the numerous independent producers and also for organizing the provision of extension and input supply services.

The approach has passed through several stages of refinement with respect to intensity of institutional service support and demographic coverage. Prior to and around independence, emphasis was on provision of agricultural extension services to peasants cultivating crops of their own choice on their own customary land, under the expectation that they would positively respond to government market advice, support, and producer prices. Input credit was only provided to a select few who were considered the more responsive farmers. Soon after, a programme of special crops schemes was embarked upon and supported by bilateral technical assistance (mainly British, Taiwanese, and Israeli). Based on the success of these largely experimental schemes, a programme comprising four regional integrated rural development projects was embarked upon in 1968 with World Bank financing. From 1978, this programme was extended to the rest of the peasant sector under the National Rural Development Programme (NRDP) and organized under eight agricultural development divisions (ADDs) with each comprising two or more development areas on the basis of which an RDP would be implemented. The NRDP was planned to be implemented over a twenty-year period under a scheme of priorities (Government of Malawi, 1977).

Institutional support services were provided through the government administrative structure (for all production related activities) and the parastatal, the Agricultural Development and Marketing Corporation (ADMARC) (for input supply and produce marketing), in a closely related manner. The two converge at the level of input credit administration, as the RDP management has both acted as credit guarantor and distributed credit inputs obtained from ADMARC to producers. Not all peasant households, however, have had equal access to these institutional services. The intensity of such services has been much greater in, and input credit has been confined to, funded RDPs. Even so, not all households within RDP areas are participants in the production scheme. Also, participants who fail to repay their credit in full are denied further credit and, in the specialist schemes, this, plus failure to comply with production procedures, has resulted in evictions (Simukonda, 1994).

The above framework suggests that the success in stimulating peasant production rests on meeting several interrelated conditions. The first is the existence of an adequate level of institutional support services for imparting the necessary knowledge of production, organizing and controlling producer behaviour, supplying the necessary agricultural inputs, and marketing the surplus output realized. The second is the need for a pricing policy that allows the generation of an income level which not only enables acquisition of the necessary inputs but also encourages higher adoption levels. And above all, there is need for a strategy that aims at raising the productivity of peasant labour particularly in the context of a land constraint. These considerations point to a close interrelationship between production and marketing.

Generally, the Malawi government has been pursuing a policy of relatively low producer prices while subsidizing agricultural input costs, ostensibly with the purpose of serving wider economic and welfare goals (Kydd and Christiansen, 1982). While subsidizing inputs may have permitted higher adoption and production levels, the overall effect of such a policy may have been to subsidize almost every section of the national socio-economy to the extent that government began to run into chronic economic problems. This, in turn, necessitated policy reform.

Overview of structural adjustment programmes in Malawi

Malawi's SAPs were aimed at improving overall economic performance, and specifically at reducing or eliminating budget deficits by raising incomes and revenues chiefly through diversification of income sources, raising taxes and duties, and improving economic management. This was in line with the general methodological objectives of SAPs. More specifically, the aim of SAPs is to alter the relative prices and structure of incentives through initiatives that raise the incentive for production of tradeables relative to non-tradeables (Sahn, Arulpragasam, and Merid, 1990). The main target of Malawi's SAPs was the agricultural sector because it was the leading economic sector. And within this sector the focus of reform was on the peasant sub-sector.

Malawi undertook three major SAP reforms and a number of complementary reform measures in the 1980s under the framework of the World Bank's structural adjustment loans (SALs). But prior to SALs, Malawi had attempted to implement short-term demand-management policies, beginning in 1981 under the IMF's stand-by loan facilities. The first of these was meant, among other things, to raise government revenue, diversify revenue sources, cut expenditure, and diversify new credit in favour of private sector growth. But when these failed, owing to government's failure to reach a credit ceiling requirement, a second stand-by loan facility was provided. However, this also failed, and so necessitated a programme of structural adjustment loans.

The first structural adjustment loan (SAL I) provided in 1982 was, among other things, directed at raising the real GDP growth rate to 4.8 percent; diversifying sources of export revenue, while increasing the role of peasant production in export revenue generation; and improving internal and external balances through better financial management of public enterprises and the government budget. To achieve these objectives, SAL I addressed problems in such areas as the balance of payments, prices and incomes, resource management and institutional building; required substantial reviews of policy, prices, and several public enterprises; and recommended such specific measures as price liberalization, increased government revenue generation, and the strengthening of several public institutions, along with measures to raise prices of export crops and to make ADMARC more efficient.

Although the prices of some crops were adjusted and the Malawi currency (Kwacha) was devalued twice during the first two years, the economy actually declined. Expenditure growth rates rose faster than anticipated, government revenue growth fell as a percentage of GDP, and the overall returns to export crops fell. As a result, not only was a second SAL (SAL II) negotiated, but also its requirements were perhaps the most controversial with respect to the effects on peasant production.

Although SAL II involved efforts to raise producer prices, it also required changes in two main areas with the potential for negative impacts on the peasant sector. One was the removal of the peasant fertilizer subsidy in gradual steps, first in terms of the price, then in terms of the transport cost element. Meanwhile, a Smallholder Fertilizer Revolving Fund was to be created with IFAD/IDA/USAID funds to ensure the availability of fertilizers. The second involved efforts to improve ADMARC's performance, chiefly by reducing its marketing costs. Measures included reducing ADMARC's marketing activities to the more economical ones, limiting its operations to marketing and processing, and permitting the entry of private traders into produce marketing. It was also hoped that this would improve marketing and distribution while serving the interests of food self-sufficiency, export promotion, and crop diversification.

Rather unfortunately, these measures did not succeed in arresting the deteriorating economic performance so what followed under SAL III and subsequent aid packages were mainly monetary policy measures designed to stabilize the economy. An Agricultural Sector Adjustment Credit approved in 1990, for instance, included measures to: (1) allow the peasantry to cultivate the higher value barley tobacco variety previously limited to the estate sub-sector; (2) discourage the transfer of customary land to the estate sub-sector; (3) privatize fertilizer distribution; and (4) raise the maize producer price to reflect ADMARC's transportation costs.

Implications and effects

From the standpoint of the peasant sector, Malawi's SAPs have to be assessed on the basis of its potential to solve the very problem it perceived and sought to tackle in terms of the likely consequences. The main objective was to improve incomes for both peasant household producers and the government through improvements in marketing, particularly by a liberalization of produce marketing and the diversification of production of export crops. The context of the pre-SAP peasant sector "problem" comprises several inter-related elements, linked to institutional organization and policy issues, and centred on the hypothesis that peasant production and incomes were unnecessarily constrained. The first is that production was constrained by being confined to only a few marketable crops. This was because only a few crops were officially sanctioned and selected for state support (for both production and marketing). The second is that producer incentives were unnecessarily constrained by low incomes. Through its monopsonistic position, the state determined the producer income rate and, therefore, peasant production decisions, by both supplying agricultural inputs and purchasing the surplus output.

However, there are other considerations about peasant production and production decisions that SAPs ought to have considered. The first is that peasants face different degrees of production and marketing constraints or opportunities, based on how far or close they are from large urban areas which are the major markets. Since the market determines what can be produced and how much can be earned from it, the closer one is to a large urban area, the more opportunities one has for higher crop diversification and incomes, as the intensity of marketing activity follows the same pattern. The second relates to the relationship between landholding size and input prices in determining production levels and crop diversification. Producers can only realize their surplus production levels after meeting food security levels. With small landholdings these goals can be better realized with use of high yielding inputs (HYIs). But use of such inputs may not be possible when their prices rise (with the removal of the fertilizer subsidy) unless producer prices rise sufficiently to achieve a higher income rate. These conditions may not apply with regard to landholders who could not achieve a marketable surplus even with the use of HYIs.

The withdrawal of ADMARC from uneconomic markets and the liberalization of produce marketing, partly to replace ADMARC, have further implications. The first consideration here is whether private traders could sufficiently replace ADMARC in areas from which it had withdrawn and actually improve marketing performance. This aspect centres on the particular interests of the private traders, which are basically related to profitability. The second is whether it is possible to mobilize, organize, and regulate the numerous independent traders for purposes of achieving the economic and welfare (distributional) roles that the state attempted to achieve through ADMARC. Would private traders adequately play, for instance, the crucial roles of supplying inputs (including on credit), maintaining and raising rural incomes (through purchasing produce at a favourable price), and supplying food crops to urban households and food deficit rural households? The last consideration concerns the question of whether the objectives of SAPs pertaining to increasing export crop diversification could be realized under a vigorously competitive marketing activity without compromising the interests of household and national food security. A vigorous export drive policy seems to conflict with one based on promotion of food crop production since export crops are mainly of the non-food type such as tobacco, cotton, groundnuts, and so on. Below we examine the implications of these considerations.

The landholding constraint

Malawi is in the unenviable position of being faced with a land shortage problem due to its large and growing population. But the peasant population itself is not homogenous in terms of land resource endowment. In this context it can be classified into three main categories based on the relevance of landholding size to capacity for use of HYIs to achieve adequate levels of production to meet food security and income requirements. (1) Those households with up to 0.74 hectares (ha); (2) those with between 0.75 ha and 1.5 ha; and (3) those with over 1.5 ha. According to the available data, the respective proportions of peasant households in these categories as of 1985 were 56 percent, 20 percent, and 24 percent, respectively (Government of Malawi, 1986), and the overall average holding size was only 0.73 ha, which is estimated to decline to 0.45 ha by the year 2000, with the greater proportion of households falling into the lower categories (Christiansen and Southworth, 1988). According to calculations based on existing levels of technologies, only those households in the upper category could ever benefit from cash crop production. Those in the middle category, considered to have moderate potential, could only achieve a marketable surplus with use of HYIs while those in the bottom category could only operate at subsistence levels with a significant number facing chronic food deficits. The data also suggests that households with no more than 0.5 ha, all of whom planted local maize, could only achieve up to one-third of the required nutritional levels unless hybrid maize were planted and adequate levels of fertilizers used, in which case it would require only 0.4 ha to reach the nutritional requirement levels, assuming all the land were planted in hybrid maize (Government of Malawi, 1986; Kandoole, 1990). Under these circumstances, therefore, the solution to inadequate production levels lies in the intensification of production. But under what circumstances would this be possible?

However, in practice, very few households, have been planting hybrid maize or have been using fertilizers. The smaller the landholding the less the proportion of the land planted in hybrid maize and the lower the rate of fertilizer use. For instance, only 0.6 and 1.37 percent of the maize planted in 1984-85 was hybrid among landholders of less than 0.5 ha and 0.5-1.0 ha, respectively, compared to 15.5 percent for holdings of over 3.0 ha (Kandoole, 1990). This situation appears to be ironic, in the sense that smaller landholders need to use HYIs to meet at least their nutritional requirements. Apparently, at the centre of this problem lies the production risk factor. The smaller the landholding the lower is the potential to realize adequate surplus levels to pay for the use of HYIs. Therefore, when HYIs prices rise it becomes more difficult to acquire them or to repay the input credit since under conditions of inadequate land size such inputs may be used only for the aim of raising food production levels.

Input (fertilizer) price increase

Available data suggest that during the 1980s when the Malawi government implemented the Smallholder Fertilizer Subsidy Removal Programme (SFSRP), under SAPs, there were both rising input prices and a generally declining performance of the peasant agricultural sector. The programme involved removal of the subsidy gradually in five years beginning in 1984-85 from the 30.5 percent level of 1983. But after four years, when the subsidy rate reached 19.8 percent, the government suspended the programme and the rate was restored to 29.7 percent in 1988-89. Although during this time producer prices sharply increased for all crops, exogenous cost effects pushed fertilizer prices well above the level that would have resulted from the removal of the subsidy. These included rising import costs due to closure of the more economical Mozambique routes, rising world market prices for inputs, and the devaluation of the Malawi Kwacha. As a result, in real terms, producer prices for maize, for instance, fell from K0.0791/kg in 1983-84 to K0.0462/kg in 1987-88. Only when the subsidy removal programme was suspended did the real producer price rise to K0.0522/kg. However, it was still below the price of the pre-SFSRP period (Sahn, Arulpragasam, and Merid, 1990).

This situation apparently had adverse effects on adoption rates and, therefore, on crop production. For instance, although the total maize production area increased slightly from 1,182,601 ha to 1,272,400 ha, that was accounted for by an increase in the production of the local maize variety, whose proportion of hectarage increased steadily from 90.3 to 95.7 percent by 1986-87. Although the hectare proportion for hybrid maize increased from 1987-88, it was too low generally, and at 6.7 percent had not been restored to the pre-programme levels. The estimated production levels were also declining during the period as well as per capita production levels and average yields (Government of Malawi, 1989). The fact that performance trends were reversed when the SFSRP was suspended points to the significance of the effects of input price increases. However, since it is the implied cost levels that are significant in input use, the suspension of the programme could only have had temporary effects. It is therefore not surprising that the situation got worse in the 1990s. During this time input credit demand declined as many producers became ineligible for further credit for failing to honour their past debts in full. This resulted from rising costs of production and falling (real) income levels which were exacerbated by the drought conditions.

Privatization of agricultural marketing

The withdrawal of ADMARC's marketing services from the more uneconomic, often remoter areas, and the liberalization of marketing by the introduction of private trader activity created several problems, both implied and real. In the first place, ADMARC not only supplied the input requirements for those who would normally not be able to obtain them on their own, from whatever source, but also it bought any surplus output offered by households, no matter how little. This had several advantages. On the one hand, the smaller producers were able to acquire inputs without incurring prohibitive transport costs. This at least avoided situations of food deficits. On the other hand, they were able and willing to sell any surplus they had and thereby enhance their income requirements. This situation also had the advantage of economies of scale. Through ADMARC the government was able to mobilize surplus contributions from numerous small producers into significant levels of national surplus to serve wider economic and welfare (food supply) goals.

Private traders could serve this function well only if they could sufficiently penetrate the countryside and offer satisfactory prices. But there are some inherent weaknesses. In contrast to ADMARC which could maintain uneconomic operations through state subsidies, private traders are driven by the ability to realize profits. As such, they will not operate in those areas where the volume of trade is not sufficient to recover transport and other operational costs. In practice they have not been able to sufficiently penetrate the remote areas, and where they have, they have normally offered prices that are too low to maintain producer enthusiasm or serve producer cash needs (Kaluwa, 1990). Also, private traders have not adequately played the input supply role because they prefer to deal with outputs from which they expect to realize higher profits on the urban consumer market. Basically, they find the input supply trade to be of a high risk due to the low income capacity of peasant households. The same is true with regard to supplying food crops to food deficit rural dwellers. By contrast, ADMARC had the advantage of maintaining depots for both agricultural inputs and food crops, all of which, however, eventually contributed to its budgetary problems.

The result of this has been a tendency towards the concentration of trading activity in areas close to urban areas. This has had some disadvantages. Due to a combination of cost and income sensitivity and imperfections in the market information system, private traders have tended to compete against, rather than complement, ADMARC, and in the process the developmental, economic and/or welfare goals may have been significantly compromised. The drive for profitability among private traders has also had several further effects. In one sense the traders pre-empted ADMARC by commencing their operations soon after or during harvest time and long before ADMARC commenced its own. Taking advantage of the peasants' desperate income needs they have offered low prices. But they have also left ADMARC with little to purchase. Although part of the intention of the liberalization programme was that ADMARC should be the buyer of last resort, it is not clear how ADMARC's operational costs could have been reduced if it ended up buying very little while maintaining large fixed administrative overheads.

Differential pricing by area, and/or by period of time, may not have helped the peasants' socio-economic situation. Unlike ADMARC's national uniform prices, private traders have taken advantage of ample supplies of crops at the beginning of the marketing season to offer lower prices, just as they have taken advantage of the low competition level in the remoter parts. But while they have continued to do this in the case of the remote rural areas, in the areas close to urban centres prices tend to rise sharply as the supplies begin to decline and ADMARC joins the market. The overall effect is, on the one hand, to differentiate the peasantry by area in terms of earning capacity, and on the other, to entice households, at times of intense trader activity, into selling more of their output than they ought to in the interest of maintaining necessary food supplies (Chilowa, Kandoole, and Musukwa, 1990). When households run out of food stocks they have to purchase them at a much higher price, if available at all. Yet, often they cannot afford to do so as they may have already spent their earnings soon after getting them.

Another effect of marketing liberalization has been the tendency to cultivate those crops with the highest private trader demand. Because these are often very few, mostly food crops, the result has been to divert attention from such crops as cotton and groundnuts which are of equal national importance. Also, it has not been easy to control private traders with respect to the disposal of the output purchased. Often traders seek the most profitable outlet and in this context they prefer to export their produce under private arrangements. This tends to compromise national economic interests because the trade is often on barter terms. It also compromises the nation's ability to secure necessary food supplies to feed the urban population and the food deficit rural households. Under this situation the government has had to import food crops, using scarce foreign exchange, or depend on food aid, both of which present a negative perception about national economic performance.

Conclusions

Although Malawi's SAPs were intended to improve national economic performance by, among other things, reforming peasant agricultural policy, they have not achieved the intended results. In fact, they seem to have done more harm than good. Cutting back on ADMARC's operations to improve its efficiency and reduce costs has created a socio-economic gap within and among the peasantry. It is perhaps true that ADMARC had been offering prices that were too low to provide producer incentives. However, the alternative, as perceived in the objective context of SAPs, has not yielded better results. ADMARC offered uniform prices throughout, and bought "every" crop offered that the producers were able and/or willing to cultivate.

By contrast, private traders being driven by the profit motive have been selective in the crops they buy, the areas in which they operate, and the prices they offer at any point in time. As a result they have not sufficiently penetrated the countryside and they have also differentiated the peasantry. They have also not played the distributional and input supply roles well, and by their specific market demands, they have promoted production of certain crops at the expense of other equally important ones and to the detriment of both peasant and national consumer welfare. Moreover, the removal of peasant fertilizer and other institutional subsidies has tended to raise production costs beyond what the producers could afford in the interest of technology adoption. Not only have producers been less willing to use such technologies, but also of more serious effect, most producers facing a land constraint have been unable to use them for purposes of raising productivity levels to achieve food security levels.

It appears that the root of the problem lay in a policy of subsidizing urban consumers in the first place. A simpler perception is that the removal of such subsidies would have reduced ADMARC's operational costs and made agricultural production more attractive. Private traders would then have taken advantage of the higher consumer prices by intensifying trading activities which would have increased producer prices, and which, in turn, would have stimulated further production. The resulting increased producer incomes would then have enabled producers to use more HYIs for even higher production and incomes. It is in that context that the input subsidy removal was to be gradually implemented, at rates that would have ensured that producer incentives were maintained. That would, undoubtedly, have served well the goals of increased marketed output and household food security.

8 Structural adjustment and the myth of its success in Ghana

Kwame Frimpong

Much has been said and written about the success story of structural adjustment programmes (SAPs) in Ghana. This is such a widely-held belief and an accepted fact throughout most of the world, that it is a difficult task to contradict it. One faces an uphill battle in trying to prove otherwise. But the truth is that all is not well with the Ghanaians, especially those at the lower socio-economic levels of the ladder.

In this chapter, a very strong case is made which challenges the so-called success story of Ghana's SAPs. It is not so much the evidence that is adduced that is so essential to the author, but rather the exposure of the falsity to the reader so that the proponents and supporters of SAPs may want to reconsider their stance and more importantly re-evaluate the framework of the whole SAPs concept.

A conscious effort has been made to avoid the excessive use of literature and data in this chapter. The facts are based substantially on participant observation during my residence in Ghana (August 1978 to October 1984), and my many visits to the country during the period 1988-94.

Ghana's economy prior to structural adjustment

In October 1979 Ghana returned to civilian rule after successive military régimes had ruled the country from 1972. The civilian government which came to power in 1979 was, by all accounts, incapable of managing the affairs of the country and there were many cases of serious mismanagement in many sectors of the economy. Many people were therefore dissatisfied and disappointed thus providing a catalyst for coup-plotters and power mongers to seize power by undemocratic means, and also making it possible for the coup to gain support among some sectors of the population. On 31 December 1981 the soldiers did indeed seize power again and the civilian government which had been in power for a little more than two years was forced out of office.

The economy before the coup was tightly monitored primarily through the use of import and export controls. Many essential commodities were difficult to acquire. One's access to these items depended largely either on one's status in the society or on one's connections to the right sources. During this period the "chit-system" became very well-entrenched in the economy. Through this system one had to obtain a piece of paper, the "chit", from the right person in authority, to enable one to purchase items. This was a system which had been introduced during the First Republic under Kwame Nkrumah's government in order to maximize both economic and political power in the hands of the ruling Convention People's Party (CPP) and to neutralize the power of the opposition forces. Every successive government also sought to use the "chit-system" to its advantage. It was therefore not surprising that the civilian government which was voted into power in October 1979 found itself relying on the same crude methods to raise funds for its party and also to entrench itself in power.

The "chit-system" unduly interfered with the normal free operation of the economy. It was an unfair system which favoured the rich and/or the highly placed individuals who by their profession or status were in a better position to have access to all that they needed. The system nevertheless worked to the benefit of most Ghanaians. At the end of the day each one would have found a way of getting access to something. However, it was not surprising that Ghanaians were popularly dubbed as "magicians". What happened was that through the extended family system and obviously through other connections, such as church organizations, social clubs and educational fraternities, one would invariably have a connection to something. Thus if "A" had rice he would make the best of it, either by distributing to others connected to him/her or, depending on the quantity, may decide to reap the highest profit from that rice by selling some to "X" and "Y" and so on. The same cycle would repeat itself if "X" or "Y", for example, were to acquire any other commodity or any other food item or clothing.

It was a popular joke in those days for the lives of Ghanaians to be likened to the fishes in the sea who survived by living on one another. The bigger fishes would eat the smaller fishes but the fishes in the sea have never been depleted. The peak was reached between 1972 and 1979 when Ghana was under a military régime. It was during that period that the term *kalabule* was introduced. Literally, it means economic prosperity by dishonest means. It simply depicted the highest form of corruption ever witnessed in Ghana.

The coup of 31 December 1981

The socio-economic and political situation in Ghana as depicted above was not pleasant for many residents and therefore some of the citizens would accept any measure which promised to bring them relief. The coup of 31 December 1981 was therefore most welcome to some of the citizens. But whether the coup was justified is a different issue. As far as this author is concerned, this was an act of treason against a lawfully constituted civilian régime. The constitutional means for changing that régime had not been lost to anyone and therefore there could be no justification for the military intervention. In support of this view, Boahen (1992: 38) states: ".....as I argued in my first lecture, under no circumstances besides a fragrant abuse of the constitution should a civilian régime that has not run its full term of office be overthrown through military action".

Basically the coup victors promised a better life for all. The most popular slogan was that "all Ghanaians were equal, and that no one was above another". For instance, it was stressed that everyone was an expert in his or her field. To carry the concept of equality beyond logical reasoning it was argued that it was not only the academics at the university who could be professors. A labourer, for example, could also be classified as a professor in his/her field just as a farmer could also be called a professor. The slogan was carried to its absurd limits when ordinary illiterate farmers, fishermen, and traders were packed together in 1992 as members of the Constituent Assembly to approve a constitution for Ghana's alleged return to civilian rule.

Some other aspects of the equality slogan were put into practice. A notion was created that the failure of a section of the population to succeed was attributable to the success of others. In order for the former to succeed economically, socially, and politically, the latter must be forced either to give up their privileged positions or to take the "never-do-wells" (failures) on board. As a consequence, ordinary messengers were insisting on being recognized as board members of corporations. For example, there is an incident which took place at the University of Ghana in the 1980s when an employee who was responsible for taking care of the animals for the research work of the Faculty of Agriculture was alleged to have refused to do his work but insisted instead that the Professor and Head of the Department should do it since they were equal. The result of the slogan was therefore "indiscipline" in the economic and social realms of the entire Ghanaian society.

Thus, two sets of opposing classes were created in the country overnight. The "successful" as opposed to the "failures". The myth was created that every successful Ghanaian had cheated in order to reach his position and was therefore the enemy of the "imaginary revolution" and must be hunted and "exterminated". On the other hand, the "failures" were the salt of the nation who must take the law into their own hands (stand for their rights) in order to defend the revolution and reap the benefits of the revolution. The most popular slogan was in the pidgin English: "we no go sit down let them cheat us again". This meant that we are not going to allow others to have the upper hand over us and it was directed at those who had been socially, economically, or academically successful. It suddenly became a crime to own a car, a house, or anything else of substance, especially if the item was of a very precious nature or classified as "posh", for example. Even one of the Secretaries of the régime officially declared that it was an offence to wear a suit. The so-called "defenders of the revolution" thus started to dress shabbily, in opened shirts, opened sandals ("charlie wotes" - a type of bush sandals), and bushy and unkempt hair. Poverty and failure in society, academically, socially, and economically became a virtue to aspire to. Very well known failures in the society were suddenly catapulted into national prominence.

The régime had initiated its economic and social policies under the notion that the country's social and economic woes were the making of the western world. International organizations such as the World Bank and International Monetary Fund (IMF) were branded as the enemies of the revolution. All those who had previously negotiated or were advocating a continuous dialogue with the those institutions were either "stooges" of western imperialism and capitalism or were enemies of the "people's power". It was, however, imperative that some form of negotiation with the World Bank and IMF should take place at least for the rescheduling of Ghana's huge international debt obligations which had resulted from the mismanagement by previous successive governments, especially by the military régimes. It was at the first encounter with the IMF and World Bank officials that the régime was awakened to the realities of the world economic order. The régime had sent some of their "ordinary supporters" for the negotiation and it is alleged that they had gone in their usual shabby costumes. The officials of the two institutions refused to meet them and stated openly that they do not recognize them. That was the turning point of the régime's avowed aim of refusing to deal with those western institutions. It dawned on them that behind the rhetoric and slogans one had to be much more serious.

Structural adjustment and economic recovery

The economic situation in the country was precarious. Ghana was being squeezed beyond the breaking point. No country was willing to give credit to a nation which had preached self-reliance and denounced all the hands that fed it. Petrol became one of the most difficult items to obtain. At times one had to spend three nights in a queue in order to have access to about two litres of petrol which might not be enough to get one back to one's home. It was as if even nature was against the very system that was being advocated and created. The country then suffered its worst drought and famine in human memory. This was followed by a massive destruction of agriculture produce as a result of an outbreak of bush fires across most parts of the nation. Most citizens were reduced to eating almost anything they could lay their hands on. There were many reported cases of people dying from eating poisonous roots and leaves. Most Ghanaians became skeletons overnight and were nicknamed "Rawlings chains".

In its desperation, the régime had to make an about turn. It was to the very institutions they had denounced and maligned that they had to turn. This time, they sent respectable members of the society and they went in their three-piece suits. In short, the foregoing explains the origins of Ghana's structural adjustment programmes. The régime was forced to accept all the prescriptions that were handed down by the IMF and the World Bank. Most analysts of the events were shocked to learn that this had happened given the régime's previous stance. If it had to remain in power, which it was desperate to do at any cost, it had to go along with the policies of the international financial institutions.

Initially, the régime's contact with the IMF and the World Bank was a guarded secret. However, the news soon started filtering out to the wider public. Once they tasted the fruits of the interaction with the IMF and the World Bank and realized that they could assist in reducing the hardships on the people of Ghana there was no turning back. In order to implement structural adjustment, the régime introduced its Economic Recovery Programme (ERP) in 1983.

Both sides found the incongruous relationship an essential one. On the side of the military régime in Ghana, they had no means of egress. They had reached a *cul-de-sac* and the assistance of the international financial institutions was a most welcome and face-saving intervention. Even though the relationship was contrary to their public utterances, they realized that if their régime was to survive they had to accept structural adjustment. For the two international financial institutions, they were now pleased to find a most willing partner. For them it would be easy for the policies to be implemented. The country was in dire need of the infusion of capital into the economy.

Secondly, and more importantly, the country was ruled under a military dictatorship which would be able to force the policies through. It was not accountable to any electorate. So long as the soldiers were in the streets it would be able to strengthen its position, sustain its power, and suppress any form of opposition either to its hold on power or to its implementation of structural adjustment. This view finds support in Amoako-Adu (1985) who stated that: "No civilian government could have devalued the cedi by that magnitude, raised energy prices, imposed heavy excise duty on beer, decontrolled all prices but 23 items, and stayed in power to implement its programmes". Thus a new relationship was born which for all intents and purposes was inconsistent with normal practices in international relations.

The first and most important flaw in that relationship was the fact that the IMF and World Bank, which under normal circumstances would have been expected to assist with the development of democracies, were the very ones who made it possible for a military dictatorship to be propped up and sustained. So long as a willing recipient had been found for the implementation of their policies it mattered less what form of government was in power. Thus, economic policies were of paramount importance rather than the political and social rights of the people of Ghana. The infant democracy initiated under the previous civilian régime was thus killed and its light faded away. The régime became more confident and more ruthless as it became a centre of attraction for the two international financial institutions. No one sees the problem better than Adjei (1994: 7) who observed:

> Contrary to all expectations, the suffering Ghanaian people have witnessed

> the world community, especially Western countries, channelling more aid to Ghana than ever before. It is estimated that about five billion dollars in aid have been pumped into Ghana over the past seven years by the International Monetary Fund, governments, and other international organizations.

He adds further:

> For some strange reason it is only when Ghana gets tyrannical leaders that it receives substantial foreign aid from the West. Could this be taken to mean that the Western governments prefer dealing with Ghanaian dictators? If the answer is Yes, then why all the hypocrisy about democracy?

A two pronged world-wide propaganda was initiated. First the World Bank and IMF wanted to prove that there had been at least one success story of its SAPs and therefore more and more capital was pumped into the system to make it work. Second, the régime needed international recognition and acceptance so it also initiated its own propaganda. The well-known and influential newspapers were inundated with advertisements of the economic growth of the country.

The nature of the success story

The most often cited basis for the acclaimed success story in Ghana's structural adjustment is the continuous growth in the GDP and GNP. It is constantly suggested, since the SAPs were introduced that the GDP or the GNP has been growing steadily between 5 percent and 10 percent. I am not in a position to dispute these figures since they are mere statistical information which emanate from the régime and we all know what statistical data can mean to the one who has the information. However, for purposes of our discussion, let us assume that the figures are correct. The most important issue for our consideration is the relationship between structural adjustment and the social and economic lives of the Ghanaians. For one can have growth in GDP or the GNP but if it is not translated into real economic value to the citizens who are the best judges of the determination of success or otherwise, then the claim of success is only in theory.

Wherein lies the success story?

The financial situation We begin with the financial situation. At the time of the coup, the official exchange rate between the Cedi (the Ghanaian currency) and the US dollar was C2.75 to the dollar. There is no doubt that the Cedi was overvalued. The black market rate was between 30 to 35 Cedis to the dollar. What is the situation now after the structural adjustment intervention? Currently, the official rate is approximately 1,500 Cedis to the dollar. The initial policy was to bring the official exchange rate to the black market level. Apart from the official exchange rate, other legal avenues have been created for foreign exchange transactions. This has resulted from the licences granted to commercial agents to open foreign exchange (forex) bureaus which have sprang up in several parts of the country. They have their own rates which are different from the official rate used by the government. Their current rate is approximately 1,640 Cedis to the dollar. In addition, there still exists the black market rate which continues to exceed both the official rate and the rate offered by the forex bureaus.

The excessive drop in the value of the Cedi has resulted from massive devaluations over the past 13 years. The devaluation exercise was initiated in 1983 when the Cedi was devalued by as much as 800 percent and by 1985 it had been devalued by 1,827 percent (Amoako-Adu, 1985). The devaluation has continued to this day with the result that the Cedi is literally worth nothing. In real terms the cumulative effect of the devaluation of the Cedi at the current rate is equivalent to over 58,000 percent.

At the time of the coup, the highest denomination of the Cedi was the 50 Cedi note. The military régime seized all of those denominations under the pretext that the state of the economy did not justify the use of that high a denomination. But now, the country has a 5,000 Cedi denomination and it is even being rumoured in official circles that a 10,000 Cedi denomination has already been printed and is to be put into circulation soon. The situation is that in Ghana today ordinary transactions done by ordinary people are in millions of Cedis.

The cost of living situation The consequences of fiscal policy on the general cost of living for the average Ghanaian is not easy to assess. However, it is in this area that one is baffled by the claim that the Recovery Programme and structural adjustment have been successful in Ghana. If the economic policies cannot be translated into any quantifiable benefits to the citizens of the country, but have rather made their lives worse off than what prevailed before the introduction of the Economic Recovery Programme, then it is hard to accept the success story. At the end of the day, any success should be determined in human terms. The question which is constantly on the lips of most Ghanaians is that it appears that only the outside world knows of our success story and not the people who are expected to be the beneficiaries of that alleged success story. If the economic policies cannot be translated into real concrete benefits then the notion that Ghana has produced a success story is only utopian. The refusal of most Ghanaians to accept the claim of a success story is based on the analysis of the social status of the average Ghanaian under structural adjustment.

Food It is virtually impossible for most households to have three meals a day. Even one decent meal is a luxury to most homes. To be able to have any decent meal for a family of four one would need about 10,000 Cedis. The daily wage was only 1,200 Cedis and has now been raised to 1,700 Cedis, which is equivalent to US$1.00. But even with this increase in the daily wage the position of the average person has not been made better. The prices of some food items are equivalent to the daily wage, or in some cases even more. One tuber of yam, a very popular staple food item, costs between 1,200 and 1,700 Cedis. The price of a simple item like a loaf of bread is 1,000 cedis. There are many who resort to having only one meal a day. And even for those people the nutritional content is questionable. It is therefore not surprising that there are serious cases of malnutrition in Ghana. The Institute of Statistical, Social and Economic Research (ISSER) of the University of Ghana in a report (1994: 153-154) states:

> Evidence that serious nutritional problems remain in Ghana, especially among children and women, is illustrated by data from the national nutrition survey conducted by UNICEF in 1986 and reports from the Ministry of Health. The UNICEF Survey showed that 58.5 percent of pre-school children suffered from acute or chronic undernutrition; i.e. were underweight (weight-for-age). This was twice the level reported in the First National Nutrition Survey in 1961; 51.5 percent were stunted (height-for-age); 40.3 percent were wasted (weight-for-height); and 8 percent were clinically classified as suffering from marasmus and kwashiorkor (that is, were severely malnourished). In relation to women, data from the Ministry of Health found 70.1 percent of pregnant women who attended antenatal clinics to be anaemic by WHO standards... The high prevalence of malnutrition in Ghanaian women from all regions reveals a nationwide problem of malnutrition in this segment of the population.

There are many outside Ghana who are unable to accept the fact that food items are expensive. There is a simple explanation for that. The pricing of items is linked to the general economic forces operating in the country. As is discussed later, the price of petrol, for instance, influences the cost of many other commodities. As labour and other inputs become more expensive for the farmer then the unit cost also increases and affects the overall pricing of the commodity produced. A vicious cycle is thus created.

Health The difficult economic situation created by structural adjustment has led to a rapid decline in the health services in the nation as a whole with the rural areas being hit the severest. ISSER (1994: 150) stresses:

> The problem of disparities between regions in the availability of health care institutions is compounded by significant under-utilization of the available services. Out-patient attendances at the MOH institutions fell from 10-11 million in 1973 to about 3.7 million in 1992 mainly as a result

of declining standards or quality of service, including shortages of drugs, as well as MOH facilities at all levels requiring extensive rehabilitation, including basic infrastructure and medical equipment.

The lack of basic health facilities for the population, particularly in the rural areas, is so precarious that it has resulted in a very high mortality rate in the country. The commonest complaint from those working in the capital city of Accra is the frequency of travelling to their villages almost every weekend to attend the funeral services of departed relatives.

Most hospitals, as ISSER (1994) indicated above suffer from severe shortages of basic medical supplies. Most hospitals lack ordinary essential items such as drugs, syringes, and hospital beds. There are severe cases where some patients have to sleep on the floor. The problem is compounded by the introduction of the fee system in respect of medical services provided by the Ministry of Health. In the past, all medical services were free. But, with the introduction of the fee system, many have been facing difficulties in paying for medical services. For example, there are many cases where people just refuse to go to hospital simply because they cannot afford the cost of the service to be provided. If we consider that the daily wage has only recently been raised to 1,700 Cedis then obviously the cost of medical service is beyond the reach of most Ghanaians. The summary of the situation is given by ISSER (1994 :150) as follows: "In sum, total coverage and hence access to health services remains low. Services simply do not reach or are inaccessible to a large proportion of the population in need".

Education This is one area which is of a very serious concern to most Ghanaians, especially the educated ones. Education is a very important tool for the development and the future growth of any nation. Serious questions are therefore asked if any government with genuine intentions can choose to ignore its own educational system. While the Western countries are spending a large percentage of their national budgets on the advancement of their educational systems, especially in the field of science and technology, in the case of the developing countries, the converse is true, especially since the introduction of SAPs.

Substantial cuts have been requested under the understanding that there is overspending in this area. The hitherto government subsidies which made education virtually free to all Ghanaians have been removed. Now, both the poor and the rich are required to pay for the education of their children. The absurdity in the system is that it presupposes that all Ghanaians can afford to pay for the education received by their children. For example, the basic annual cost for sending a child to a Junior Secondary School (JSS) is approximately 230 000 Cedis. Even the highest paid civil servants, such as the Permanent Secretaries, find this cost prohibitive. At the universities, the government has introduced a loan scheme to maintain the students while tuition remains free. The amount of the loan which is provided, however, makes a mockery of the whole system. During the 1993-94 academic year the loan was 50,000 Cedis. It has since been increased to 150,000 Cedis per annum but it remains inadequate in relation to the real needs of the students.

The government's callous neglect of the education system can also be judged by the extensive deterioration of the infrastructure and the facilities which existed before the emergence of the military régime. The facilities and infrastructure had not been properly maintained. Further, government expenditure, even though in monetary terms it may appear to have increased, it is mainly for recurrent costs, especially for the payment of salaries and wages. The acquisition of basic items, such as books, does not fall within the government's priorities. The budgets submitted by educational administrators have always been substantially cut by the central government, thus making the running of the institutions virtually impossible.

While other nations are making education one of the key areas in their development programmes, in the case of Ghana, the position appears to be different. ISSER (1994: 147) states:

> In a fundamental sense, education is the key to human development and to widening the options of life for the individual and society as a whole. The 1991 UNDP Human Development Index (HDI) which is calculated on the basis of three highly interrelated variables - life expectancy, education and income - categorized Ghana as having "low human development" i.e. below 0.50. (This is within the index range of 0 to 1.0)... Thus, according to the World Bank, one area where there is a very clear difference between Ghana and the more successful fast-growing countries is in education... According to the World Bank, most successful countries had achieved near-universal literacy as a pre-condition to rapid economic growth compared to Ghana's literacy level of about 55 percent. Functional literacy is estimated to be only 35-40 percent.

One result of the restrictive measures on the funding of the education sector has been the high rates of drop outs from the formal educational system. There are many who cannot afford to send their children to school and there are many instances of the non-availability of facilities, such as classrooms, to cater for the education of the children. All of these factors have had negative effects on the academic standards in the country. The results from the first batch of the JSS examinations revealed a very serious weakness in the system when nearly 70 percent of the children were not successful.

The neglect of the educational system by the government can be judged further by the closure of all three of the country's universities from April until December 1995. The salaries for the academic staff were so low that they embarked on a strike to back their demands for better conditions of service. This resulted in the closure of the universities. Instead of responding to the demands, the government allowed the universities to be closed for that long a period. The result was that students who were scheduled to graduate in 1995 had to do so in 1996. This also disrupted the administration of the universities, in that the students who were to enter the universities for the 1995-96 academic year had to wait for one whole year for their admission. Eventually, when a settlement was reached, the highest annual salary agreed upon for the academic staff was a little more than 6 million Cedis for those with the rank of Professor. This was equivalent to US$4,000.

Housing and rentals Structural adjustment has also adversely affected the cost of housing and rentals. Items for building are too expensive. An average three bed-room house is estimated to cost about 80 million Cedis. This state of affairs also affects the rental costs.

The price of petrol Ever since the régime came to power, petrol has been one of the areas constantly subjected to price increases as a result of the imposition of very high taxes. The short-sightedness of the policy of increasing the price of petroleum products is that it has a spiral effect on all sectors of the economy. Many Ghanaians rely on privately-owned commercial vehicles for the transaction of most activities including commercial activities such as the conveying of agriculturally produced commodities from the rural to the urban centres. Expensive petrol therefore affects the pricing of other commodities.

The unemployment situation Another destructive outcome of structural adjustment has been the massive public sector retrenchment. In addition, the economy has not been expanding in order to absorb new trainees. University graduates spend at least two to four years before they are able to find employment.

The situation is worsened by the fact that the private sector, which under structural adjustment is expected to play a significant role in providing employment, has also been neglected. This neglect has arisen from the fact that the régime, from the early 1980s, deliberately fought a war against imaginary enemies - the local businesses - as part of its campaign and slogan that all successful Ghanaians were deemed to be responsible for the non-progression and failure of a section of the Ghanaian community. In the process, local entrepreneurship was destroyed. For example, successful businesses, such as B.A. Mensah Group of Companies and Appiah Minkah, were destroyed. The net effect is that very few Ghanaians have had the courage to remain operative in the private sector. Ghanaian ownership of businesses in the private sector amounts to only 1 percent. The remaining 99 percent is owned by foreigners. It thus raises doubts as to the sincerity of the government in restructuring the economy.

Migration The economic, social, and political situation has forced many Ghanaians to leave their country either to seek greener pastures, to escape persecution, or just to avoid any contamination by the régime. The escape from persecution and the refusal to collaborate with the régime was quite prevalent in the 1980s. This problem seems to have subsided since the alleged return to civilian rule in 1992.

The threat is, however, still there since the economic hardship has not abated.

The exodus has created a very serious case of brain drain and has affected many sectors of the economy, particularly in the area of education and health services. In the case of the health sector, ISSER (1994:150) states: "Ghana has trained fairly impressive numbers of medical personnel. Unfortunately, however, the years of economic decline have led, in the recent past, to a mass exodus of qualified people both from the public sector and private sector from Ghana". Such an exodus has detrimental consequences for the nation as a whole. Again, ISSER (1994:150) stresses that "About 965 doctors currently work in Ghana (one for 16,000 people) of whom 628 are in the public sector...."

Appraisal and comments

The problem with Ghana's recovery programme is that while the cost of its implementation is measured in foreign currencies, the effects are determined by the local currency. The expected beneficiaries do not receive their salaries measured in terms of foreign currencies. As a result, the hardship, both social and economic, has been exceedingly severe. The lot of Ghanaians has thus been worse than before the implementation of structural adjustment.

The problem is further aggravated by the maintenance of social, educational, and health facilities which require substantial importation of equipment from outside. Even agriculture, which can be said to be labour intensive, also requires a substantial importation of items such as tools, fertilizers, and insecticides. These items are also priced in foreign currencies. With the substantial devaluation of the Cedi, all of these items are too costly to acquire, and, as a consequence, there is not just stagnation in terms of national development, but a progressive deterioration.

Conclusions

There is a strong belief that both international and local propaganda has been orchestrated on the alleged success story of Ghana's structural adjustment. But to the average Ghanaian the alleged success story still remains a dream. The experience under structural adjustment has been a nightmare because of the untold hardships and sufferings both in human and material terms. Until there can be clear-cut concrete evidence that the very people for whom the policies are being pursued can claim to have any tangible benefits, this author and most Ghanaians do not understand why Ghana is alleged to have been a success story under structural adjustment.

The fact that the so-called success story of Ghana's ERP is not quite so has been corroborated by President Rawlings himself in his address to the nation on 2

January 1990 in which he stated:

> I should be the first to admit that the Economic Recovery Programme has not provided all the answers to our national problems. In spite of all the international acclaim it has received, the effects of its gains remain to be felt in most households and pockets. Many families continue to experience severe constraints on their household budgets. Notwithstanding the vast improvements in the supply of goods and services in the markets today, there are many who have found it difficult, during the past holiday season, to manage a modest celebration with a chicken for a meal or a new dress for a child or a bottle of schnapps for the folks back home. Meanwhile, we are now thinking of how to meet our rent, the next term's school fees, and all other routine expenses. These everyday difficulties which ordinary Ghanaians have to face make it hard for us to appreciate the significant gains we have made under the Economic Recovery Programme.

Part Three

ASSESSING THE IMPACT OF STRUCTURAL ADJUSTMENT PROGRAMMES: THE SOCIAL EFFECTS

9 Structural adjustment and the poverty principle in Africa

Gloria Jacques

The structure of the African economy is the underlying determinant of the continent's central condition of underdevelopment. The major problems of mass poverty, food shortage, low productivity, weak productive base, and backward technology are pathological issues arising from the structures of production, consumption, technology, and socio-political organization (UNECA, 1989). It is necessary, in order to address such issues, that structural analyses of the political economy of Africa be studied so that measures may be introduced to change the delinquent structures. It would seem that past and current policies for adjustment have, in most cases, neglected this vital element.

This chapter examines the situation of four countries in Africa (Malawi, Mozambique, Zambia, and Zimbabwe) with regard to economic privation and structural adjustment programmes (SAPs) and will also consider the concept of "adjustment with a human face" which arose out of the perceived deficiencies of adjustment programmes worldwide. Positive aspects of structural adjustment will be postulated as will two alternative approaches to the methods of the international financial institutions for getting struggling developing nations "back on track."

The conditions of poverty and structural adjustment programmes in Africa

In the 1970s African countries began experiencing a serious crisis which grew in magnitude and effect, particularly with respect to poverty and its concomitant problems (UNECA, 1989). Towards the end of that decade it was generally acknowledged that the situation had reached drastic proportions due, to some extent, to the world recession, the decline in prices for exports on which these countries depended for their foreign exchange, the rise in oil prices, and the decline in African food production. The situation was exacerbated by the dilemma inherent in external borrowing which assisted as crisis intervention but, in the long term, plunged the countries concerned into deeper and deeper debt.

Malawi

Malawi's real economic growth was favourable in the fifteen years following its independence in 1964. The economy registered an annual growth rate of 6.1 percent between 1964 and 1978 but this fell to 1.3 percent between 1978 and 1980, and all but stagnated between 1980 and 1982. The declining economic trend was also evident in decreasing employment creation, reduced export growth, unfavourable balance of payments, slow industrial capacity utilization, and a high rate of inflation (CSR, 1990).

External shocks contributing to this situation included rising import prices (especially for fuel) and falling export prices, rising transport costs due to the disruption of traditional sources through Mozambique, and severe drought which affected agricultural and export output and increased the importation of maize. Internal weaknesses in Malawi's economic structure such as the narrow export base, stagnant smallholder agriculture, heavy import dependency in the industrial and energy sectors, and inefficient public enterprises also contributed to the depressing scenario of decline (Kutengule, 1993).

From 1981 to the present time structural adjustment programmes have been implemented in collaboration with the World Bank and the International Monetary Fund. Their major instruments sought to reduce or eliminate subsidies on fertilizers, education, housing, health services, and food (especially maize meal); enhance the role of private traders and decontrol and liberalize prices and licensing measures; diversify the export base; devalue the currency; promote efficiency in parastatal organizations; enhance the marketing of smallholder agricultural produce; and reduce fiscal and balance of payments deficits (Sahn, Arulpragasam, and Merid, 1990).

Despite poor monitoring arrangements, some studies reveal that the structural adjustment policies have exacerbated the declining socio-economic conditions of the poor, especially in urban areas, in Malawi. This is evidenced by growing unemployment; declining real wages; rising fuel, housing, and food costs; and the deteriorating quality of social and physical infrastructure especially in the poverty-stricken areas. All of these conditions have undermined the already depressed living standards of the poor (CSR, 1990).

Mozambique

The negative trend of the national economy in the 1980s was deleteriously influenced by the civil war which had been raging in the country since 1976. One quarter of the total population of sixteen million people were driven from their homes by the fighting and more than one and a half million of them became refugees.

During the 1980s domestic food production per capita declined by 23 percent and the Gross National Product fell by 1.1 percent annually. Average annual inflation was 38 percent and more than half the population lived below the poverty line. Between 1983 and 1992 the country imported US$425 million worth of arms and at the end of the 1980s there were one hundred and eighty military personnel in Mozambique for every one doctor (UNDP, 1994).

A structural adjustment programme, internally known as the Economic Rehabilitation Programme, was instituted in Mozambique in 1987. Its objectives were to reverse the decline in production and to improve income levels (especially for the rural population); reduce financial imbalances and strengthen foreign reserves; enhance efficiency in economic structures; and restore normative relationships with trading partners and creditors (Dava, 1993).

Although there were some encouraging economic indicators during the initial years of the SAPs and although there are factors unrelated to SAPs, such as colonial structures, drought, war, limited technical capacity, population growth, economic stagnation, and unemployment which contribute to poverty in the country, it is the opinion of some analysts in Mozambique that the SAPs had many negative social effects. These include higher prices, reduction in basic services, increase in unemployment (with outcomes such as health hazards, accidents, child labour, crime, prostitution), and a negative impact on women who have to care more for the sick, the elderly, and children (Dava, 1993).

Zambia

Zambia's economic problems began with the Arab oil embargo in 1970 which coincided with falling copper prices and seriously affecting the country's major industry. As a result, the economy went into a state of decline and foreign exchange became drastically limited (Tembo, 1993). In the late 1970s and throughout the 1980s, as the recession deepened and revenues shrank, the government of Zambia found it difficult to reduce spending correspondingly (Masiye, 1993). Since 1978 Zambia has made several efforts to correct the situation. The first International Monetary Fund package involved devaluation of the currency, liberalization of prices, and other fiscal and monetary restraints. It resulted in high debt-service charges, increased inflation, and reduced government spending on the social services sector.

In spite of these measures budget deficits worsened and further programmes of deflation, devaluation, and currency auctioning were introduced. In 1987 Zambia broke away from the International Monetary Fund which resulted in the donor community withdrawing or reducing aid to the country. However, in 1989 Zambia agreed to the IMF's conditions and opted for structural adjustment which included the removal of subsidies on food and agricultural imports, decontrol of prices, reintroduction of fee-paying structures in education and health institutions, increased interest rates, and promotion of cash crop production (Masiye, 1993). The human costs of these measures have been considerable in terms of rising levels of hunger and malnutrition, cuts in education and health spending, declining real wages, and increasing poverty. The 1991 Preliminary Results Report of the Prices and Incomes Commission showed that progressively larger numbers of the middle-income group in the population were joining the ranks of the low-income group in real terms.

The sharp decrease in public spending has affected health and education provisions in particular. Large numbers of children from low-income households cannot attend school as fees and transport costs are beyond the families' means. In the 1970s 40 percent of the national budget was allocated to education but by 1992 this had been reduced to 16 percent. There has thus been a decline in expenditure per pupil and a reduction in the quality of education offered. Low literacy rates exacerbate the conditions conducive to absolute poverty as the vicious cycle is perpetuated. Gender issues are also adversely affected as female education is neglected in cases where it is necessary for the family to make a choice in the education of girls or boys. This leads to further disadvantage for women in the employment sector (Tembo, 1993).

The health sector too has suffered with persistent shortages of drugs, the imposition of user changes which are prohibitive for the poor, increases in child mortality and diseases in children, and deterioration in women's health especially in relation to pregnancy and childbirth. There have even been incidences of non-performance of emergency operations because of lack of rubber gloves which were not available due to government cuts in health expenditure (Musumali, 1992). Overcrowded, unsanitary, and inadequate housing conditions produce high rates of disease such as diarrhoea, dysentery, cholera, and tuberculosis, and consequent high rates of morbidity and mortality (Tembo, 1993).

Zimbabwe

The post-independence era in Zimbabwe saw the expansion of social services in an attempt to improve the situation in relation to the indigenous population, especially in the fields of health and education. Because of this, the allocation of investment in the productive sector was inadequate and could not create economic growth which matched population growth. Many secondary school-leavers could not be absorbed into the shrinking economy which was characterized by foreign exchange and price controls, rigid parastatal organizations, controlled employment, and unresponsive investment practices. In addition, there was a new government in place composed of relatively inexperienced administrators and there was also political unrest and instability. As a consequence, there was a lack of growth in the economy, inadequate investment, a high level of budgetary deficit, and increasing subsidies. The result was high unemployment and lowered standards of living leading to growing poverty which was further exacerbated by intermittent drought and poor commodity prices on the international market during the 1980s (Kasere, 1993).

In 1991 Zimbabwe introduced the Economic Structural Adjustment Programme which aimed to focus on productive sectors so as to promote economic growth.

This process embodied a competitive mode of production where market forces were of paramount significance. This was achieved through liberalizing trade; removing controls on foreign exchange, labour, prices, and parastatals; and creating an enabling environment for local and foreign investment providing for absorption of informal sector workers. Consequently, prices of basic foodstuffs increased, retrenchment through competition in industry grew, and the poverty status of urban and rural dwellers worsened.

Social dimensions of adjustment programmes

From the foregoing examples it is evident that structural adjustment programmes, focusing, as they do, on economic rather than social factors, may prove effective in the long term but can produce some distressing effects in the short term especially for those sections of the population in African countries who are already living in poverty. The living standards of the poor can be eroded by measures which raise the prices of consumer goods and services. Job losses, through redundancies in public enterprises or privatization, are also a threat. It is thus necessary for the programmes to ensure that the poor are not subjected to needless deprivation and that any benefits generated are reasonably shared. This is an obligation which both the International Monetary Fund and the World Bank now acknowledge. There is currently a requirement that the Policy Framework Papers prepared in relation to SAPs should "identify measures that can help cushion the possible adverse effects of certain policies on vulnerable groups .... in ways consistent with the program's macroeconomic framework" (IMF, 1991). As a result, an increasing number of SAPs now contain safety-net provisions.

The 1990 *World Development Report* admitted that "when structural adjustment issues came to the fore little attention was paid to the effects on the poor" (World Bank, 1990). In 1987 a special programme of activities known as "Social Dimensions of Adjustment" was introduced and this was given greater impact by the creation in 1993 of a Vice Presidency in the World Bank with responsibilities in the area of human development and poverty reduction (Killick, 1995; Ekpo, 1992).

Social Dimensions of Adjustment Programmes have been introduced in some of the countries in Africa with a modicum of effectiveness. In Malawi, micro level interventions are being initiated with a view to learning about projects that can assist the poor during periods of adjustment. In urban areas, under-five and home-craft shelters have been established but the bulk of the projects have aimed at assisting the rural poor (Kutengule, 1993). In Mozambique, the project aims at alleviating poverty through a programme of safety-net provisions and cash transfers to people in low income groups in urban areas and at establishing some social services such as the provision of water supplies in rural and urban areas. The urban cash transfers comprise food subsidies for vulnerable groups such as pregnant women, malnourished children, female-headed households, and households with minimal incomes. Salary subsidies for civil servants with large households and earning the lowest salary in the public service have also been implemented (Dava, 1993).

In Zimbabwe, the Social Dimensions of Adjustment Programme focuses on employment creation and training and on social welfare provisions targeting food security, education, and health matters. In urban areas, cash transfers are made to needy individuals and families while in the rural areas there is supplementary feeding for the under-fives, lactating mothers, and the elderly as well as food relief in the form of "food for work" and free food handouts. Educational assistance also targets those who need help with the payment of school and examination fees. As far as health is concerned, people in rural areas have been exempted from paying medical fees and in urban areas individual and geographical targeting exempts those in low and high density areas who have financial problems. Price decontrol and deregulation is being implemented in such a way that vulnerable groups such as the unemployed, female-headed households, the elderly, the chronically ill, the under fives, and pregnant and lactating women will be safeguarded (Kasere, 1993).

Adjustment: A positive perspective

To understand clearly what is happening let us identify the process of adjustment relevant to this discussion. It comprises two phases - stabilization, generally the domain of the International Monetary Fund, designed to put a floor under the downward spiral in key economic indicators such as budget deficits; and structural adjustment, generally the sphere of the World Bank, designed to restructure the economy and ensure longer term economic efficiency (Haddad et al, 1995).

Towards the middle to late 1980s the realization that the welfare impacts of adjustment could be negative was experienced by the designers and implementors of adjustment programmes and positive action, such as Social Dimensions of Adjustment, began to be considered. Measures to protect the poor were introduced in a considerable number of involved countries in 1992 and 1993, particularly, but the negative welfare impacts of adjustment still remain to some extent.

However, there are positive aspects to the structural adjustment scenario. A significant factor to be borne in mind is that different population groups are affected in different ways by adjustment programmes, some more positively than others. For example, import liberalization is likely to harm the urban working poor by forcing the closure of inefficient import-substituting industries whereas the cash-crop smallholders may benefit from lower prices and a more dependable availability of inputs (Killick, 1995). As far as social services are concerned, cutbacks affect the urban poor more than those in rural areas (where the most poverty-stricken of the population usually reside) because of lower utilization rates by the rural poor, especially in the fields of health care and primary school enrolment. On the other hand, agricultural reforms, part of most structural adjustment policies, are likely to have positive impacts on the poor in the rural areas. For example, the promotion of cash crops can certainly help the rural poor even where subsidy removal increases the cost of inputs as this can be offset by reduction in export taxes (Haddad et al, 1995).

Unfortunately, one of the most insidious truths about structural adjustment and its relationship to poverty is that there is insufficient dependable data which renders many of the criticisms of externally engineered adjustment somewhat suspect. Poverty is difficult for government statistical services to come to grips with and also there is a suspicion that some governments do not give high priority to data collection in this area. Again, economies are often in crisis immediately prior to the adoption of structural adjustment programmes and some researchers fail to take this into account. They impute to adjustment all deleterious effects some of which are possibly attributable to the initial crisis situation.

The importance of building a more reliable database is highlighted by Bourguignon and Morrison (1992) who suggest priorities such as five yearly household consumption surveys (augmented by smaller yearly surveys); annual census of formal sector enterprises (augmented by sample surveys of informal sector enterprises); and improvements in the quality and regularity of standard social-indicator statistics. This is an area where national governments have prime responsibility but donors, such as the World Bank and its Social Dimensions of Adjustment Project, can assist with resources.

The responsibility of national governments cannot be over-emphasized and effective political measurement of the economic design is imperative. Addison (1993) suggests that "many African countries present a difficult political environment for any donor agency that is intent on reducing poverty .... many governments are reluctant to define a poverty agenda ... in order to avoid sacrificing political patronage". It has been suggested that Malawi provides such an example in that the government showed little concern for some years for the interests of 55 percent of the population living in absolute poverty with a system of policies and institutions discriminating against poor smallholders in favour of the owners of large estates (Chipeta, 1993; Campbell and Parfitt, 1995). Given a positive attitude by governments, then structural adjustment could proceed in a more meaningful way.

Some countries have introduced their own adjustment programmes with little recourse to international financial institutions (IFIs), and the East Asian economies, particularly, have proved exemplary with regard to pro-poor policies (Parfitt, 1995). Countries such as Singapore, Malaysia, Thailand, and Indonesia adopted flexible economic programmes, adjusting continuously and of their own volition to circumstances as severe as those in the developing countries of Africa and, through diversifying and transforming productive structures and experimenting with policy interventions, found the best solutions to economic and social problems. Most importantly, they were able to achieve positive results while reducing inequalities and absolute poverty (Killick, 1995).

Killick (1995) also argues that for effective policy in the field of adjustment to be formulated, four principles should be given cognizance: modifications to adjustment programmes need to be placed within the context of a comprehensive country-level anti-poverty strategy; a balance has to be struck between the need for economic adaptation and the desire to protect the poor; adjustment policies should be designed so as to minimize the costs and maximize the benefits to those in poverty; and defending the interests of the poor necessitates considerable intervention by the state.

In order to implement these principles, it is necessary that the programmes are tailored to meet the needs of individual countries with their unique economic and social structures and their specific nature and severity of the initial situation. Also, anti-poverty strategies should be integrated into adjustment programmes from the outset in a two-way relationship with the strategy guiding design and adjustment needs feeding back into periodic modification of the strategy. Positive measures are better than ameliorative responses to the extent that they give priority to maintaining infrastructure and various forms of public investment, such as rural feeder roads, health clinics, the provision of treated water, and primary schools, from which the poor can benefit. Such investments also generate employment in the construction sector which employs a large proportion of unskilled workers (Killick, 1995).

Export promotion measures also can contribute to the welfare of the poor through employment generation and the raising of the incomes of smallholder cash crop producers (Paus, 1994). The reform or, where appropriate, privatization of relevant public enterprises can also help, with regard to employment, in some instances. The new poor and those who lose their jobs through public sector retrenchment may, through training, technical support, and assistance with initial capital, become successful entrepreneurs which would be beneficial to both the individual and the economy as a whole.

In tandem with adjustment programmes, short-term "safety-net" provisions are often necessary, particularly for the protection of the urban poor. This may comprise the creation of special packages (such as Ghana's Programme for the Alleviation of the Social Costs of Adjustment) and may include projects for the rehabilitation of roads, clinics, and schools; slum upgrading; retraining schemes; and targeted food programmes (Addison, 1993).

An alternative approach to safeguard the poor is the creation of special social funds which have been used in some countries to support labour-intensive infrastructure projects, producer co-operatives, and the improvement of nutrition and health services. Notable, internationally, in this regard is Mexico's Solidarity Fund. Zambia has also moved in this direction but it is too early to assess the effectiveness of this and other such funds (Killick, 1995). Care needs to be taken, in adjustment programmes, in the imposition of indirect taxation (such as a sales tax) which can and should be designed to impact mainly on the consumption expenditures of the relatively well-to-do in the population rather than, as often happens in developing countries, backfiring on the poor. Similarly, user charges in service delivery, especially education, while often more beneficial to the poor than subsidies which may be regressive, might discourage those in straitened circumstances "from sending their children to the very service which offers the best avenue of escape from the culture of poverty" (Killick, 1995).

Targeted schemes tend to eliminate the participatory factor of the undeserving poor but often at the cost of missing many of the deserving poor, predominantly the poorest of the poor. Killick (1995), however, found that in a survey of thirty Latin American countries targeted schemes were more progressive than general subsidies and much more so in the case of food subsidies and somewhat more for health and education. Behrman (1988) also offers that, notwithstanding their inefficiency, food subsidies have generally increased incomes and improved nutritional status among the poor, particularly the urban poor.

Alternative strategies

"Development should not be undertaken on behalf of a people, rather it should be the organic outcome of a society's value system, its perceptions, its concerns, and its endeavours" (UNECA, 1989). The United Nations Economic Commission for Africa, in its document on an alternative framework for structural adjustment in Africa with emphasis on socio-economic recovery and transformation, goes on to state that, in order to achieve and sustain development, the education, training, health, wellbeing, and vitality of people has to be promoted and ensured in order that they may participate effectively and fully in the process of development. Thus, programmes of economic and social development should emanate from the societies in which they are to be implemented. Some pessimists even allude to the fact that Africa, through structural adjustment, is being recolonized (Himbara and Sultan, 1995). It is partly for this reason that the International Monetary Fund and World Bank projects have often achieved disappointing results.

UNECA (1989) states that the alleviation of mass poverty and the raising of living standards on the continent can only be achieved through the pursuit of a policy of self-sustained development which seeks to maintain ongoing economic growth, transform typical economic and social structures, and establish a supportive resource base. Essential in this context is regional self-reliance which involves integration of physical, institutional, and social infrastructures; production structures; and African markets, and this can be achieved through establishing food security; through the production of goods such as iron and steel, machine tools, fertilizers, pharmaceuticals, building materials, and equipment for construction, agriculture, and transport; and through promoting inter-African trade. This will all have to be achieved through the implementation of effective development strategies and policies.

UNECA's framework is based on three modules or sets of macroentities, namely the operative forces, the available resources, and the needs to be catered for. The operative forces (which could be positive or negative; internal or external; temporary or permanent) are economic, political, technological, scientific, environmental, sociological, and cultural and together they impact on the general pattern and rate of development. The available resources include human resources, especially in terms of mixes of quality and skills; natural resources, such as land, water, and forests; domestic savings; and external financial resources. Needs include vital goods and services and the ability to acquire them (UNECA, 1989; Ekpo, 1992).

UNECA (1989) suggests major policy directions for the three modules. For the first module they include enhanced production and efficient resource use which must sometimes resist balancing the budget at the expense of growth and production; greater and more efficient domestic resource mobilization through plugging financial leakages and relying less on external resource inflows; improving human resources and building technological capacity and capabilities through ensuring that reductions in budget deficits are not accomplished at the expense of social sector provisions, predominantly education, health, and other social infrastructure such as law and order which is essential for the maintenance of an enabling environment; and vertical and horizontal diversification through producing essential goods and services to meet the needs of the majority of the population in all sectors and widening the range of export earning products focusing particularly on African markets.

Policy directions for module 2 include establishing a pragmatic balance between the public and private sectors through ensuring optimum rates of return on investment for entrepreneurs, although there are areas such as building the physical, human, and institutional infrastructure, environmental protection and conservation, and the provision of essential services in which the public sector has a distinct role to play, especially in Africa; creating an enabling environment for sustainable development through facilitating participation in decision-making, consensus building, maintenance of justice and equity, elimination of civil strife, access to opportunities for all, and the creation of a favourable investment climate; shifting of resources through minimizing non-productive expenditures and excessive military spending and prioritizing health and welfare allocations; and improvements in the pattern of income distribution among different socio-economic groups through ensuring that the poor and disadvantaged will have increased access to the means of production, especially land.

Module 3 policy directions include food self-sufficiency through achieving a proper balance between the food subsector and the agricultural export system which is often favoured through the policy of price incentives; lessening import dependence through local production and discouraging the growth of an "import culture"; realignment of patterns of consumption and production so that locally produced food, clothing, and other necessities will be readily accepted and national and subregional self-reliance will be fostered; and managing debt through establishing strong debt management systems including continuous assessment of payment capacity in the short and long term and deliberately concentrating external loans on productive projects with high and fast returns and a substantial foreign exchange component.

UNECA (1989), though perhaps an improvement on policies of the international financial institutions, is somewhat apologetic in nature and also relies largely on appeals to the concerned countries. The African Alternative Framework certainly focuses on a clear elucidation of Africa's predicament and makes suggestions qualitatively superior to the programmes which have been introduced thus far but to date its implementation in Africa appears to be minimal (Ekpo, 1992).

Worthy of attention and serious consideration in the search for alternatives to the process of structural adjustment is James Midgley's (1995) definitive work on social development representing a summation of many years of research, collaboration, philosophical debate, and pragmatism leading to a conceptualization of a process which, in its purest form, can produce optimal conditions in societies, both developing and developed. He defines social development as "a process of social change designed to promote the wellbeing of the population as a whole in conjunction with a dynamic process of economic development". The goal of social development, he argues, is "to promote social welfare - a condition of social well-being which occurs when social problems are satisfactorily managed, social needs are met, and social opportunities are created". It is thus a process of change fostered through deliberate human action or social intervention.

The process of social development comprises three stages. These are the pre-existing social situation which it seeks to change; the social development process itself; and the end state or goal which the process seeks to attain. Strategies for implementing this process of harmonizing social interventions with economic development activities may be formulated on three levels - where the primary responsibility for social development is placed on individuals; where the role of local communities is stressed; and where the contribution of governments is emphasized.

The underlying belief in the first strategy is that the welfare of the whole society is enhanced when individuals strive to promote their own welfare. There are two schools of thought in this regard. The first is the laissez-faire approach where individuals determine their own destiny. The second is the interventionist philosophy which argues for the specific involvement of government and other organizations to promote social development in the context of a market economy through adopting measures that enhance individual functioning, create a more vibrant enterprise culture, and facilitate the productive use of the market by ordinary people.

The emphasis here is on investment in large-scale industry and enterprise to stimulate economic growth, create jobs, and, through a strategy of employment, raise incomes. It is believed that this will also provide jobs for people in the subsistence agricultural sector who will be absorbed in new industrial and commercial enterprises. This is a move away from the international financial institutions structural adjustment programmes which are, for the most part, anti-statist in concept. Many people now believe that governments *per se* have a critical role to play in institutional development through which an enterprise culture may evolve.

There is also the argument for the creation by governments of conditions conducive to the emergence of small-scale enterprises which provide opportunities for poor people to generate resources to meet their own needs. Such conditions include easing restrictions on small-scale enterprises (many developing countries have regulations making much informal sector enterprises illegal); improving credit facilities for small businesses; building infrastructure such as industrial estates and markets which can support these enterprises; training entrepreneurs in small business management; and providing extension services to help small businesses with, *inter alia*, marketing, product design, and financial planning. Integration with the formal sector is also important through subcontracting by government and non-governmental organizations and by commercial banks and private sector businesses interacting and providing services to small enterprises.

It is also important to enhance individual functioning by those who are unable to operate competently in the market-oriented system due to low self-esteem or a proliferation of social problems which impedes their coping capacity. Social work is well placed to provide assistance of this kind and social workers are now being employed in several developing countries to teach the poor to function effectively as economic actors in individual income generating projects or micro-enterprises.

Social development by communities is, of course, closely related to the concept of community development. In most cases, community development has adopted a materialist approach encouraging the construction of community centres, schools, clinics, roads, and sanitary and water supply projects but other aspects, such as enhancing community identity, strengthening democratic participation, and fostering self-help and self-determination are also often emphasized.

Although these projects have not always realized their potential, community development offers an effective means for promoting social development within the context of economic growth through raising the levels of living of people as a result of infrastructure in the form, for example, of networks of feeder roads which enhance communication and easier access to markets and the importation of materials and technologies. Also, irrigation and fertilization schemes have often fostered local economic development.

Through community action or community participation local people are urged to take matters into their own hands and create their own community development activities, with possible funding from government or other donor agencies. This highlights the concept of employment which also includes emphasis on the role of women and marginalized groups within communities and focuses on bringing them into the mainstream of community structures and functioning.

Social development by governments embodies the principle that economic growth and social welfare can be fostered by government planning and this has been implemented by many countries around the world. However, much of this planning has focused on economic issues and has not always made reference to social conditions. As a result, many Third World countries began, during the 1970s, to incorporate social planning divisions into their central planning agencies. However, several of these countries fell into debt for reasons discussed earlier in this chapter and resorted to structural adjustment programmes with the concomitant loss of commitment to unified socio-economic planning, although this is now returning in several of the affected countries.

Unified planning involves governments setting specific goals for development; channelling resources to targeted low-income groups; and expanding education, health, and other social programmes. This necessitates the redistribution of resources through progressive taxation policies, the removal of regressive measures that place an unfair burden on the poor, and wasteful expenditures (especially in Third World countries) on conference centres and other non-essential facilities as well as excessive military spending.

The basic needs approach in the field of social development urges governments to address the urgent needs of the poorest groups in developing countries. These cover survival needs such as nutrition, safe drinking water, and shelter; social rights such as education, health care, and social security; and non-material needs such as participation in the political process, protection against discrimination, and provision of equal opportunities for advancement. This basic needs strategy involves needs assessment studies; the identification of target groups; the development of specific programmes that are low cost, relevant to local conditions, and participatory; and a firm commitment by leaders, planners, and international agencies.

Finally, with regard to government involvement in social development, the concept of sustainable development must be acknowledged with particular regard to the formulation of policies and programmes that promote the economic and social welfare of populations in ways that do not harm the environment. They should also link environmental policies to local development initiatives through relevant education, creating incentives, and promoting a sense of ownership of resources.

In conclusion, Midgley (1995) states that the various social development strategies must be harmonized and synthesized so as to facilitate their implementation in ways that are compatible rather than competitive. Such a process is embodied in what he calls "The Institutional Perspective", which requires that governments play an active role in managing and co-ordinating the implementation of strategies for social development. This can be achieved through creating formal organizations that can assume responsibility for managing social development efforts in ways that maximize the participation of communities, markets, and individuals. They exist at different levels but should be co-ordinated at the national level. The style and approach of the co-ordinating body should be one of managed pluralism.

As a final word, Midgley (1995) propounds three ways in which the social development approach seeks to harmonize economic and social policies to enhance social welfare for all. First, it seeks to create formal organizational and institutional arrangements by which the policies can be integrated. These are located at national, regional, and local levels and must be coordinated to ensure that the standards of living of all sections of the population are raised. Second, it seeks to ensure that economic development has a direct impact on the social well-being of all citizens. This must be done through encouraging investments which will create employment or self-employment opportunities on a significant scale so that the incomes of ordinary people are increased. This will also involve the introduction of cost-effective appropriate technology and redistribution of resources through fiscal rather than punitive measures.

Third, it seeks to formulate social policies and programmes that contribute positively to economic development such as investments in human and social capital in the fields of education, health, nutrition, housing, maternal and child welfare, drinking water, sanitation, income subsidies and support, and others. While some economists view these as consumption expenditures others argue that they enhance and support economic development. Community development programmes should not only improve physical and social amenities but should also help people to engage in positive economic activities. Also, programmes for people with special needs should not rely on maintenance approaches but should seek to integrate the differently abled into the economy through vocational training, job placement, and the creation of micro-enterprises, co-operatives, and community-based projects which encourage economic self-sufficiency.

There is a clear linkage between Midgley's social development and the United Nations Development Programme's (UNDP, 1994) concept of sustainable human development which it defines as:

> Development that not only generates economic growth but distributes its benefits equitably; that regenerates the environment rather than destroying it; that empowers people rather than marginalizing them. It... gives priority to the poor, enlarging their choices and opportunities and providing for their participation in decisions that affect their lives. It is development that is pro-people, pro-nature, pro-jobs and pro-women.

Conclusions

There are few simplistic generalizations which can be made about the impact on poverty of adjustment programmes as formulated by the international financial institutions. There remain many problems associated with the collection of relevant data and research methodology and outcomes are varied and complex. People in poverty often are harmed by adjustment programmes, especially the urban poor, but emphasis on negative outcomes should take into consideration also other influences on poverty which compound the problems in an adjustment scenario.

Adjustment programmes should, ideally, develop within the societies which have need of them but, whether internally or externally engineered, the primary responsibility for achieving anti-poverty objectives must lie with national governments, which do not always themselves display much real concern with the poor. However, the international financial institutions must share some of the responsibility and should continue to do more to design structural adjustment programmes within a cost-minimizing framework. The major policy tasks are to formulate a long-term anti-poverty strategy and ensure that adjustment programmes are consistent with that strategy without moving away from the imperative of adapting the economy to changing circumstances.

Alternative practice in the form of the Economic Commission for Africa's statement on adjustment and James Midgley's social development perspective are perhaps much more relevant to the needs of Africa but lack the compulsive edge inherent in the tradeoffs offered by the World Bank and International Monetary Fund. Given the intrinsic nature of political states, wherever in the world they exist, the "greatest happiness of the greatest number" is a cry much vented but seldom achieved and the motivation to bring about positive economic and social change from within a society often lacks that dimension of commitment necessary to uplift a nation and its populace.

Perhaps the political planners of Africa would do well to utilize a concept from the world of architecture in the form of "telesis", which is the opposite of serendipity, and denotes planning which is in harmony with the natural, physical, economic, and social environment. If societies could focus on a co-ordinated, systems approach to economic and social planning and work with dedication towards regional cooperation and support, the need for external prescriptive measures for their very survival might diminish making way for a new order containing a meaningful place for all their peoples.

10 The social impact of structural adjustment programmes on the smallholder irrigation farmers in Zimbabwe

Dumisani Magadlela

Zimbabwe's agriculture is currently divided into two sub-sectors: large-scale commercial farms (4,500 of them, occupying 10 million hectares of prime agricultural land), and smallholder communal farms (850,000 in number, occupying low agricultural potential areas) (Rukuni, 1994: 15). More than 75 percent of the entire population lives in rural or communal areas where a majority of the people are at the mercy of erratic rainfall patterns and poor market organization to secure their livelihoods.

Most communal area farmers cultivate their land mainly for subsistence purposes (sizes of their holdings range from 0.4ha to sometimes 4ha). One of the major reasons for this is that the prices of farming inputs continue to rise without sufficient complementary increases in producer prices for crops to offset production costs and encourage growth. Smallholder communal area farmers have had seasons where production could not even meet their basic subsistence needs, for example, the 1991-92 drought season. They have to rely on government drought relief food hand-outs in such circumstances. The hope that the following season will be better keeps them working, but still they are forced to source capital for farming inputs from relatives who provide cash remittances from towns or, if possible, they get loans from credit institutions whose conditions, such as high interest rates, may make loans inaccessible to most smallholder farmers.

Smallholder irrigation schemes in communal areas provide places where farmers have relatively more secure water supplies than their rain-fed counterparts and can grow enough food for themselves and their relatives, and still be able to sell surpluses to meet their cash needs. With drought spells that seem to be gradually assuming a more permanent presence than before, irrigation schemes have become food resource bases not only for the plotholders in such schemes, or those who benefit from sales of their produce in towns, but for increasing numbers of rural villagers around the area who either rent pieces of irrigated land to produce food, or work in the irrigation scheme for food and cash. The unfortunate aspect of this sector is that smallholder schemes do not have enough potential to have a nationwide impact on food security. They are distant from markets, face water shortages, and continue to depend on government subsidies for daily operation and maintenance (Rukuni and Makadho, 1994: 137).

This chapter offers a micro-level view of how aspects of policy changes at the macro-political and economic levels affect the lives of smallholder irrigation farmers in a government managed irrigation scheme. The focus is on how farmers in communal irrigation situations are affected by policy changes that are made at top government levels, and especially how structural adjustment policies of market deregulation, price decontrol, and trade liberalization create conditions where the smaller farmer (in terms of scale of production and capacity to compete) is marginalized and pushed deeper into a situation where the only aim is to produce enough food to survive, and not to break into new markets or expand the production base.

Structural adjustment programmes in Zimbabwe

Structural adjustment programmes (SAPs) were introduced in Zimbabwe in 1990 through the initiative of the World Bank and the IMF. The initial objectives of SAPs in Zimbabwe were to deregulate the economy, decontrol prices, and introduce trade liberalization. The aim was to gradually make the whole economy more open to internal and external competition. This was not an easy road to take in light of the government's avowed belief in a socialist ideology to transform the lives of the poor. However, an important aspect of this shift was the fact that Zimbabwe's economy had not really become socialist after independence in 1980, it had remained inherently semi-capitalistic and in-ward looking. The problem lay in the fact that government soon after independence spent more than it earned, and had to borrow money to make up the difference. SAPs were accepted with the belief that it would "re-start the process of economic growth by liberalizing the economy, cutting down and reshaping the role of government, and encouraging domestic and foreign investment, this would be complemented by deregulating domestic prices through the removal of subsidies" (Chisvo and Munro, 1994: 1).

Before the implementation of SAPs, and as a result of the country's socialist policy, 'too much state money was spent on uneconomic social projects which impoverished the country' (Gerber, Nel, and van Dyk, 1995: 196). Most of these social projects were a political necessity and were meant to go some way towards satisfying the high expectations of the majority Black Zimbabweans who expected independence to yield tangible results such as access to productive land, more lucrative jobs, and construction of more schools and clinics around the country. A minimum wage level was legislated for different industries soon after. Most of these social concessions were not immediately productive and they took a big chunk of the national budget.

The decision by government to finally embrace SAPs was based, among other things, on what critics of the government's socialist stance termed a triumph of economic rationality, and a realization that economic decisions must be "based on business principles and not political rhetoric" (Gerber, Nel, and van Dyk, 1995: 197). But this was by no means an easy decision. The government had to face the conflict between the need to redress inherited social imbalances and external pressure to allow market forces more freedom in the economy (Kadenge, Ndoro, and Zwizwai, 1992: 170).

The government's acceptance of World Bank and IMF prescriptions to revamp the economy were regarded by some as a sell-out by top politicians to capitalist forces and a coup for the local White minority which controlled a large stake of the economy. There were heated debates in the local media about how the government had finally given in to pressure from the World Bank and IMF at the expense of the poorest sections of the population. Some of the arguments had racial and class overtones, with some commentators believing that the new Black political élite was allying itself with the economically powerful White group to benefit from SAPs. Some local businessmen and most commercial farmers felt that the lack of legislative protection from external competition would introduce powerful foreign competition which would steal local markets from them. How these changes would affect smallholder communal area populations, who constitute the majority of the population, was not directly dealt with or discussed in detail. They, like everyone else in the country, would have to carve out their own niche, create their own space for survival, and devise their own strategies to earn a living if conditions became less conducive to growth.

The communal areas

Zimbabwe's communal Areas (CAs) cover about 16.4 million hectares, which is 42 percent of the total land area of the country. This is the residential area for approximately 75 percent of the country's total population. Agricultural production for this sector increased dramatically between 1979 and 1981, and kept rising steadily after that, dropping only during the dry seasons. Although there was a rapid increase in smallholder farmers' maize production and participation in local markets between 1979 and 1981 (Mashingaidze, 1994: 209-14), their capacity to sustain or improve this position has increasingly become more and more restricted with droughts and structural adjustment.

Forty percent of communal area households are female-headed as a direct result of male labour migration. Inflation-induced declines in real-incomes in the urban formal sector, where most men from CAs work, impacts negatively on supplies of cash remittances back to the communal areas (Chidzonga, 1993: 201), and loss of jobs as a result of the streamlining of parastatals can only worsen the problem. Most communal area farmers are not fully aware of what SAPs really entail. A survey by Kadenge, Ndoro and Zwizwai (1992) revealed that peasants and people in mining communities around Zimbabwe were not fully aware of SAPs. However, it was evident that the re-introduction of primary school fees and the removal of price controls were better known than, for example, inflation and foreign exchange rates among these groups.

It should be pointed out that government did not altogether forget about, or sacrifice, poor sections of the population for the hope of revamping the economy through SAPs. Seemingly appropriate measures were put in place to cushion them against the worst effects of the programme. The Social Development Fund (SDF) was established in 1991 and in conjunction with the Department of Social Welfare (DSW) provides assistance directly to households who are disadvantaged, have no source of income, and have to apply for help for either school fees, health care, or food (Chisvo and Munro, 1994: 20). However, the targeting strategy leaves out some most deserving groups such as communal area farmers who are situated too far away from the SDF or DSW offices. Some of them do not even know how to apply for assistance, and the cushioning appears to be urban biased in its targeting of the needy because rural residents cannot afford to board buses and find places to sleep in the urban areas if their applications are not processed on the same day. They find it cheaper, and it makes economic sense, to stay at home and make the most of whatever is available.

Marketing boards

Marketing boards have assisted smallholder communal area farmers to sell their produce in a more or less guaranteed market since 1980. Infrastructure support and related services were put in place to support smallholder farmers soon after independence. In 1980, there were only 3 grain marketing board (GMB) depots in the communal areas. By 1990 there were 37 of them (Rukuni, 1994: 31). The most notable success record for CAs farmers was in the production and marketing of the staple crop of maize through the GMB. Rohrbach (1988: 315) states that government increased the real producer price of maize by 80 percent, and the ratio of the producer price to the price of maize fertilizer increased 50 percent. However, the total percentage deliveries to the GMB dropped with the advent of SAPs and that has resulted in grain collection depots closing and maize deliveries becoming more cumbersome.

The privatization and streamlining of the GMB meant that smallholder farmers had to seek new markets and be able to bargain with new buyers on competitive prices for their produce. The GMB has been trying to rationalize or liberalize its functions since the launching of SAPs. From the early stages of SAPs, the GMB retreated from its monopolistic policy and closed some of its collection depots around the country. Also, the Cotton Marketing Board (CMB) changed its name to the Cotton Company of Zimbabwe (CCZ) in 1994, when it became a private entity, and has since been trying to rationalize its operations. Cotton is one of the main cash crops in the CAs and there is a CCZ depot at the irrigation scheme. CCZ staff said that prices of inputs (seed, fertilizers, and chemicals for pesticides) have gone up by more than 30 percent at different times since 1991. Producer prices of cotton have also gone up by about the same rate during the same period.

The irrigation scheme area

The irrigation scheme is a 442 hectare government managed project located in Nyanga district of Manicaland province in Eastern Zimbabwe. There are more than 400 households with irrigated plots in the scheme. The managing agency is the department of Agricultural Technical and Extension Services (AGRITEX). The project was constructed between 1956 and 1960 and started operating soon after completion. The irrigation area has an altitude of 850m. A series of dry spells over the years have resulted in poor harvests in the scheme, but in good years dryland farmers in the area have managed to do better than irrigators because of generally good soils. The average plot size is 0.8 hectares, but there are farmers who have access to more land through renting other farmers' land. Local businessmen rent plots from some of the plotholders, most of whom are now too old to work on their plots full-time. The majority of farmers put their land under food crops in order to secure themselves from food shortages and avoid buying food which is very expensive. The scheme is situated in Natural Region II which has an average annual rainfall of 800mm, but in some seasons rainfall averages drop to as low as 228.6mm.

According to the farmers, 1992 was the worst season since the construction of the irrigation scheme in the early 1960s. This was soon after the launching of SAPs and the farmers' position was compromised by a gradually rising cost of living. An interesting perception of SAPs emerges from the coincidence their launching had with this disastrous season. When asked what they understood by SAPs, two out of three irrigation farmers said that they remember well the year of SAPs when they did not harvest anything and were forced to pay irrigation fees. This was the year they got drought recovery assistance from government, and to them SAPs are identified with starvation, the shortage of water, and suffering.

This linking of SAPs with hard times is common even in urban areas as a result of job losses and the increasing cost of living. AGRITEX reported a zero harvest for some crops in the 1991-92 season. Farmers literally begged management and the government to exempt them from paying their annual irrigation fees, but to no avail. With their small plots and hardly any capital resources or credit sources, it was difficult for most smallholder farmers to recover from such a crippling drought after investing their earnings in expensive inputs and getting nothing in return.

As far as production is concerned, it seems that the majority of farmers produce more subsistence and food crops than they do cash crops such as cotton and tobacco. Hectarage figures show that subsistence and food crops are more popular in the irrigation scheme than cash crops. The 1991-92 and 1992-93 seasons had poor production levels because of the drought which reduced water flows in the irrigation scheme. After the severe 1991-92 drought, hectarage for main food crops of maize and wheat increased.

The small sizes of irrigators' landholdings, the insecurity of both markets and tenure, compounded by inaccessible credit, rising input costs attributed to SAPs, together with recurrent droughts, force farmers to be resistant to any moves that increase their risks (Magadzire, 1995). Some government officials deny irrigation farmers drought relief aid because they have irrigation water to produce enough food to survive, this then drives them to first secure their families' food requirements before they can venture into the risky business of commercial or market crop production in which they also have vested interests.

The irony here is that they are constantly being pushed from all angles, by government through AGRITEX, their union, and the credit organization - the Agricultural Finance Corporation (AFC), to go commercial so that they can reap higher returns from their farming activities. To many farmers, being a more commercial-oriented producer implies buying more chemical fertilizers and sticking to recommended scientific methods of production, which is generally regarded as expensive. There is limited participation in markets and a creation of what one may call a low level spiral that borders on poverty. Smallholder farmers do think of producing enough to market, but their priority is not to generate cash to support national programmes like SAPs, but to sustain their livelihoods and at least have enough to produce more food in the following season. If the cash crops do well, fine, there will be good cash, but if there is a shortage of water, food crops get priority usage, to sustain their livelihoods until the next rainy season.

Some of the main actors in the irrigation scheme are irrigation and dryland farmers, AGRITEX, and interested outsiders such as the Air Cured Tobacco Association (ACTA) which markets its tobacco in auction floors in towns and marketing boards. The needs of smallholder farmers, pitted against assumptions and objectives of intervenors, exposes the vulnerability of this agricultural sector in a deregulated free market environment.

Some farming practices

Farming in the irrigation scheme has been generally described by farmers there as a gamble and a big risk. Farmers say that each season is different and there is no guarantee that one will produce enough crops to sell and get sufficient cash to afford inputs for the next crop. Irrigation schemes have rules about use of irrigated plots and expected levels of production per crop per season which farmers have to try and achieve.

Also, there is some form of competition among the farmers to prove that they are the best. To achieve their goals, farmers strive to stick to recommended farming methods including such things as the amount of fertilizer to apply per crop and per unit area. Most farmers said that they cannot afford to use the recommended amount of fertilizers every season because inputs have become much more expensive than they were before.

AGRITEX recommends specific amounts of each type of fertilizer per crop, but they are not as strict as the management was during the colonial period about coercing farmers to follow recommended farming practices. Use of organic fertilizers is encouraged and there has been a general increase in their usage. A few farmers use crop residues, but this is almost an insignificant number compared to the majority who believe in chemical fertilizers as the solution to their low production levels. Farmers believe that burning crop residues destroys pests and diseases that may linger in the field until the next crop.

Labour is scarce in some CAs as a result of outward migration. But this issue has its complications and contradictions. The existing labour of the unemployed youth is unaffordable for many farmers. Cheap labour from Mozambique has since disappeared after the peace settlement in that country saw the repatriation of most Mozambicans back to Mozambique. The main source of labour now, as was the case historically, is the extended family.

Family members who increasingly find it difficult to maintain their families in towns, as basic commodity prices rise, move them back to their homes in the CAs and join them there when they lose their jobs. While this has its negative implications in the form of increased pressure for arable land, it provides the elderly residents of the CAs with a form of respite from some of the hard work.

More rainfed communal area farmers are now dependent on the irrigation scheme for their food requirements. When the summer rainy season is not a good one, it is almost guaranteed that the following winter irrigation season will be invaded by rainfed/dryland area farmers who strike 'draft power and labour for irrigated land' deals with irrigators and come to claim them in winter to grow wheat for food (Magadlela, 1994b). There is a silent (because it is illegal to lease or rent state land) scramble for irrigated land deals. Extension staff have estimated that in 1994 more than 50 percent of irrigated crops in winter belonged to farmers from outside the irrigation scheme. With some relatives losing jobs and coming back, and dry spells continuing, there are serious potential conflicts in the making on this issue.

Input prices

Increases in prices of inputs such as chemical fertilizers, and seeds and pesticides since the launching of SAPs have been identified as some of the main causes of the decline in communal area production since 1990. SAPs-induced price decontrols have increased most fertilizer and seed prices to levels where farmers say they cannot help but reduce the number of bags of fertilizer they apply per unit area, for example. With dry spells continuing throughout the region, the risk for investing in agricultural production has increased dramatically for smallholder farmers. To produce a reasonable crop of maize from one hectare requires inputs which cost approximately US$130.

Discussion and conclusions

Smallholder communal area irrigation farmers are not directly under the spotlight of assessment on how they are being affected by SAPs, or any other political, social, and economic changes taking place or initiated by government. Communal area villagers have locally designed mechanisms for withstanding external pressures to change their lives. Irrigation farmers are now aware of SAPs. They have listened to it being discussed on radio, and have heard people talk about the current tough times of expensive consumer prices of basic commodities being a direct result of SAPs.

The farmers' comfort is that they can produce most of their food themselves and they rearly buy commodities like bread and vegetables. But they cannot make their own fertilizers, and although they encourage each other to use organic manure, they still cannot entirely do without chemical fertilizers and chemicals for pests and diseases, some of which are imported. Farmers still have to buy tested seed for crops like maize, tomato, cotton, and tobacco. This factor alone, of gradual increases in input costs soon after the implementation of the initial phase of SAPs in Zimbabwe, accounts for most of the impact that SAPs have had on smallholder irrigation farmers in the communal areas of Zimbabwe. They have not escaped the net of being drawn into yet another of the trends that depicts the world as moving towards what has been termed "the global village".

It would seem that SAPs, if meant to revamp the agriculture-driven economy, have come at the wrong time. That is, just when rains were not falling favourably which resulted in recurrent droughts and constant uncertainty and insecurity for the farming industry. Although the smallholder farmers' recorded contribution to national food stocks and to the generation of revenue through exports has been irregular since 1980, it cannot be denied that their production has not only shown signs of growth but has also contributed immensely to sustaining the majority of the country's population which is generally located in the dry communal areas.

From the farmers' point of view, SAPs have resulted in many people losing their jobs and they are now returning to their roots in the communal areas, straining even further the already crowded land resource. Chakaodza's (1993: 67) contention that SAPs and the drought joined hands to compound the suffering of poor sections of the Zimbabwean population is very much in order here. What may not be, however, is the argument that SAPs and the drought have pushed people from communal areas into towns where they are now squatters. This may be true of some but not many of the areas around Zimbabwe. Some people's movement from towns into CAs may be characterized by a realization of the potential to earn a living from the land. The main catalyst here is the potential availability of water, and this could explain why in irrigation schemes there are people who lost their jobs in towns and have returned to settle and farm.

Improved and more vigorous water harvesting methods such as dam and borehole construction could help develop rural economies which can support urban areas and contribute to national growth. If some of the retrenched people cannot find land to make a living for themselves, they will seek other means to survive. There is no scientific basis for this, but the increase in crime in communal areas, perpetrated by young people, may be accounted for by this factor. They may feel that they 'have to steal' for survival because they cannot find jobs in towns or have lost them as a result of their employers restructuring their companies and are frustrated by land shortage and droughts.

Another sore point among most smallholder producers in CAs is that they seem to fail to time markets in such a way that they can sell their crops without creating a glut in the market. There can be said to be a general lack of understanding of market changes or trends among some rural smallholder producers. A common cause of marketing problems is the lack of unity among producers when it comes to planning which crops to grow and how to sell them especially in co-ordinated units of production such as irrigation schemes. The lack of market surveys before deciding what and when to plant results in glut situations where buyers end up imposing prices because farmers subsequently find themselves in weak bargaining positions. Furthermore, smallholder farmers have a reputation of being less organized when it comes to seeking and securing markets, especially when compared to their larger-scale and more commercial counterparts, although they both have their respective unions.

On the whole, the effects of SAPs on smallholder farmers have not been fully researched and documented. This chapter attempted to highlight some of the indirect social impacts of SAPs on this section of the population by alluding to price decontrols for farming inputs and basic commodities, market deregulation, and some implications of retrenchment and streamlining of the civil service. The movement of people back to the land after job losses can be seen as one of the last straws of seeking a basic livelihood. Migration into towns is for some a final attempt to escape the inevitable starvation in barren unproductive land in communal areas. This makes smallholder irrigation development one of the prerequisites for implementing SAPs especially in regions which have been hit by recurrent droughts. Agro-based economies like Zimbabwe's are unfortunate in that their SAPs, while dependent on World Bank and IMF magnanimity, are virtually at the mercy of the weather. The survival of the smallholder farming sector in the Zimbabwean context is crucial for both political and social stability. This is not merely because it houses more than 75 percent of the country's total population, but also because it has the potential to offer subsistence to urban victims of SAPs. Nevertheless, some significant gains made in developing this agricultural sector have been put in limbo by the threat of their collapse under deregulated high input prices, open market and 'unfair' competition, removal of support and infrastructural services (grain collection depot closures), and increased risks of farming in distant communal areas.

11 The social impact of structural adjustment programmes on the youth in Zambia

Kwaku Osei-Hwedie

The role and process of structural adjustment programmes (SAPS) in reviving the economies of developing countries as part of the efforts to promote social development has attracted much attention. Socio-economic development remains a central issue because individuals as well as governments subscribe to it. However, there is always some controversy surrounding whatever methods are chosen to pursue socio-economic development. The question is how to reorganize the economy, and civil society as a whole, in order for people to have a meaningful and satisfying life. In Zambia, efforts are well underway towards liberalization of the economy and democratization of the political process. SAPS are being undertaken to bring the economy back on sound footing, and give people more say in socio-political and economic issues.

The main purpose of this chapter is to examine the impact of Zambia's SAPs on one social group, youths; to identify and discuss the socio-economic difficulties associated with SAPs which those youths face; and to discuss the strategies adopted to cope with these difficulties. The emphasis is on the period from the mid-1980s to 1991.

There are several problems associated with making assessments of the impact of SAPs on any social group. These include lack of substantive information due to non-disaggregated data and scarcity of comprehensive household surveys. Another relates to interpretation of existing data. It is difficult to separate the effects of normal adverse changes from those of SAPs (Commonwealth Secretariat, 1989); and hence no specific effort is made to do so in this discussion. Thus, some of the effects described may well be attributable to general changes in economic circumstances than to SAPs *per se*.

For the purpose of this discussion, the focus will be on youths who are enrolled in colleges and universities as well as those in resettlement and skills training programmes. This choice enables us to focus on two contrasting youth groups. On the one hand, the college and university group have been fortunate enough to progress through the educational system and, hence, have better employment opportunities and life prospects. On the other hand, most of those in skills training have had a feel of the educational system but had to drop out for one reason or the other. Hence, they have had to readjust their educational expectations and employment prospects.

The definition of youth chosen is one based on age, and the age range is 14-25. This age based definition enables us to capture students in both the non-formal training programmes after grades 7 and 9 and university and college students. Generally, most students dropout of the school system at grades 7 and 9 which correspond roughly to ages 14 and 16, respectively. The majority of university and college students are between the ages of 18 and 24, although there are some students who enter the university as mature age students.

University and college students

Burawoy (1972) argues that, in the past, students were usually ignored and many scholars did not make major attempts to study them. However, with the expansion of education in Zambia, especially university education, and the rising consciousness that education was not only for the privileged few but was one of the keys to the egalitarian society, the position of the student has altered accordingly. Burawoy (1972) contends that three factors are noteworthy in helping us understand the increased importance of students.

Firstly, increased numbers of students have led to increased competition for jobs, the devaluation of diplomas, and the depersonalization of education. Secondly, students have become increasingly self-conscious, possibly because they are now more conspicuous by virtue of their numbers and their being defined as a distinct group. Third, the enhanced self-consciousness, alongside an inflated view of their importance, engendered by the nature of their education and their experiences in wider society, has contributed to the development of specific student interests despite the transience of the student status. Many scholars who have analyzed students in Zambia have concentrated more on university students than college students. Perhaps, this is not surprising because the former are relatively more vocal and radical than the latter who, except in a few instances, have assumed a conservative profile. In this chapter, therefore, more emphasis has been placed on university students for no other reason than that there is more information on, and interest in, university students than their college counterparts.

The University of Zambia was established on 23rd November, 1965. There were 312 full-time students in Natural Sciences, Humanities and Social Sciences, Education, and Social Work. In 1979, the full-time student population stood at 3,339. This rose to over 4,000 in 1990. In 1987, the university federal structure, which was comprised of the Lusaka Campus and the Ndola Campus was abolished, and instead a new university called Copperbelt University was inaugurated, in place of the Ndola Campus, with a student population of about 1,500.

Since 1971 relations between university students and the government have not been very warm. There have been repeated conflicts and clashes over policy between students and the government. The former considered themselves stalwart Marxist-Leninists and were opposed to the philosophy of "humanism" of the ruling United National Independence Party (UNIP). They felt that they were intellectuals of the Zambian society and should therefore be afforded the opportunity of interpreting national and international issues to the masses (Lulat, 1981). It is not surprising that since the economic condition of the mass of Zambians has worsened as a result of the country's economic quagmire, university students have been provided with an opportunity to express their solidarity with the masses in even more concrete terms than before.

We note that students were catalysts in the riots which rocked parts of Zambia, including the capital, Lusaka, precipitating the shortlived coup staged by Army Lieutenant Mwansa Luchembe on June 30, 1990. The students called upon the populace to rise and protest against the sharp increase in the price of maize meal. Lulat (1981) extends this argument by stating that the continued comparatively high level of radical student political activism among Third World countries is an outcome of the failure, to date, to achieve meaningful levels of development in those countries so as to enable them to wean themselves away from dependence. Thus, major student demands have been either in terms of increases in their subsistence allowance or improving the quality of meals in the cafeteria.

Despite the remarkable expansion in education, there are still some problems. Available data indicate that about 20 percent of pupils enrolled in grade 4 in rural areas do not proceed to grade five due to lack of facilities (ILO, 1981). Thus, the progression rate has remained very low, the student teacher ratio is very high, and investment in education has declined drastically (Osei-Hwedie, Mwansa, and Mufune, 1991). These have been compounded by the economic crisis and rising population growth. For example, the progression rate for secondary schools has dropped from 23 percent to 18 percent. The implications have been a growing inability for a large number of students to continue in formal education and the need to find other avenues to prepare them for employment.

Settlement schemes and skills training programmes were seen as the answer to the mounting problem of youth unemployment. These were also identified as the tools to effect rural development; to spearhead modern farming methods and training in socio-economic innovation; and to improve land tenure, cooperative working, and credit arrangements which were seen as more difficult to achieve in old established farm areas (Kalapula, 1985). Over the years, the government has laid down objectives and strategies aimed at addressing the problem of unemployment among the "out-of-school" youths in the country. As a result, special school leaver projects have been set up throughout the county. The need to expand these projects increases as the numbers of unemployed school leavers rise and the economy increasingly fails to expand to create more jobs for the masses of job seekers. The government has, as a matter of policy, emphasized that the most obvious alternative to wage employment is employment on the land. Hence, the frequent "go back to the land" exhortations (Kalapula 1989: 33). Some of the strategies adopted by the government to cater for the employment needs of the school leavers and drop outs include:

1 *Land resettlement schemes* These have been inaugurated with the intention of creating employment opportunities. This is in addition to other existing land resettlement schemes such as rural reconstruction cooperatives, Zambia national service camps, and state farms (Republic of Zambia, 1988).

2 *Youth development skills programmes* These are coordinated by the Ministry of Youth and Sport. Every year, 4,000-4,700 youths are trained in youth training centres in various provinces. They participate in activities such as carpentry, agriculture and farm management, tailoring, mechanics, tannery and leather works.

3 *The national youth resettlement scheme* This was launched on April 15, 1988 by the government through the Ministry of Defence. The objective of this scheme is to settle unemployed youths, aged between 16 and 35 years, irrespective of their marital status and educational attainments (Kalapula, 1989). According to Kalapula (1985), the settlement schemes have not been able to achieve their objectives and the centres have been plagued with several problems including the location of the schemes, provision of social services and other necessary infrastructure, the internal organization of the centres (in particular the social and productive relations between the settlers and military supervising staff), and low production rates despite the large scope of investment and controlled selection of settlers.

Crisis and adjustment

In order to understand the economic crisis and related adjustment and coping strategies, one must also understand some of the macro changes in the Zambia political economy. Burdette (1988) maintains that Zambian society reflects two worlds - one based on indigenous culture and the other on foreign culture; that there is social and personal dislocation due to rapid cultural transformation; and that the confusion associated with the changes create tension for people and social problems for the government. Since independence, close to one-half of the population have migrated to urban areas. By 1980, the Lusaka, Central, Copperbelt, and Southern provinces contained over 55 percent of the nation's population (Burdette, 1988).

Post independence Zambia has seen a rapid stratification of people into classes. By 1980, according to Burdette (1988), distinct social classes were identifiable and the earlier myth that Zambia was an egalitarian society in which upward mobility was based on hard work and merit had been shattered. In general, a wealthy class, a working class, and a petite bourgeoisie class are all observable. The emergence of an extensive and highly sophisticated material culture makes stratification more pronounced, especially in the urban areas. By 1976, 8 percent of the income was shared by the poorest 40 percent of the population while 35 percent of the income was shared by the richest 5 percent (Burdette, 1988).

Political independence gave the nationalists the mandate to restructure the political system and with it the economy of the nation. This mandate was entrusted to Kenneth David Kaunda. In restructuring the political and economic system, it also changed the national social framework. First came administrative reorganization and localization of posts, finally culminating in a policy of Zambianization. The civil service saw accelerated expansion. For example, it rose from 22,511 civil servants in the 1963-64 period, to 51,497 civil servants in 1967. Zambians were promoted to high level positions to meet the personnel requirement for expanded services which had been openly neglected under colonial rule. For example, expenditure rose sharply in the early years with remarkable achievements in education (Burdette, 1988).

Educational policies in Zambia have been implemented through several strategies. The 1966 Education Act integrated the hitherto racially segregated school system. Through this act, all educational systems were integrated into one national system of education. Furthermore, tuition was made free in all government and government aided institutions through to the university level. In 1978, the government embarked on educational reform. The goal was to provide fee-free and compulsory nine year universal primary education (Simson, 1985). These reforms also provided for continuing education for adults and youths who had left or had never entered full time education. In 1975, the government launched a programme designed to make educational institutions engage in production. This was meant to inculcate manual labour and the love of agriculture into the youths. The economic crisis and the need to cut spending on social service brought the third major policy change into the Zambian education system in the late 1980s. Tuition was introduced and examination and boarding fees were imposed on students. However, by any standard of measurement, educational improvements have been rapid and impressive.

The civil service, also went through significant changes. The civil service was politicized through political appointments to reflect and satisy entrenched interests. President Kaunda also devised the system of 'reshuffling' - frequently changing holders of senior party, bureaucratic, and parastatal posts, sending them to other posts and at times restructuring the jobs involved. Reshuffles were done without prior warning or consultation. The result was that many ministries and departments were constantly going through change of identity and personnel (Burdette, 1988).

During this period, there was an increasing growth of the personal power of the President. With the increasing power of the President came a corresponding decline in the power of other institutions such as the cabinet and the national assembly. Despite the consolidation of power, it became necessary to pacify party loyalists by finding posts for them. Thus, as part of the reorganization of the economy, a new economic era for Zambia was launched, backed by the ideology of humanism and socialism. It has been argued that the intention was to socialize control in order to bring it closer to the people of Zambia (Tordoff, 1974).

Zambia is a mono-economy based on copper mining. Copper has always accounted for over 90 per cent of the country's export earnings; 40 per cent of GDP in the early 1970s; and around 19 per cent of national employment. Mining was not so much of a liability immediately after independence. Firstly, copper prices were very high at nearly twice the average world production costs (Kydd, 1988). Secondly, Zambian mineral output was rising, and thirdly, the new government managed to recapture the mineral rent from the British South Africa Company. Eventually, the government effected some nationalization to gain complete control of the mine. This situation enabled a high rate of investment of about 30 per cent of GDP. The 1968 and 1969 economic reforms ushered in the era of nationalization. This nationalization brought in revenues which enabled the creation of parastatals under the Zambia Industrial and Mining Corporation (ZIMCO). This boom situation of the 1960s and early 1970s also contributed to rapid urbanization. Thus, the urban share of Zambia's population rose from 20 per cent to 45 per cent between 1963 and 1980 (Daniel, 1985).

The boom years also came with real wage demands between 1964 and 1970. Within this period, the real earning of employees more or less doubled. In the same period employment in the public sector increased significantly. There developed a corresponding growth in social services to support public employees and other categories of the expanding urban population. All of these contributed to the growth of the non-productive, non-tradeable, and consumption-based sectors. According to Daniel (1985), between 1965 and 1970, total public expenditure grew at an average annual rate of 19.3 per cent. Between 1966 and 1973, 53 per cent of new recorded wage employment was generated in the public sector, and about 40 percent in government services alone.

The turning point in Zambia's economy came in the mid-1970s. This was marked by an enormous fall in copper prices. Colclough (1988) indicates that the average real price of copper on the London Metal Exchange fell by one-quarter during 1974-76, and that by 1984-85 it stood at only 40 percent of its real 1970-72 value. This was compounded by declining ore grades and technical production difficulties. In an economy which still relied on copper the price drops had serious adverse effects including the following:

1 Manufacturing which relied on foreign inputs started declining (Daniel, 1985);

2 Real domestic income was cut by one-quarter by 1975 (Colclough, 1988);

3 The national debt increased due to inability to pay on the one hand, and the need to sustain consumption on the other (Colclough, 1988; Makgetla, 1986);

4 Merchandise imports declined to about one-third of the 1970 volume, falling by almost one-half between 1980 and 1985 alone (Makgetla, 1986);

5 The real value of exports (adjusted for changes in import prices) was halved between 1974 and 1975, and it was halved again by 1983 (Colclough, 1988) and;

6 General living conditions deteriorated and institutional decay developed.

All of these developments were exacerbated by the oil shocks starting in 1973. In the 1970s the government reacted to the situation by instituting mechanisms of protection of urban interests through subsidy maintenance. It also instituted mechanisms of control of the economy through pricing, marketing, foreign exchange, and trade measures. The government considered the difficulties as temporary and hence did not institute any major policy changes. Instead, the major thrust of policy became that of trying to see to it that consumers were protected from what would otherwise have been inevitable price increases given the declining supply situation in the country (Musokotwane, 1989). In light of this, price controls were placed on a number of essential commodities such as the national staple - maize meal - as well as on petroleum products. Such a policy measure to control prices had far reaching implications, especially on the agricultural sector. For example, this policy discouraged the growth of the agricultural sector and at the same time fuelled the rural-urban migration process since the domestic terms of trade were deteriorating against the rural areas.

In December 1982, the prices of all commodities except maize and wheat were decontrolled. Monopolies in agriculture were also to be phased out. Zambia broke off with the IMF in May 1987 and promulgated the New Economy Recovery Plan (NERP). The objectives emphasized agricultural exports, import-substitution, and creation of employment among emergent farmers. Policy instruments included the use of appropriate technology such as oxen draught power; promoting regional cooperative advantage, for example, encouraging certain crops in appropriate provinces; and the reduction of input costs to make agriculture competitive.

Despite the reform measures adopted, the downward turn of the economy continued. By 1982, the economy had reached an all time low ebb with no sign of picking up. Realizing that formative efforts to revitalize the economy had not reached fruition, the government tried an alternative package of policy changes. These were primarily aimed at allowing more market forces to control the economy. Hence in 1982, efforts were made to liberalize the economy. The decontrol of the price of beef was considered a step in that direction. The local currency (Kwacha) was also linked to a basket of other currencies, and this entailed more flexibility in the exchange rate policy than was previously the case.

Perhaps the most radical move towards liberalization was instituted in October, 1985 when the government adopted SAPs under the sponsorship of the International Monetary Fund (IMF) and the World Bank (Republic of Zambia, 1987: 3). The hallmarks of this programme were: (1) foreign exchange auctioning - this meant that foreign exchange was to be distributed by auctioning it to the highest bidders. Hence, the foreign exchange rate was to be market-based (Chanda, 1990); (2) decontrol of prices of most commodities. This was aimed at improving the profitability and viability of enterprises operating in the economy so as to forestall redundancies; (3) upward adjustment of interest rates; (4) wage freeze; (5) decontrol of imports; and (6) restriction on government expenditure aimed at reducing the budget deficit.

In the face of the crisis, policy makers viewed the youth situation as a case which needed special attention through the mobilization of resources. For example, school leavers were seen as comprising the largest unskilled and unemployed collective and hence special school leavers' projects became the answer (Kalapula, 1989). As a matter of policy, the government insisted that the most obvious alternative to formal employment is employment on the land. Hence, the future of the youth was related to the processes of agricultural and rural development (Kawonga, 1981). The belief that youth unemployment was due to lack of skills led to the conclusion that settlement schemes would eventually turn into self-sustaining communities, capable of employing all the settlers in the long run (Mulengu, 1989).

The impact of structural adjustment on youths

Despite the good intentions, the impact of SAPs on youths, just like on other social groups, has been very severe. SAPs discouraged the expansion of the agricultural industry, especially peasant agriculture and encouraged rural-urban migration. This is more so because agricultural inputs were beyond the reach of ordinary or peasant farmers. The contraction of the agricultural industry meant dwindling opportunities for employment in that sector. Its expansion would have meant more young people finding their livelihood on the land, and with that it would have been possible to encourage them to remain in the rural areas. Peasants were not able to take any serious advantage of increased producer prices for these were off-set by increases in the prices of inputs, especially fertilizer. In addition to this, late payments for produce disadvantaged the peasants. Thus, at best, the rural areas remained constantly unattractive for the youths as a place to seek better opportunities. At the same time, capital-intensive production processes requiring relatively little manpower reduced employment opportunities for most of the young people who had migrated to the cities.

Furthermore, SAPs reduced the purchasing power of consumers and occasioned a profound drop in living standards. This was more severe for the youths who had to depend on others for their livelihood (Musokotwane, 1989). This is especially so when we consider the fact that unemployment is higher among young people. Hence, the youth have had no means to cushion themselves from the rise in prices. Students at the University of Zambia, for example, were subjected to high prices for meals and books at the institution. In 1988, meal prices at the University of Zambia went up by 100 percent which the Dean of Students said had been necessitated by the high cost of food stuffs (*Zambia Daily Mail*, 1989).

The declining purchasing power, in turn, meant a fall in demand for commodities. As a result many small scale industries closed down. According to Republic of Zambia (1987), investment in unsold stocks increased and parastatals suffered liquidity problems. The result was that thousands of workers were laid off. The inflation rate which rose from 20 percent in 1984 to 60 percent in 1988 adversely affected investment and employment both in the formal and informal sectors of the economy. The consequence was that unemployment and underemployment, particularly among the youth in urban areas, emerged as a serious problem. Employment in the formal sector declined from 365,190 in 1984 to 360,540 in 1986 (Republic of Zambia, 1987).

Musokotwane (1989) indicates that the rise in prices manifested itself in increased cases of malnutrition, poor health, and falling living standards all due to increasing poverty. Income related criteria is seen as perhaps the most important method for measuring poverty (UNICEF, 1986). Zambia, in general, experienced a drop in income due to falling terms of trade beginning in the mid-1970s (Reinikka-Soininen, 1990). Using income indicators, the Price and Incomes Commission (PIC), in 1985, estimated that 35 percent of urban dwellers were living below the poverty datum line (PDL). The figure for those living in high density housing in urban areas was 50 percent. For the rural areas the PIC estimated a figure of 40 percent of existing households as living below the PDL. In the last decade or so, Zambia has experienced a general drop in national income and consequently it has been reclassified as a low-income country having been dropped from middle-income status (Reinikka-Soininen, 1990).

Malnutrition is a well known symptom of poverty. Household food security and nutritional status highly correlate in Zambia. Food security and nutrition are affected by the amounts and kinds of food available at a given place and time; the ability of the household to obtain food; and the desire on the part of the household to obtain food that they can access through the market, home production, and other mechanisms (Cogill and Zasa, 1990). A study which compared nutrition figures from the early 1970s and the early 1990s found that 20 years of change and development in Zambia have not resulted in any significant improvements in the nutritional status of children living in rural areas. What is clear, for example, is that stunting has certainly not improved and may possibly have worsened in the last

20 years (Cogill and Zasa, 1990).

The policy measures also led to uncompetitive salaries not only between the civil service and the parastatal and private sectors but also between those salaries offered in the country and neighbouring countries. The resulting loss of skilled manpower to parastatals, the private sector, and neighbouring countries as people sought "greener pastures", meant that the institutions for youths could no longer maintain high standards. The falling standards affected the morale of the youths and students at the University of Zambia and other institutions of learning were greatly hit by the exodus of lecturers as a result ofthe poor incomes they earned.

The departure of excellent academics has had a demoralizing effect upon those who remained, many of them junior members of staff who should not be expected to cope with the kinds of heavy responsibilities they were given at such early stages of their careers (Moody, 1989). As a result of continuing staff shortages at the University of Zambia, very little research is done and new programmes such as post-graduate courses cannot be designed or implemented, thus restricting opportunities for youth to improve themselves academically. To cope with the low wages many lecturers are engaged in part-time work. Moody (1989) observes that many lecturers have tended to have part-time consultancies which interfere with their academic duties and also result in friction with their colleagues who may have to shoulder more responsibilities.

Production in the economy has also been severely affected. For example, in the agricultural sector, bank borrowing has become prohibitive. The effect on youths, especially those in skills training schemes who wish to enter the informal sector upon graduation, is obvious. As Mulengu (1989) points out, one factor which is linked to youth unemployment in the country is that they lack starting capital and are therefore unable to enter the informal sector. They also lack the collateral which may enable them to borrow from commercial institutions. The high interest rate on bank loans also puts loans beyond the reach of many people.

SAPs have created a plurality of hardships for the youths as government expenditure on social welfare services have been curtailed. An example is the introduction of school fees to make parents share in the educational costs of their children. Most people have expressed fear that these types of measures would result in mass illiteracy because most youths would not be able to afford to go to school. In fact, as a reaction to the measure, over 1,500 students at the Copperbelt University rioted to show the public that they disapproved of the scheme. Protest commentary also appeared in the national dailies against the fees and their possible impact on lower class students (*Zambia Daily Mail*, 1989; *Pasha Magazine*, 1989).

Reduced funding to the University of Zambia, for example, has adversely affected the running of the institution. According to the Commissions of Inquiry appointed to look into problems of the institution, the university was provided with adequate funds to enable it to run all its programmes effectively from its inception until 1973. Student requirements such as food, books, allowances, and accommodation facilities were sufficiently provided for and the University was able to make available all the materials necessary for teaching and research. Since 1974, however, following the rapid deterioration of government finances as a result of the fall in copper prices, the flow of financial resources to the University did not keep up with the expansion that took place in the number of schools and students (Republic of Zambia, 1986: 39).

The unsatisfactory under-financing engendered a critical cash flow problem for the university. For instance, because of limitations in finances, the university authorities, in their allocation of funds, were forced to place emphasis on student catering at the expense of the library and bookshop both of which are key to any university education. The lack of scholarly materials in both the bookshop and the library was another way by which the economic conditions prevented academic excellence. In fact, the university had to cut down on the number of courses offered due to inadequate funding which led to reduced educational facilities. At one point in time, the university had to rely on a substantial overdraft facility from the Zambia National Commercial Bank to meet its obligations.

College students were not spared from these problems either. The quality of college education declined mainly because of reduced government financing which manifested itself in such problems as poorly furnished and dilapidated buildings, and a scarcity of textbooks and other essential items. During the period 1979-1984, student enrolment in technical education institutions remained stable but had dropped by 21 percent by 1988. The policy objectives to increase enrolment in each college, especially the teachers' colleges, from 300 to 500 students was also not realized due to financial constraints.

The impact of the harsh economic climate on university and college students was summed up by the former Minister of Higher Education, Professor Lameck Goma, who observed that the economic crisis has had a profound impact on the provision, development, and progress of higher education and science and technology in that students and researchers lack materials; buildings and equipment are not maintained; laboratories cannot be used for lack of supplies and spare parts; researchers cannot follow developments in their areas due to lack of current journals and other essential publications; and lack of funds to attend professional meetings (*Zambia Daily Mail*, 1989).

For those youths in resettlement and skills training schemes the problem was even more acute. Lack of sufficient funds to run these schemes effectively was the order of the day. In one of the daily papers it was reported that Twange youth skill-cum-production project was closed due to lack of adequate financial resources even though it was one of the most progressive programmes in the country (*Times of Zambia*, 1988). The high cost of inputs has also been a big set back for youths who graduate from skills training schemes. It is said that out of the 4,000-4,700 youths, who are trained in various provinces every year, only about 30 to 40 percent are placed in self-employment. This is due to the high cost of inputs such as building materials and equipment.

Some coping mechanisms

A common strategy among university students is that of preparing their own meals as opposed to eating all their meals from the university dining halls where meals are expensive. Many students, at the beginning of a new term, form cooking clubs, with memberships ranging from two to six, and pool their funds together. They appoint a treasurer who is responsible for keeping the money and buying foodstuffs. Most students say this measure is not only cost-effective but also convenient since they prepare meals of their own choice and cook at their own time. It is also felt that students become responsible by managing their own ration system. The ability to regulate meals and choice of food means possible savings for other pressing needs.

It has also been observed that there is a proliferation of small businesses on college and university campuses. These businesses deal in several items including soft drinks, bread, scones, rice, eggs, cakes, clothing, and beer. Students sell such items either from their rooms or from canteens situated at various strategic places within the students' residences. Through such strategies most university and college students have been able to handle some of the problems occasioned by the economic crisis. The supplies come from relatives and friends or they are bought from the cheapest source and resold. The commodities sold are mainly based on demand and availability.

For university and college students, the introduction of boarding fees as a result of government measures to reduce public expenditure has meant scouting for alternative means of income. This measure has hit students more directly than any other in the educational sphere. Some university students who were previously sponsored by the government have sought new sponsors to enable them to complete their studies. Since the measure to reduce the amount of money given to students does not affect those students who are sponsored by individuals and private companies, searching for additional sponsors is more prominent among government-sponsored students. For example, in the 1989-90 academic year government-sponsored students were asked to contribute to their sponsorship. Such contributionss are usually sought mainly from donor agencies. It has also been observed that during vacations, most students seek employment to enable them to save some funds for the next academic year.

It also became very common for students to go from office to office seeking research assistantships from faculty members likely to conduct research during vacations. It was also not unusual to find close to 100 students responding to advertisements for one or two research assistantships. Students were known to have taken up to a week off from studies to conduct interviews in far away parts of the country. Most of them realized that they could not rely solely on their parents and relatives any longer because those individuals were also affected by the crisis. Those students who managed to secure permanent jobs continued to work even during the course of the academic year (Osei-Hwedie et al, 1992).

For those youths in skills training and resettlement schemes, it was often very frustrating when they were unable to enter into the informal sector even after training due to the high cost of inputs such as equipment. They survived on petty activities such as selling cigarettes, and others resorted to criminal activities. For example, it was reported that most of the youths who had undergone training as mechanics at skills training centres were behind the rampant thefts of spare parts from motor vehicles which they later sold. Mijere (1989) who analyzed the creativity of "mishanga" (cigarette) sellers reported that most of them had failed to find employment and "mishanga" selling was the only alternative employment for them.

Mijere (1989) also contends that the youths in the informal sector instituted several informal market strategies such as repackaging of commodities in quantities affordable by the poor. In addition to this, they delivered commodities to customers, sold on credit, and allowed customers to bargain. According to Chan (1989), some youths were also organized into groups with leaders assisted by secretaries, treasurers, and publicity secretaries responsible for recruitment. They also had elaborate systems of protection during times of police raids, and they conformed to a special code and street language.

The other coping strategy that has been used by youths in skills training and resettlement schemes is the formation of cooperatives. Even the government recognizes the importance of cooperatives as a coping strategy for youths. The youths themselves have, at their own initiative, created clubs and cooperatives as a means of survival. These enable them to pool their resources together and purchase inputs which would have otherwise been beyond their reach had they worked individually. This mechanism has proved to be a success for most of them and many are participating in it.

With the increasing economic difficulties, more and more youths ventured into informal and black market activities. According to Todd and Shaw (1980), approximately 10-15 per cent of urban working males are located in the informal sector and when both sexes are considered, the proportion rises to about 20 per cent. The importance of the informal sector as a coping strategy for youths increased in the 1980s. Although no hard data exist, there has been a considerable increase of youths in the service sector. The streets of Lusaka and other cities bear witness to thousands of youths selling soap, cooking oil, tooth paste, and cigarettes; and washing and servicing cars. Even the police "clean up campaigns" could not stop them. Concomitant with this has been the astronomical increase in petty theft and other crimes in city centres and bus stops.

Conclusions

The discussion has focused on the changes in the political economy of Zambia; the ensuing crisis; efforts at restructuring; and reactions and coping strategies by some segments of the youth. From the discussion it is evident that the youths are not disinterested parties in the changes that are taking place and that they have sought measures to adapt to the changing socio-economic conditions; and to improve their circumstances of living, or at least to ensure their survival within the context of the economic crisis.

It is apparent that a new type of youth, more vocal, aggressive and aware is emerging, one who plunges into social, economic and political issues as they emerge, and participates, first hand, in order to survive in the society. Not that the pre-crisis youths have been passive. However, their participation has been more of vocal reaction and mere demonstrations against policies. The post-crisis youths have continued with this opposition against official policies and have added another dimension, that of taking positive and concrete measures, also at the individual level, to meet the ever changing social and economic demands as a result of SAPs.

It must also be noted that, whereas the changing character of the youths has had positive aspects, there are negative consequences that one must be aware of. The youths have been emboldened by the crisis and have become aggressive. Thus, some of the unemployed have transferred this energy into criminal activities such as gang attacks, robberies and auto thefts, a situation which earlier youth policies tried to prevent. Finally, on the whole, the extent to which the youths have changed due to the crisis and economic restructuring needs further systematic investigation.

12 Migration as a consequence of structural adjustment in Africa: The impact on Botswana

Gwen N. Lesetedi

Botswana is one of the few countries in Africa not to have implemented structural adjustment programmes (SAPs). Despite this, Botswana still has been affected by the consequences of SAPs on other countries in the region. Zambia and Zimbabwe, for example, are two countries in the region that have implemented SAPs. These countries share geographical boundaries as well as socio-cultural and economic ties with Botswana and there has been considerable migration from these two countries, as well as the rest of Africa, to Botswana primarily to seek employment.

This chapter focuses on the consequences of international migration which one could say, in some ways, has been intensified by SAPs. Most of the data used are from the *1991 Botswana Population and Housing Census*. Censuses are conducted in Botswana every 10 years and the most current one was conducted in 1991. The census data provide information on sex, age, occupation, and type of income of the migrants. The other source of data is the migration statistics collected at border posts entry points. Foreign nationals entering or leaving Botswana are required to complete a form at gazetted entry points.

The context of migration

Migration in Africa can be seen in the context of people movements that have taken place in the past as well as the present (Adepoju, 1988). Such movements from one place to another, for various reasons, has always occurred in Africa. The causes and patterns of international migration in Africa are rooted not only in the historical process but also in the social, political, and economic processes in the region.

In practice, it is necessary to treat international migration and internal migration separately. However, there are linkages between internal and international migration. For example, most prospective migrants tend to move around internally before they graduate to moving across borders to other countries. International migration can be further categorized into four types of movement (Oucho, 1988).

The first category consists of permanent immigrants or emigrants which is considered part of a historical process. The second category is that of legal labour migrants and these include both skilled and unskilled labour movements between countries. The third category is the illegal or undocumented migrants. The final category consists of refugees, which is characterized by movement due to civil, political, or environmental strife. Africa is second only to the Middle East and Asia in terms of the number of refugees (Parnwell, 1993: 42).

In Africa, the use of migrant labour has been a long standing and pervasive feature. South Africa, for example, had the most complex system of labour control. Workers from Zimbabwe, Malawi, Botswana, Mozambique, Lesotho, and Swaziland provided labour to the country's industries. However, this is changing as Botswana has now become one of the primary destinations for immigrants because of its booming economy and the poor economic performance of the other countries in the region. Most migrants to Botswana are skilled and educated unlike the unskilled labour which went to South Africa in the past. Also, there are no bureaucratic arrangements for recruiting labour as was the case in South Africa which had set up employment offices in the source countries in order to recruit labour for its mines, farms, and so on.

Population movements, whether it is internal migration or international migration, can be of central importance to the development process. Such movements provide a benchmark of the success or lack thereof of the process of development. At times development may be so uneven that it results in people moving away from areas where there is no progress to places where they perceive there is greater progress. Migration is also part and parcel of human development. It has also played a role in the spread of technology, in the process of industrialization, and in urbanization. Migration does contribute both negatively and positively to the development process and it remains one of the key factors in the process of social change and development.

The causes and patterns of migration, be it internal or international, are quite varied. There are several factors influencing people to move. These include demographic factors such as age, sex, education; and economic factors such as jobs and better incomes. Basically, migration is largely the result of economic motives. People migrate when they are unable to satisfy their economic aspirations within their own societies.

Structural adjustment programmes in Africa

Sub-Saharan Africa has the world's lowest rate of economic growth. This has been compounded by rapid population growth and the political instability experienced in most of the countries. By 1989, thirty-five countries in sub-Saharan Africa had adopted SAPs (Sandbrook, 1991: 95). These SAPs were designed to redress stagnant economies and stimulate economic growth. Not only were more jobs supposed to be created but more industries and private companies also as a result of increased private investment. Unfortunately, SAPs, to date, have not achieved all of that. In actual fact, in some instances the programmes have led to a rise in unemployment, a stagnation of wages, and falling standards in the provision of social services. As Sawyer (1990: 36) puts it, "unfortunately, of those who remain in employment, even the best paid, particularly in the public service, are subject to severe erosion of the real values of their earnings". Though some jobs have been created through SAPs, the wages are not high enough to sustain the workers and, consequently, these workers move on to greener pastures.

However, SAPs have registered some success stories. In some cases their implementation have resulted in key reforms which have helped the poor. The poor were hit by the general decline in economic activity but they benefit from improvements in price incentives that result in the better off rural households employing more workers, for example. In addition, they are able to purchase locally produced goods and services. SAPs have also brought about improved rural infrastructure and greater rural credit which has contributed effectively to the growth of the agricultural sector. Taking the example of Nigeria, during the oil boom, the agricultural sector suffered great neglect. As a result, food production declined and Nigeria became a large net food importer. Since the implementation of SAPs in 1986, there has been an increase in cash crop output.

Another success has been the growth of the informal sector. The number of people engaged in the informal sector has increased significantly in most of these countries. In Zimbabwe, there are around 1.6 million people in this sector accounting for 27 percent of the total labour force (Brand, Mupedziswa, and Gumbo, 1993: 250). In Tanzania, between the period 1985-86, the informal sector contributed 30 percent to GDP (Shao, Kiwara, and Makusi, 1992: 97). This contribution rose to 50 percent by 1990.

In the Southern African region, countries like Malawi, Zambia, Zimbabwe, and Tanzania have all embarked on SAPs. Zambia implemented SAPs as far back as 1985 while Zimbabwe implemented them in 1990. In Zimbabwe, the government announced a five year plan to stimulate economic growth in a different direction. The new direction was that economic activity would be less controlled by government. What has occurred instead is an increase in unemployment which has resulted in the migration of both skilled and unskilled manpower to seek employment opportunities in other countries. This is a trend not only peculiar to Zimbabwe but also to some of the other countries implementing SAPs. It is important to look at the consequences of implementing SAPs in some of these countries because that is where the migrants in Botswana originate from.

In Zambia, despite the implementation of SAPs, the economic situation did not improve. The country has experienced a deterioration in the health and education sector. The delivery of medical services has drastically declined due to the shortage of drugs and equipment. Education has also suffered the same fate as funding declined and thereby resulting in poor conditions of service for teachers and a general deterioration in the infrastructure to the point where pupils sat on floors without textbooks and other school facilities.

During the period 1985-90, unemployment stood at over 60 percent (Mwanawina, 1993: 77). The capacity of the economy to generate more jobs decreased over the years. The government had tried to redress the situation by absorbing more labour into the civil service. This resulted in the government becoming the largest employer in the country. However, even with such steps, formal employment increased by only one percent between 1988 and 1990 (Mwanawina, 1993: 76).

The consequences of migration

Migration is a dependent as well as an independent variable depending on the circumstances. As a dependent variable it can be a response to social, political, economic, and cultural changes within society. It can also be viewed as an independent variable since it can initiate change itself. In this chapter, migration is considered as a dependent variable since it is responding to changes within society - those changes which have been brought about due to the implementation of SAPs.

Migrants are usually categorized according to whether or not they have crossed geographical boundaries. These boundaries could be district, county, or international. In the case of internal migration the motivation to move is stronger than international migration. This is so because international migration may involve a change of language, customs, politics, and so on. Migration is associated with the redistribution of the population and a contribution to the population growth of a given place. It is also viewed as an efficient adaptation to changing economic circumstances. Migration has made it possible for countries of migrant destination to experience more rapid economic growth in that such countries attract skilled labour.

On the other hand, it has been argued that this type of migration prevents the establishment of a permanent industrial labour force. It discourages the acquisition of skills by the locals in the recipient areas. This may lead to social problems in the recipient areas where migrants find jobs and increase the rate of unemployment amongst the locals. Migration is also selective. For example, only a selected proportion of the population migrates. Usually it is those in the younger ages and the majority of migrants tend to be males. It is easier for the younger migrants to find jobs as they are in the economically active ages.

The case of Botswana

Due to the favourable economic climate in Botswana the number of foreigners coming into the country has been increasing and, inversely, the migrant labour to South Africa has declined. Botswana now attracts more migrants in the form of skilled and semi-skilled workers mostly from its neighbouring countries. In 1971, there were 10,800 non-citizens in the country. This increased to 15,700 in 1981 and 29,500 in 1991. Among the non-citizens, 63 percent came from other African countries, with citizens from Southern African countries accounting for over 90 percent.

The majority of non-citizens are concentrated in the urban areas. It is one of the societal consequences of migration (both internal and external) that there is a redistribution of the population particularly in the direction of the urban areas. The younger and more skilled members of society are much more concentrated in towns than in the rural areas. In 1991, 64 percent of the non-citizens resided in urban areas with 41 percent in the capital city, Gaborone. It is only in the 1970s that the majority of non-citizens were concentrated in the rural areas (Republic of Botswana, 1994). However, this could be explained by the fact that Botswana was not that urbanized at that time.

As stated before, migration is selective, not everyone moves and males tend to move more than females. In 1991, males made up 61 percent of the non-citizen population. Of these, 45 percent were between the ages 15-29 and 37 percent were between the ages 30-44. Those aged 15-44 are the more economically active. The data confirm that there has been considerable migration to Botswana during the period 1985 and 1991. This period coincides with the poor economic performance in the countries of migrant origin and their implementation of SAPs.

One of the consequences of international migration is that it can help in the stimulation of economic growth in the receiving country. The excellent performance of Botswana's economy also coincided with the poor economic performance of most African countries and their implementation of SAPs. This, in turn, led to the migration of skilled manpower from the latter countries to greener pastures such as Botswana. Undoubtedly, international migration has brought skilled manpower to Botswana. The shortage of skilled manpower in Botswana, especially in the public sector, resulted in a large number of vacancies and a heavy reliance on expatriate manpower. The majority of the manpower shortage is experienced in the professional and technical categories.

The 1991 census indicated that the majority of the working non-citizens are in cash employment and they comprise 4.6 percent of the total working population in the country. Of those non-citizens working for cash, 88 percent are employees while the rest are self-employed. This further indicates that the shortage of skilled manpower is in the professional and technical categories. Non-citizen workers are comprised of 27 percent professionals followed by craft and trade workers who comprise 23 percent.

It is said that the influx of migrants tends to increase the demand for infrastructure, facilities, and social services such as schools and hospitals. Moreover, access to housing, education, transport and other facilities will be limited and thereby result in the lowering of living standards. However, these issue do not seem to arise in Botswana because non-citizens comprise a small proportion of the population. The 1991 census revealed that only 2.2 percent of the population are non-citizens. They are therefore not a burden on housing, education facilities, and so on.

It has also been argued that the acquisition of these foreign skilled workers discourages the local acquisition of skills because it is more cost-effective to employ those who already possess skills than to train personnel. However, this is also not the case in Botswana because the government has a manpower training policy which is supposed to address this problem. The government has also been making an effort to vigorously implement a localization policy whereby trained and skilled citizens replace expatriates in an orderly fashion.

Conclusions

International migration cannot be solely attributed to SAPs. It has always been there but it is has become much more intensified with the implementation of SAPs. The small foreign population of about 2 percent in Botswana, mostly from Africa, has contributed to the country's economic growth. Though it can be seen as a vicious cycle, the favourable economic climate is what attracted the migrants in the first place. Therefore they found an already well performing economy. At the same time, these professionals, undoubtedly, leave a gap in their home countries.

What should be noted is that migrants do contribute positively to the economy of Botswana and they do not pose a threat nor do they contribute to socio-economic problems. Such problems probably occur with the so called "invisible labour force" or illegal migrants. The legal non-citizens are employed in positions which can be easily monitored unlike the illegal immigrants tend to be relatively unskilled and contribute to the high rate of unemployment. It is difficult to determine the latter's impact on the economy because there are no official or unofficial statistics to even indicate how many there are in the country.

Finally, another important issue to consider is that SAPs might, in the long-term, result in the stimulation of economic growth in some of the currently failing economies. That would result in a reverse in the trend of skilled manpower migrating to Botswana and some of those who are already in the country may return to their countries of origin.

Part Four
ALTERNATIVE APPROACHES TO RECONSTRUCTION AND DEVELOPMENT

13 Better assessments of structural adjustment programmes in sub-Saharan Africa: The quest for more qualitative measures

Arnon Bar-On

From their inception, sub-Saharan Africa's structural adjustment programmes (SAPs) have been criticized, mainly on the grounds that they distort development more than advance it. Such distortions set in, it is suggested, because what economic development these programmes achieve is not accompanied by an attendant degree of social progress, defined usually in terms of more egalitarian income distribution. Armed with this thesis, analysts then assemble much convincing data to prove their point, such as the financial enrichment of the business, political, and administrative élite at the expense of the people, an ever increasing proportion of whom are relegated to living in poverty.

This chapter assesses the thesis that sub-Saharan Africa's SAPs were introduced, among other reasons, in the name of egalitarianism. Its main argument is that in order to prove that these programmes fail to distribute income progressively, it is necessary first to show that they sought greater income equality and, second, that they define equality as their critics do. If these assumptions are incorrect, then structural adjustment programmes might have failed on their critics' terms, but not on their own terms. Subsequent examination will then suggest criteria by which to assess the success or failure of SAPs. It will be argued, however, that this latter exercise is critically impeded by many of the current socio-economic indicators which are insufficiently sensitive to capture the essence of such success or failure.

Background

For most of its years of independence, and especially since the early 1980s, sub-Saharan Africa registered the smallest gains on most human development indices compared to other regions. Also, it is the only region where per capita food production has been declining regularly (IFAD, 1993). It is partly in response to this situation that African governments, often at the instigation of international agencies, have been induced to re-examine their development policies and to pursue new strategies to revitalize their economies.

Although there are many, often conflicting, explanations of the origins and nature of Africa's development difficulties - ranging from structuralist schools of thought to neoclassical monetarist analyses (Mkandawire, 1989) - there is virtual consensus on how these difficulties should be tackled. Mainly, these ideas revolve around modernization theory. This theory contends that the traditional and largely authoritarian systems of stratification of most African societies impede the emergence of the Western idea of man (rational, motivated by self-interest, competitive, and self-managing) which, in turn, thwarts the development of the entrepreneurial and capitalist class-system which is deemed as the cornerstone to achieving progressive change (Midgley, 1995).

It is in interpreting the primary objectives of this modernization or progressive change, however, that cardinal disagreements emerge and, consequently, give rise to different prescriptions for action. In light of the fact that all sub-Saharan African SAPs are heavily influenced by the International Monetary Fund and the World Bank, on whose assistance in implementing these programmes governments have become totally dependent, most of the disagreements are argued along either the New Right or the Liberal Left world-views.

The perspective of the new right

For the New Right, one central objective of structural adjustment is to unleash markets, which *ipso facto* engenders productivity. This productivity, in turn, generates capital and savings which can then be re-invested to further economic growth. New Right policies aim, therefore, to stimulate production, mainly by getting the prices of commodities right. This generally includes devaluation of artificially strengthened currencies, privatization of economic activities, tax reductions, curtailment of public spending on unproductive consumption, elimination of state subsidies for services and goods, and abolition of minimum wage legislation.

The critical property of these policies, from the perspective of this chapter, is that progressive income distribution features in none of them. Indeed, given that the New Right accepts inequality as an absolute value, fundamental to the free market's sheer existence, egalitarianism as a matter of policy negates the objectives of structural adjustment. Of course, this does not mean that advocates of the New Right reject more progressive income distribution as a possible outcome of the free market. As countries get wealthier, everyone should benefit, but the way this wealth is distributed, according to neoclassical economic theory, is of little importance. Criticism of the failure of SAPs to achieve greater income equality, at least from this perspective, is therefore misdirected.

The liberal left perspective

If we cannot criticize SAPs for failing to promote egalitarianism on the terms of the New Right, then it is to the Liberal Left interpretation of these programmes' objectives that we must turn. This is no easy task, however, for much Liberal Left thought is hard to pinpoint. In part, this is because Left Liberalism covers an extremely wide range of socio-political thought, and so its ideas are often muddled. Also, these Liberals are guided by few, if any, predetermined constructs. What concerns them is the functional efficiency of societies as they are rather than realizing some abstract good, and so their analyses and subsequent prescriptions for action are more a matter of pragmatism than of principle.

The Liberal Left shares with the New Right a fundamental faith in the free market, but their faith is equivocal. As Keynes pronounced, "The world is not so governed from above that private and social interest always coincide" (George and Wilding, 1994: 69), or as Patten (1983: 105) remarked that "Adam Smith's 'invisible hand' can get up to a great deal of mischief on its own". Primary among these mischiefs is the free market's potentially destructive implications for social order and stability, which in the Liberal Left view is the basis of all social life. In the words of Harold Macmillan, "if capitalism had been conducted all along as if the theory of private enterprise were a matter of principle we should have had civil war long ago" (Gilmour, 1978: 168).

The Liberal Left's response to civil disorder is to use society's organs of governance to create among its members a sense of "community", which Liberalism generally interprets as One Nation. "Society, is held together only by the moral bond of mutual obligations" (Walker, 1987: 45). Similarly, but from a more institutional position, Gilmour (1983: 224) argues that "a free state will not survive unless its people feel loyalty to it". Liberals are deeply concerned, therefore, with poverty and inequality which threaten conflict, and consequently with measures to reduce them. People will not feel loyalty to the state unless they gain from it protection and other benefits (Gilmour, 1983: 225). In short, the answer to reconciling society's need for social stability with the social consequences of capitalism, that is, class divisions, rests with social policy and so with the social services.

Conventional thinking holds that social services promote equality. As Le Grand (1982: 3) notes, it is "wholly or partially in the name of equality that most governments subsidize in some way the provision of medical care, education and housing". Yet, this political rhetoric aside, the question must be asked: precisely what kind of equality are Liberals concerned with, which is to ask what objectives do they demand of the social services? The answer, like much Liberal Left thinking, is never clear, but generally can be subsumed under three headings. These are (1) social integration; (2) social security; and (3) equal opportunities.

Social integration

Primary among the Liberal Left's objectives for the social services is enhancing people's commitment to their system of governance and inculcating them with a sense of equal worth in order to incorporate them in a common culture. The practical expression of this equality of status is the Liberal Left's adoption of universal service allocation in preference to selectivity, although selectivity clearly is more effective in redressing poverty and income inequalities by omitting upper income groups from benefits. Selective service provision, however, is socially divisive. This is because it differentiates sharply between those who receive benefits and those who finance them. In contrast, universal service, which operate by equality of non-differentiation (O'Higgins, 1987: 13), treats all recipients alike, and supposedly is more effective at reducing social distances. This equality of entitlement and use (which clashes inherently with the principle of distribution) is a price worth paying to secure the greater goal of social integration.

Social security

The second Liberal Left objective for the social services is to make accessible to all, irrespective of their income, occupation or social position, the conditions of civilization which, in the absence of such measures, can be enjoyed only by the rich (Tawney, 1964: 122), or as Walker (1987: 45) phrased it: "society has the obligation to guarantee to even the humblest the means to live and enjoy a decent life". This objective follows largely from the first because to feel part of their social heritage, and to live by its prevailing standards, people require a sense of security against unavoidable ill-fortunes, such as old age or disease, against disruptive market exchanges, such as unemployment, and against discrimination based on their ethnic origins, religion, and lifestyles.

Much disagreement abounds about what is meant by the "civilized" or "decent" life that the social services are meant to ensure, and like many social situations, these ideas are more easily identified when lacking. It is partly for this reason, and partly because of their general view that it is the role of the social services only to cushion free market exchanges, not ameliorate them, that the Liberal Left equates social security with minimum standards that focus on manifest wants, or the absence of ill-fares rather than the promotion of well-fares. To paraphrase Bradshaw and Deacon (1986: 84), want, squalor, disease, ignorance, and idleness are evil giants; welfare is not. This becomes even more apparent in the Liberal Left's third objective for the social services, namely the equalization of opportunities.

Equal opportunities

The final objective for the social services is the promotion of equality of opportunities by which the Liberal Left means that everyone should have an equal opportunity to compete. To this end young and old require some minimum standards of health, education, and shelter, and sufficient peace of mind to make good their individual potential. In short, it is up to what Lowe (1993) aptly calls "the opportunity state" to enable people to be unequal if they so wish after being given similar opportunities to reach the same starting line.

In summary, the Liberal Left's view is that the state should promote institutions which foster social stability and effective market participation but must refrain from income redistribution that not only negates individual freedom but sustains expectations which cannot be satisfied. Also, according to one of Liberalism's most important proponents, John Galbraith, the achievement of economic growth much reduces people's concern with income inequality, and so makes its amelioration redundant (Reisman, 1980). This is because economic growth increases social mobility and so diminishes the importance of class. Also, it encourages more equitable consumption, and so lessens interest in the position of the rich and the inequalities they represent. Finally, economic growth promotes greater social pluralism by introducing additional forms of social prestige to wealth. Consequently, and for all these reasons, gauging the structural adjustment programmes by measures of distributional equality is inappropriate.

If not income distribution, then what?

If neither New Right nor Liberal Left standards can be used to assess the success or failure of SAPs in terms of distributional equality, then what measures are appropriate? For the New Right, the answer is simple: we must use purely economic indices to assess the programmes. From the Liberal Left perspective, on the other hand, the answer is more complex. This is because few of the current socio-economic indicators successfully gauge the Liberal Left's notion of social equality, and because of structural limitations in Liberal Left thought on achieving genuine social service universality.

Social equality

As demonstrated above, the Liberal notion of equality is concerned with the nature of social membership in political collectives, and especially with integrating the poor into their wider community. This idea goes beyond counting money, calories, years of education or the number of rooms per household. Such quantitative measures and statistics have their merit, but miss the point. What is required are more qualitative data that reflect people's sense of being part of their society. We can compose these data from three interrelated measures: (1) a measure of communal standard of living; (2) a measure of security that this standard of living will be maintained in the future; and (3) a measure of people's expectations about improving this standard of living.

Communal standard of living pertains to the prevailing physical and social living conditions of a particular people with reference to sufficiency rather than to satiety. It sets the ground, therefore, for the minimal requirements of feeling a sense of belonging to a given society, and accounts for the fact that all resources above a minimum amount have diminishing returns. The pioneering work in this field was conducted by Peter Townsend (1979) who tried to assess the extent to which the poor can live up to the mundane standards of their society and to partake in what are considered normal activities such as being able to afford to hold a wake after the death of a relative. More recently, UNDP (1993; 1994) has taken a similar path. It showed that different people in the same country live in different circumstances. Generally, however, there are still very little data of this nature, other than the distinction between rural and urban populations and, to a somewhat lesser extent, between the genders.

The second measure, security, refers to people's legitimate expectation that they will maintain their present-day standard of living and opportunities in the future. To date, the idea of security has mainly been interpreted in national terms. Yet for most people, security pertains more to worries about their daily life: Will my family and I have enough to eat? Shall I keep my job? Will my street and neighbourhood be safe from crime? Will I be discriminated against because of my gender? Will I be prosecuted because of my religion or ethnic origin? (UNDP, 1994).

At their most abstract, one could argue that structural adjustment programmes cover much of this issue in seeking social and economic stability. Yet apart from making inroads into the most basic human needs, such as food, health, and income, the idea of social security in its wider sense is still little referred to in analyses of the overall state of societies. One possible reason for this is that the way different individuals define security depends much on their immediate situation and culture. The difficulties in gauging such diverse attitudes must not blind us to their importance. Also, they reiterate the critical significance of ensuring that data collection is culturally relevant, although this too poses considerable difficulties, especially in the African context.

Finally, any measure of social belonging must include people's expectations about improving their standard of living. A pertinent method to gauge this variable is suggested by relative deprivation theory. This theory suggests that people seek the standard of living of the people they compare themselves to, and that these comparisons are socially upwards, following a largely triangular number series. Thus if we divide society into ten income groups, beginning from the poorest to the richest, this theory suggests that persons in the poorest group want to live like the group immediately above them, the second group wants to live like the group two levels above them, the third group wants to live like the group three levels above them, and so on. Consequently, if we know the standard of living of all ten groups (a relatively simple matter), we have a ready-made measure of each group's expected standard of living.

Social service universality

In keeping in line with the free market system, Liberals assume that what is principally required to equalize the use of the social services among the social classes is some degree of geographic equity and the removal of budgetary constraints to the offering of such services. In other words, it is assumed that the mere availability of services and their provision free-of-charge at the point of entry or at a subsidized level are sufficient guarantees of their universality. It is becoming increasingly evident, however, that such formal accessibility is a far cry from *de facto* accessibility. For example, in many African countries, children's health care lags even where health facilities are present and services are provided free-of-charge. Consequently, many of the indices which we currently use to assess the social services, such as the number of doctors per given population, are inadequate since the proof of accessibility is the use of a service, not its mere presence. Also, most of these indices do not take account of the full range of need-meeting services which people in non-Western societies have available to them. Thus, all present-day medical statistics are oblivious to traditional medicine, for example. Similarly, the data on social services disregard the plethora of indigenous and religious arrangements that provide similar forms of assistance to communities.

To be more meaningful and relevant, therefore, we must expand our stock of social services indicators. In particular, these indicators must account for the fact that need-meeting is not a one-way endeavour, but that it places numerous demands both on the people with needs and on the institutions which are meant to satisfy these needs. Both parties must be able to reach out to each other and work together. The difficulty in everyday life, however, is that such capacities are often lacking. This is due to a range of personal, social, organizational, and other factors which cumulatively may be called supply and demand accessibility. Supply accessibility denotes an institution's capacity, ability, and will to provide required resources. Demand accessibility relates to the elements that determine the individual's resource-utilization patterns (Aday and Andersen, 1974).

Supply accessibility is characterized by two elements: resources and organization. Resources are the capital and labour which are devoted to a particular field (health, welfare, education, housing). Included here are the personnel and structures and materials which are used in service provision along with their volume and distribution. Other than for traditional social services, much of this information is already available although usually not conveniently located. The second element of supply accessibility is organization. This describes what the system does with its resources. The components of organization are entry and structure. Entry refers to the processes and conditions that are involved in gaining entrance to a system, and includes factors like the provider's criteria of eligibility, administrative ritualism and physical location. Structure, on the other hand, concerns the characteristics of the system which determine what happens to users after entry. Included are variables like who attends to the users; how they are treated; the time they must wait; and the actual type, level, and quality of assistance they receive.

The other side of the service provision equation are the individual determinants of utilization. These are divided into predisposing and enabling components. The former consists of variables such as the age, gender and ethnicity of users, and their values and beliefs about appropriate states of well-being. These and other such variables describe the propensity of individuals to use services. For example, in cultures where self-reliance is a dominant value, people often find it more difficult to ask for external assistance than in cultures that put a premium on collectivity. In contrast, the second component of demand accessibility - enabling - refers to the practical means people have to use the services at their disposal. Among others, these include people's knowledge of what resources are available and how to use them as well as language skills, physical mobility, and time. Again, as with supply accessibility, barriers to any of these elements detracts from universality, or to use the economists' terminology, universality is predicated on equality of cost, that is, that no individual faces higher costs in using a service than another (Le Grand, 1995).

Conclusions

This chapter has argued that to meaningfully assess sub-Saharan Africa's structural adjustment programmes we must use the terms of reference of these programmes. Given that these terms of reference seem to be ideologically grounded, we cannot, therefore, use income distribution alone to measure their success of failure, but must rely on other criteria instead. For proponents of the New Right this is relatively simple. The universally available economic indicators are sufficient. For the supporters of Liberalism, on the other hand, assessing structural adjustment programmes is more difficult. This is largely because most of the socio-economic indicators that are currently used are insufficiently sensitive to gauge the notion of social belonging, or because such indicators are lacking altogether.

To overcome this lacuna, we must refine the nature of the data we collect and analyze. To this end, two sets of indicators are suggested. One pertains to the notion of social equality which can be assessed by combining measures of a communal standard of living; the sense that this standard of living will be maintained in the future; and people's expectations about improving this standard of living. The second set of indicators suggests how to more sensitively assess the means by which social equality is attempted, and consists of a variety determinants of demand and supply accessibility which have to be fulfilled to ensure that social services are genuinely universal.

14 The limits of privatization as a development strategy in Africa

H.P.B. Moshi

A World Bank (1994b) study on the overall impact of structural adjustment programmes (SAPs) in Africa came to three important conclusions. First, policies have improved in some countries but progress has been uneven, and in some countries policies are worse. Furthermore, no country in Africa has established what are internationally regarded as good macroeconomic policies or an adequate "policy frontier". Second, in general, countries that improved their policies had improved growth, while those with deteriorating policies suffered further declines in growth. Even so, overall growth for the region remains very low and even the best reformers are not yet growing fast enough to reduce poverty.

Third, much effort has been expended on public enterprise reform. The results are difficult to assess, but the available data suggest that there is great need for more accelerated divestiture. The data show that about 20 percent of public enterprises have been privatized or liquidated. Further, there is little evidence in any country of a major reduction in the value of government asset holding. Over half of the countries have not undertaken significant privatization activities.

This chapter is focused on the third conclusion mentioned above. It points out that the slow pace of privatization should have been expected, and thus, should not be a surprise to anyone who is familiar with the economic and political environment in Africa. That environment, in turn, limits the privatization exercise in Africa as an alternative strategy for African development.

What are public enterprises (PEs)

If we use the World Bank's (1993) definition of a "state-owned enterprise" or a "parastatal" or a "public enterprise", then we could define such enterprises as those enterprises which are owned, by majority shares, and operated by the government. Such enterprises include agricultural marketing boards, industrial and commercial firms, mines, utilities, and transport companies as well as financial intermediaries.

The public enterprises are thus distinguished from the rest of the government because their revenue comes from the sale of goods and services and because they are self-accounting and have a separate legal identity.

What is privatization

As would be expected, privatization has come to mean different things to different people. In the broadest sense, privatization has been referred to as a process to increase the efficiency of the public sector or any policy move to foster private sector development (Naya, 1990). This view encompasses a wide range of policies as a way of developing and nurturing the overall private sector.

Further, privatization could be seen as a process of corporatization (Boston, 1992; Rohdewohld, 1993) or commercialization. This process involves the internal restructuring of a public enterprise as well as improving the regulatory environment under which it operates with the objective of overcoming those problems which make such an enterprise perform unsatisfactorily. The commercialization process, therefore, aims at raising the operational efficiency of a public enterprise without changing its ownership structure. Nevertheless, in some cases this process is seen as a precondition or a preparatory stage for privatization.

Furthermore, in a narrower sense, privatization can be defined as a sale of part or all of a public enterprise to the private sector. For the purpose of this chapter, we will define privatization from this narrow perspective of change in ownership structure. Further, this narrow definition is in line with the neoclassical economic theory and thinking of reducing (rolling back) the entrepreneurial role of the state in an economy.

The growth of public enterprises in Africa

During the past three post-independence decades, there has been a rapid growth in the number and size of public enterprises in African countries. The public enterprise sector expanded rapidly, particularly in the early 1970s, and came to dominate many key sectors. Statistics on the number of public firms, their share of formal sector employment, and their share of value-added are limited and unreliable. However, they do provide some insight into the importance of the public enterprise sector in the pre-SAPs period. Ghana, Kenya, Mozambique, and Nigeria, for example, had more than 300 public enterprises each. In Tanzania, the number of public enterprises increased from 42 in 1967 to 425 by 1984 (Moshi, 1994). In a 1983 report the World Bank estimated that there were 2,956 public enterprises in some thirty African countries (World Bank, 1983). This figure, however, is likely to have been underestimated, particularly if the municipally owned and operated enterprises were not included in the calculation.

Commenting on the all-embracing nature of state involvement in the economy in Africa, the United Nations Economic Commission for Africa (UNECA) (1994) observed that:

> Each government in Africa has fingers in every pie. Its interests range from banking and insurance through oil refineries, air and road transport, to looking after agriculture and social welfare. Central government bureaucracies are no longer content with mere shuffling of papers from desk to desk, they now brew beer, distribute cement, and sell meat.

The performance of African public enterprises

A World Bank (1981) report concluded that:

> It is now widely evident that the public sector is over-extended, given the present scarcities of financial resources, skilled manpower, and organizational capacity. This has resulted in slower growth than might have been achieved with available resources, and accounts in part for the current crises. Without improved performance of public agencies, stepped-up growth will be difficult to achieve.

The report thus warns that "unless there is a change in the operating effectiveness of parastatals, particularly in industry, they will not take their proper place as growth points. They will, instead, continue to be fiscal drains and major contributors to slow growth" (World Bank, 1981).

The tone of the World Bank's *World Development Report 1987* was quite similar. It observed that: "The performance of state-owned enterprises (SOEs) varies widely between countries, but their record has frequently been poor, particularly in developing countries. They have clearly failed to play the strategic role in industrialization that governments had hoped for".

Such unfavourable assessments of public enterprises have also been echoed by other scholars. However, it is important to bear in mind that this poor performance should not be generalized. Performance varies across countries, sectors, and periods. For example, empirical evidence suggests that PEs in market-oriented countries were better performers than in socialist-oriented countries. Furthermore, the performance of public enterprises in the pre-debt crisis in Africa was quite favourable when compared to the subsequent years.

Apart from the issue of performance variations across countries, sectors, and time periods, one should recognize the fact that public enterprises cannot be regarded as non-performers in all aspects. Indeed, in some cases they promoted competition where they existed alongside private enterprises; they produced goods and rendered services and thus satisfied demand which would have remained unsatisfied; they raised the technological capacity of some countries in certain sectors; they nurtured a class of indigenous managers and businessmen; and they promoted private initiative by supplying infrastructural facilities and intermediate goods as inputs to upstream industries.

Further, one should not negate the fact that public enterprises played a significant role in the economies of the highly successful Newly Industrializing countries (NICs) in East Asia such as Taiwan, Hong Kong, Singapore, and South Korea. It has, of late, become fashionable for the World Bank to play down this fact, especially when they are urging the African countries to emulate the Asian path to development.

Without going into the details of the debate on the controversy surrounding the appropriateness of the methodology and indicators used in the assessment of relative efficiency between public and private enterprises, it suffices to point out here the following: There seems to be a general agreement that profit maximization, the yardstick of success of private enterprise, is not acceptable as a measurement of performance of public enterprises, especially in countries where these enterprises have many social rather than only economic or political objectives (Tambunan, 1993). This caution points to the need to widen the spectrum of indicators to be used in such an assessment. One such indicator could be that of productivity which reflects the ratio between the quantity of goods and services produced and/or costs of production resources consumed.

In addition, even if the issue of measurement indicators were to be resolved, there are factors which would affect the performance of public enterprises negatively by destroying or undermining the commercial ethic of an enterprise. Indeed, a significant part of the problem is that of politicians who influence the objectives of public enterprises and, in particular, less compelling non-commercial objectives are substituted for economic and financial objectives. Hope (1996c) argued that political interference in decision-making and bureaucratic failure are probably the principal sources of inefficiency associated with public ownership. This aspect tallies with the concept of double management in public enterprises which refers to the relationship between the enterprises and the regulatory framework.

Other factors associated with the inefficiency of public enterprises are those of easy access to capital. Thus, borrowing takes place at rates below market prices and quite often with government guarantees. Also, in quite a number of sectors, public enterprises operate as monopolies. This accentuates the "comfortable life" phenomenon and destroys even further the commercial ethic.

Leaving the debate on the measurement of performance and the factors affecting such performance aside, the International Financial Institutions (IFIs), namely the World Bank and the International Monetary Fund (IMF), are convinced that the privatization of public enterprises and the rolling back of the role of the state in economic affairs would improve the performance of public enterprises in particular and the African economies in general.

The objectives of privatization

Privatization hinges on the neoclassical hypothesis that private ownership brings greater efficiency and more rapid growth. As already discussed earlier, public ownership itself is often held responsible for a great number of different types of inefficiencies. For example, legally granted monopoly status, political and administrative protection against customers' complaints, and the absence of clearly defined property rights - all subsumed under the general rubric of "bureaucratic failures" as opposed to "market failures" (Hemming and Mansoor, 1988).

During the 1980's, privatization was actively advocated by major international bilateral agencies and the IFIs. Many developing countries, especially African countries have followed this advice, although the extent of their philosophical agreement as opposed to the financial pressures exerted by these agencies and institutions remain unclear. In addition to the belief that privatization improves efficiency, increases output, and lowers costs, proponents argue that it curbs the growth of government expenditure, raises cash to reduce public and external debt, and promotes individual initiative while rewarding entrepreneurship. Finally, supporters of privatization see it as a way of broadening the base of ownership and participation in an economy.

Theoretically, each country can be expected to have its own privatization objectives, depending on its level of development and the social goals it may wish to pursue. In reality, however, African countries can hardly formulate home-made privatization objectives because of the standard conditionalities imposed on them by the IFIs through SAPs. An important ingredient of SAPs is the privatization of public enterprises. The main objectives being those of fostering competition, increasing efficiency and productivity in the public sector, and reducing budget deficits and public debt. Nevertheless, wider objectives of private sector development are part of privatization policies as illustrated by the Tanzanian case which spells out the privatization objectives as follows (Republic of Tanzania, 1993):

1 To improve the operational efficiency of enterprises that are currently in the parastatal sector and their contribution to the national economy;

2 To reduce the burden of parastatal enterprises on the government budget;

3 To expand the role of the private sector in the economy to enable the government to concentrate public resources on its role as provider of basic public services, including health, education, and social infrastructure; and

4 To encourage wider participation by the people in the ownership and management of business.

In implementing privatization programmes many countries in Africa had to embark on a classification exercise in order to decide which public enterprises would be either retained, liquidated, or privatized. In Nigeria, for example, enterprises were classified into four major categories: Category I included those more strategic enterprises in the service and manufacturing sector which should be partially privatized and where ownership by the government and its agencies should be limited to a share of between 30 and 70 percent. Category II consisted of enterprises slated for full privatization. Category III listed enterprises slated for partial commercialization. Category IV consisted of enterprises which in future should operate on full commercial terms (Rohdewohld, 1993).

The categorization exercise in most African countries has usually been carried out by a central organization responsible for privatization such as the Technical Committee on Privatization and Commercialization (TCPC) in Nigeria, the Presidential Parastatal Sector Reform Commission (PRSRC) in Tanzania, and the Zambia Privatization Agency (ZPA) in Zambia. In carrying out their activities these organizations tend to be assisted by a number of local and foreign consultants.

Any review of the African privatization experience is made difficult either because of lack of data or data inaccuracy. In spite of this, the available data provides some insights into the progress made so far. The evidence suggests that the 1980s implementation record of privatization does not indicate success. This is illustrated by the fact of a sample of 14 countries only 29 actual sales had taken place by 1987 against a planned number of 308 sales. However, liquidations and closures were more frequent, with 105 cases being reported (Shirley and Berg, 1987). The overall record (excluding Nigeria) is 93 cases of privatizations out of 331 planned, which is just below 30 percent. If one adds privatizations "under way" the ratio of success reaches 37 percent (Fontaine, 1993).

More recent evidence indicates that to date less than one-fifth of Africa's state firms have been sold off. However, not many of the important ones like airlines, mining, telecommunications, and electricity are usually sold. Ghana, for example, sold part of its stake in the Ashanti Goldfields Corporation, its top export earner, in 1994; and Zambia its copper mines (*The Economist*, 1994). Nigeria, on the other hand, has privatized less than 5 percent of its total portfolio. It has also been observed that "in ten years, Kenya sold almost nothing at all" (*The Economist*, 1994). Tanzania planned to conclude 73 cases of privatization by the end of 1994. However, by 1995 only 20 cases were completed. In sub-Saharan Africa, the number of privatized state-owned enterprises during the period 1980-91 was 373 which accounted for 17 percent of developing country sales with close to one-fifth of those occurring in Guinea (Kikeri, Nellis, and Shirley, 1992). Although the number and type of privatized enterprises differ across countries, the overall experience has been of lower numbers than initially anticipated and a few generalizations do emerge from that experience.

First, most of the privatizations were re-privatizations of the earlier nationalized private enterprises. This is quite evident particularly in Ghana and Tanzania and especially in their agricultural sectors. Second, privatizations have concentrated on, and have been successful only for, small enterprises. Finally, most of the privatization cases were in the manufacturing sector.

The implications of these generalizations for the financial and fiscal performance of the economies of African countries have been marginal for three main reasons. First, initially, the implementation of public enterprise reforms, for example, in Ghana was accompanied by an improvement of the fiscal situation but this was short-lived as fiscal deficits appeared again later. This experience is also shared by other countries like Niger, Malawi, and Tanzania. Second, being over-ambitious, the reforms had to be reversed. Third, the reforms did not touch the inner mechanisms of the public enterprises and failed to improve efficiency in a long-lasting way. These reasons essentially represent the obstacles faced by privatization programmes in the African context.

Constraints and obstacles

As already noted above the experience of privatization in Africa has been dismal. The World Bank (1994b) associates this poor performance with the inability of some African countries to adjust. The Bank thus observes that "adjustment has not failed, but some countries have failed to adjust". It then concludes "Adjustment can work in Africa - and it does work in Africa". Two important criticisms can be levelled at this observation and conclusion. First, the failure of some African countries to adjust is not a refusal by these countries to take an additional dose of the reform medicine in order to reach the so called "adequate policy stance", but rather their inability to take an added dose because of the structural inadequacies in such economies.

Second, the assumption that if adjustment or reforms have worked elsewhere, then they should also work in Africa is wrong. The dominant view within the World Bank that Africa is not different from other continents is ill-conceived. Indeed, Africa's economic structure, and the nature of its politics, entrepreneurial culture, human and technical capacity, are different. A policy reform programme which overlooks these differences, both during its design and implementation stages, is bound to fall short of the expected results. This is more so if such a programme is imposed on a society rather than being a process of internal evolution in response to the changing internal and external environment. In the ensuing sections we look in some detail into the factors limiting privatization in Africa.

Underdeveloped capital markets Africa has much weaker formal domestic capital markets than other developing regions. At present there are less than five countries in sub-Saharan Africa which have stock market facilities. Without such facilities privatization becomes problematic.

Paucity of capital In Africa private wealth is extremely limited and fairly unequally distributed across households. The largest household group in Africa is comprised of the peasantry and, given their meagre incomes and consequently poor savings propensity, it is unlikely that they can actively participate in the privatization process as owners of privatized assets. Also, the unequal distribution of income across households or ethnic groups and geographical areas mitigates against privatization. In Tanzania, for example, the major entrepreneurial group is of Asian origin. Because of this, there is a very strong opposition to the selling of public enterprises to this already wealthy group.

Scarcity of entrepreneurial skills There are very few Africans experienced in entrepreneurial activities such as identification of a niche for a new firm, assembly of inputs, organization of key functions in the firm, and allocation of risk among different actors. Although the situation may vary from one country to another, especially between socialist- and capitalist-oriented countries, experience in Africa shows that personal connections rather than ability or competence do dominate business transactions.

Poor regulatory and institutional frameworks Generally, Africa lacks regulatory and institutional capacities to carry out successful privatization programmes. In some cases the problem of human capacity could be solved through training. This, however, takes time and requires financial resources which might not be available when needed. In the short-run, technical assistance could be the solution. However, all depends upon its availability and the attitude of a government towards such assistance. Institutional capacity building is also a costly process both in terms of time and finances.

Corrupt civil services Despite the fact that the majority of civil servants in African countries are well trained, most of them are corrupt. This is so primarily because most of them are not being paid living wages. In the event of privatization there is the likelihood that corrupt tendencies will increase such that the transparency of the process is jeopardized. This will, in turn, increase the resistance to privatization.

Attitude towards foreign ownership This aspect has to be analyzed from two perspectives: the imposing of policy (conditionalities) instruments by foreigners and the ownership of national assets by foreigners. The former refers to policy prescriptions to African countries by IFIs as well as other international agencies and the donor community. Given the extent of the crisis facing the African continent since the mid-1970s, countries may, out of "desperation", agree in principle to implement some imposed policies in order to get access to international financial resources and to win international support and sympathy without necessarily being convinced that such policies will work. This manifests itself at the level of implementation as observed by the lack of political will and the partial commitment accorded to such policies by the nationals of the countries concerned.

In some cases privatization could have been possible if foreign ownership would have been welcomed. This is not always the case. One should recall that the nationalizations which characterized post-independence Africa were partly geared towards Africanization of national economies. Public enterprises were thus the product of the economic nationalistic movement. This movement is still dominant in many African countries, especially in certain sectors of the economy. Foreign ownership, therefore, is seen as a danger to economic nationalism and the sovereignty of a country (Moshi, 1994).

Dilapidated enterprises The physical and financial conditions of public enterprises in most African countries are in very bad shape. Financially, such enterprises are highly indebted to both domestic and international financial institutions. Due to this state of affairs they hardly attract buyers. The would-be buyers often demand that the balance sheet of such enterprises should first be "cleaned-up" (should be free of debts). Further, they usually demand that the enterprises should be physically rehabilitated before they buy them. All of these demands, which nonetheless are justifiable, have huge financial implications for African governments. To circumvent this problem, a number of countries, for example, Nigeria, have privatized the "easy cases" first and the "difficult cases" continue to remain in public ownership.

Inadequate supportive infrastructure A successful privatization programme requires, among other things, an adequate and functioning economic infrastructure. That is, a network of communication systems, electricity, water, and so on. Experience in Africa shows that the network of roads, rail, water, and airways is too underdeveloped to form what one could call an "integrated market". This explains, to a greater extent, the continued existence of dualism in the African economies. That is, the existence of both a modern (exchange) and a traditional (subsistence) economy.

Furthermore, the supply of electricity is mostly confined to urban areas and most of the rural areas remain unelectrified. Apart from this urban bias character, the supply to both households and business entities has been inadequate. Countries like Tanzania and Nigeria, for example, have been experiencing frequent electricity cut-offs and rationing. The same phenomenon and problems face water supply. These economic infrastructure bottlenecks not only inhibit the development of markets, but also discourage potential investors and entrepreneurs from actively participating in the privatization programmes.

Political risk-aversion The reforms being carried out in Africa in the context of SAPs are highly vulnerable to political instability. One should bear in mind that the advent of multi-party democracy in Africa is a recent phenomenon and a product of the collapse of communism in Eastern Europe. The democratic reforms have indeed destabilized a number of African countries.

Privatization, with some of its negative effects on employment and poverty, increases even further the already existing political instability. Thus, risk-aversion strategies, on the part of politicians, are adopted. It needs to be pointed out here that African countries lack a "web" of social organizations or social safety nets which would have mitigated against some of the negative social effects of privatization. Without such safety nets it would be very difficult, if not impossible, to reduce or to avoid the negative popular and political reactions provoked by privatizations that result in unemployment and a decline in real wages.

De-industrialization effects The experiences of Latin American and Asian countries show that trade liberalization and privatization enhanced the industrial capacity of those economies. That is, the manufacturing component (ratio) of exports increased with the adoption of such policies. In Africa, the opposite has been the case. The manufacturing sector contribution to GDP in Tanzania, for example, has fallen drastically from 14 percent in the 1970s to around 8 percent by 1994. The concentration has thus shifted from production to commerce. These de-industrialization tendencies indicate that the continent's chances of rapid industrialization are weakened instead of being strengthened. Yet, industrialization remains a crucial indicator of economic development.

Conclusions

The main theme of this chapter has been the limits of privatization in Africa. We have emphasized that the physical, cultural, social, and institutional environment is so different from that of developed countries such that a policy of massive privatization cannot be implemented with the anticipated speed, extent, and economic impact.

This caution does not imply that privatization is totally irrelevant in the African environment. Indeed, all depends on the sectors and the countries involved. However, privatization cannot be the panacea for improving macro and micro efficiency in Africa and there are some important lessons to be learned from this.

First, privatization can work in Africa if the theoretical efficiency considerations take on board the on-the-ground realities in Africa. That is, efforts should concentrate in matching the aspirations with the feasibility of policy instruments. Second, efficiency is not necessarily an ownership issue. Under an improved regulatory framework or environment, increased competition, and an overhauled internal structure of the public enterprises, higher efficiency standards can be achieved. This being the case, these modalities of efficiency improvement should be given more weight in Africa's structural adjustment programmes.

Third, structural adjustment programmes are too narrow in their objectives and too short in their time horizon to address wider socio-economic development issues in Africa. These characteristics of SAPs tend to overlook the important role the state has played and will continue to play in the economic development process. The demands that the state must "roll itself back" might be justifiable in developed countries. On the contrary, in Africa, if the state has to play its developmental role, then "rolling back" is not justified. However, a better realignment between the private and the public sectors is necessary.

15 Barriers to reconstruction and development: A brief view of corruption and economic crime in Southern Africa

Dave Macdonald

There can be little doubt that what has been labelled crimes of the powerful (Pearce, 1976) has been a neglected area of public and political discourse. In Southern Africa, the "new South Africa" has been responsible for placing accountability and transparency in both government and the commercial world on the regional agenda, partly in recognition that both corruption and economic crime are serious obstacles in the path of democratic socio-economic development. However, both corruption and economic crime are umbrella concepts that cover an extremely diverse and complex range of human activities and as such demand clarification.

The context of corruption and economic crime in Southern Africa

There are, for example, at least three senses of what is meant by corruption, particularly in the context of Southern Africa. Colonialism itself was a corrupt system which subverted traditional cultures and structures through domination and the imposition of foreign values and ideologies. In many of these traditional systems clientelism, familialism, nepotism, and gift-giving were normative behaviours and it is ironic that these all constitute some form of corrupt activity as defined by modern moral codes.

Perhaps the most commonly used contemporary definition of corruption is that it refers to unethical activity in government such as abuse of office or public mismanagement, especially as these interact with unacceptable activities that take place on the deviant fringes and margins of the business and commercial world. The problem with this type of definition, however, is that it helps to rationalize and legitimize corruption as a non-criminal activity. Corruption becomes an issue of ethics and morality rather than crime and criminality. While there is an obvious overlap between crime and morality the consequences of holding either view are very different in terms of the perceptions of offenders and strategies for controlling the problem.

Although corruption takes many shapes and forms we can distinguish between two main types that can be identified as criminal: (1) official corruption, and (2) commercial corruption, whether in the more limited sense of contravening any penal code or in the broader sense of a social justice definition of criminal behaviour. It can be argued that both of these types of corruption need to be controlled and regulated through the criminal justice system rather than through other regulatory agencies.

Official corruption can be defined as the taking of bribes by relatively minor government officials in return for a service. A recent international comparative crime victimization study carried out by the United Nations Interregional Crime and Justice Research Institute (UNICRI, 1993) shows that this type of corruption was the second most frequently reported crime victimization experience in developing countries in 1991, particularly in Northern and sub-Saharan Africa. In answer to the following question, for example, 41 percent of respondents in Kampala and 31.9 percent of respondents in Cairo responded with a yes: "In some areas there is a problem of corruption among government officials. During 1991 has any government official, for instance a customs officer, police officer or inspector in your own country, asked you to pay a bribe for his service?". This leads UNICRI (1995: 20) to suggest that among the types of crime covered by their survey, "consumer fraud and corruption stand out as the most frequent in all the regions of the developing world and in most of the cities within the specific region".

The importance of this research cannot be overemphasized as it provides substantial empirical evidence that refutes the myth that crime is predominantly predatory. That is to say, street crime carried out by the lower classes and marginalized groups within society. It also suggests that the impressions, stereotypes, and commonly held perceptions about endemic levels of official corruption in developing countries are largely true and have a basis in fact. Furthermore, it emphasizes the centrality of corruption in the development process and the citizen's position *vis-á-vis* government and the commercial sector. In particular, it illustrates the general lack of citizen protection and the ways in which people are coerced while trying to satisfy their legitimate needs and rights.

As UNICRI (1993) points out, this apparent malfunctioning of the public sector is complemented by the malfunctioning of the tertiary sector where consumer fraud also appears to be endemic. In the same study, 70 percent of respondents in Kampala, 30 percent in Dar es Salaam, and 23.5 percent in South Africa answered yes to the following question: "Last year, 1991, were you the victim of consumer fraud? I mean, has someone when selling something to you or delivering a service cheated on you in terms of the quantity or quality of the goods/services?".

Certainly there may be good reasons why people engage in these types of petty criminal activity in developing countries where scarcity is the keynote of social existence. This is particularly true in the case of official corruption, "for the lowly-paid official in the Third World, unlike his counterpart in the West, labours under the burdensome demands of kin and friends; demands to feed, clothe, house and pay school and college fees for brothers and sisters" (Theobald, 1990: 81). As Palmier (1983: 209) has argued, it is likely that this type of corruption "will be most prevalent when salaries are low, opportunities great and policing weak". Indeed, in many African countries where the state has been perceived as the "milk cow", official corruption has become institutionalized and normative largely because it is seen as a necessary activity for day-to-day survival. It is no longer perceived as a question of morality, never mind illegality, and could almost be conceptualized as some type of a personal structural adjustment strategy.

Within Southern Africa one of the problems in making any general statements about patterns of corruption and economic crime is that the region consists of countries with very different political and socio-economic conditions. From the more prosperous middle-income countries of Botswana and Namibia to war torn "Fourth World" countries like Angola and Mozambique; from socialist-oriented countries like Zimbabwe to overtly capitalist countries like Mauritius and South Africa. However, whatever the level of economic or socio-political development, there can be little doubt that, for the vast majority of the region's population, scarcity is a keynote of social existence.

Even within this context of regional scarcity is to be found what can be termed commercial corruption which involves high-ranking officials, usually politicians or civil servants, in collusion with individuals or corporations from the commercial sector and involving large amounts of money, often centered on the contract and tendering process. It is commercial corruption that we will focus on here, that is, the nexus between the public and private sectors that provides such a conducive context for criminal activity. We should note that commercial corruption is different from that specific form of élite corruption that has plagued Africa for so long - the plundering of public funds by corrupt and criminal political leaders.

In the case of commercial corruption there can be little doubt that this form of criminal activity is common, if not endemic, in the Southern African region, although, by definition, it is perhaps one of the most secretive and well-protected forms of corruption and therefore difficult to obtain accurate data about. It should be noted that with or without public sector collusion, economic crime covers a wide range of activities including foreign exchange swindles, counterfeiting, bank scams, and business frauds. A recent report by the Council of Southern African Bankers (COSAB), for example, suggests that "corruption has reached intolerable levels in our societies; and we believe that business can and should take the lead in fighting corruption and restoring fundamental values" (*The Southern African Economist*, 1995: 9). An analysis by the Department of Criminology at the University of South Africa shows that during 1994 there were 58 major cases of fraud in South Africa each with a value of over US$100,000 reported to the police (Forensic Accounting, 1995). This is, of course, a gross underestimate of the true incidence of serious fraud as many cases go undetected and others discovered by commercial organizations go unreported and are dealt with in-house to save possible embarrassment; harm to public image; questions about organizational competence; and to retain investor/customer confidence. Another report suggests that Mozambique in 1994 lost US$3.5 million in uncollected revenue from the department of customs and excise due to corruption and that in Zimbabwe, in 1992, the government lost a total of US$3 million due to fraud by public officials (SAPEM, 1995).

While these examples suggest the complexities of trying to unravel commercial corruption within such a diverse and heterogeneous region of the world as Southern Africa, there are indications that this type of criminal activity, as opposed to official and élite corruption, is likely to substantially increase throughout the region in the coming decades. As South Africa, the dominant economic player in the region, re-affirms itself globally and the region becomes more fully integrated into the new world economic and socio-political order, development is likely to be subsumed under the dictates of the policies of international organizations like the IMF, the World Bank and its private sector division, the International Finance Corporation (IFC), as well as the transnational corporations. Indeed, it is a cultural imperative that development within such a context may be based on "an ideology of greed and selfishness, passed off as self-sufficiency, and of untrammelled individual aspirations passed off as ambition, which cannot fail to have an effect upon upper world crime" (Brake and Hale, 1992: 116). Commercial corruption along with other types of economic crime, in other words, is a natural and logical extension of the pursuit of profit within an all encompassing global capitalist system where the urge to individualize success and personal gain is the preferred method of advancement and where private, extensive, and limitless individual accumulation of wealth, otherwise known as greed, is the structural norm and primary economic driving force.

As Southern Africa develops over the next few decades within this context of global capitalist expansion, it would do well to learn lessons from the consequences of inculcating and incorporating such a spirit of free enterprise and venture capitalism that were the hallmarks of Western European societies throughout the 1980s. The policies of Margaret Thatcher's conservative government, for example, were designed explicitly to encourage "individualism, free enterprise and the pursuit of profit" (Brake and Hale, 1992: 134). This resulted in moving privatization on to the centre-stage of policy making; the introduction of market economies into the spheres of health and social welfare; and deregulation in a laissez-faire commercial environment allowing financial institutions to regulate themselves in the interests of economic profitability. A recent report published by the Public Services Privatization Research Unit in London claims that in developed countries privatization has enabled a group of transnational companies to dominate public service provision "resulting in cartels, combines and corruption", and that "corruption goes hand-in-hand with contracting out and privatization" (*Mail and Guardian*, 1996a). In other words, privatization has helped to encourage the bending of rules, a carpet-bagger mentality, and a cavalier attitude to the law by entrepreneurs. Indeed, as Brake and Hale (1992: 122) point out, this "anti-collective, individualistic morality of the pursuit of money in the enterprise culture has led to a belief by some speculators that they can take risks which are criminal".

It should be noted that this is not, of course, a new phenomenon but an extension of the essential nature of the capitalist enterprise stretching in particular from 19th century Victorian England to the present day. The imprecision of Victorian commercial law, the laxity of enforcement, the rising scale of financial organizations, increased free trade and an ethos of rugged individualism and venture capitalism all contributed to a climate of moral erosion that was incompatible with strict integrity. "The entrepreneurial culture of Victorian England had aggressive businessmen who were impatient with ethical codes, and whose pre-occupation with material success led them to fear failure more than fraud" (Robb, 1992: 181).

The nature of this type of commercial corruption, however, is that it is perceived almost as normal business practice within a context of capitalist enterprise and its expansion into developing countries. German companies, for example, that bribe clients overseas can write off the bribe against tax as a legitimate and necessary expense. Transparency International (TI), an NGO aimed at building international and national coalitions against corruption, estimates that, "15 percent of the amount involved in all international transactions is paid in bribes and kickbacks to heads of states, government ministries, and other senior civil servants involved in business negotiations" (SAPEM, 1995: 8). Certainly, there has been an increasing public awareness that influence peddling is a normal corporate business practice. During the 1970s a series of revelations in the United States confirmed that transnational corporations regularly made payoffs to foreign government officials in order to secure business contracts. For example, Gulf Oil executives admitted paying US$4 million to the South Korean ruling party and Lockheed Aircraft admitted paying a staggering US$202 million in overseas bribes (Siegel, 1986). In developing countries, such as those in Southern Africa, transnational corporations frequently try to corrupt government officials who can facilitate contracts, capital exports, market monopolies, and cheap and docile labour (Szeftel, 1983). This can be a result of the expansion of transnational corporations into the region or the expansion of South African companies into other countries in the region. The latter case raises concerns about the continued dominance and control of the South African economy by mainly white capitalists such that, according to one commentator, "South Africa is trying to perpetuate the old ideas of apartheid South Africa, trying to make its neighbours into satellite economies and markets for its goods" (*New African*, 1995: 34).

It can be demonstrated that although post-election South Africa has meant the arrival of external markets with the relaxing of trade barriers and the development of a more open economy, one downside of this new entrepreneurial spirit is corruption, crime syndicates, dishonesty, embezzlement, and bribery. Economic crime has become a big and lucrative business in South Africa. Not a day goes by without reports of corruption, bribery, company mismanagement, or foreign exchange contravention.

However, as we have noted, there is a paucity of accurate and reliable information on commercial corruption in Southern Africa. The corruption scandals that have surfaced in Southern Africa over the last decade have revolved around three aspects of the development process: land; building and construction; and banking and finance. A recent submission to the first African Congress on Economic Crime suggests that to combat economic crime we need to have efficient financial systems and that unless there is greater control over financial systems in Southern Africa, particularly bank supervision and exchange control, "our efforts to prevent and combat economic crime in a regional context will not succeed" (Alant, 1995: 1).

Conclusions

In conclusion, it has been suggested that corruption "is not an aberration, but rather the way the system works in the typical African state" and that "the most propitious conditions exist in countries that have both large public sectors and relatively indulgent policies towards the activities of private enterprises" (Harsch, 1993: 37). Within the Southern African region, structural adjustment programmes, promoted by the World Bank and IMF through policies of privatization, the abolition of state marketing monopolies, and the provision of credit and other support for the private sector, are likely to increase these activities of private enterprises and "spur a shift from parasitic to nurture capitalism" (Harsch, 1993: 41). This is based on the belief that the private sector should be the main engine of economic growth, that a large public sector is prone to corruption, and that "privatization offers the only viable prospect of curtailing corruption in the Third World" (Theobald, 1990: 158). While this may be true of the petty criminal acts of official corruption and the large scale looting of public coffers through élite corruption, as in Kenya and Zaire, it is unlikely to be true of commercial corruption and parallel economic crimes. The experience of the 1980s would suggest that a socio-economic context of free market entrepreneurial capitalist development is, in fact, the ideal climate in which these types of criminal activity flourish. There can be little doubt that these activities are systemic and systematic in nature and not the individual acts of a few corrupt and corruptible corporations, business executives, and public officials.

Although arguments have been proffered about the benefits of commercial corruption in developing countries, for example, that it assists capital formation, fosters entrepreneurial abilities, and saves time and money by oiling the wheels of the bureaucracy, these in no way mitigate its real costs. Corruption in general is essentially socially divisive, undermines both democracy and stability, and is "associated with a pathological political style, an ethos of mistrust, subterfuge and conspiracy" (Theobald, 1990: 130).

Certainly there should be little doubt about the seriousness of corrupt activities and the necessity for a criminal rather than an ethical definition. As Levi (1987: 29) has pointed out, it is almost impossible to calculate their economic and physical impact for "it may bear no relation to the value of any bribe involved, for a bribe of a few hundred pounds may cover the failure to insert vital structural supports that may cause a building to collapse". A recent case in South Africa illustrates this point only too well. In 1994, in Merriespruit, the Freestate gold fields, seventeen people died as a result of a slimes dam collapsing. It also caused considerable damage and injured another six hundred people. The negligent corporation found guilty of culpable homicide in this disaster, Harmony Gold Mine, was asked to pay a fine equivalent to one-fifth of one percent of the mine's post tax profits for 1995 (*Mail and Guardian*, 1996b).

This exemplifies one of the main problems in dealing with commercial corruption. Even if it is defined as a criminal activity it is likely that perpetrators will only receive a derisory sentence or a negligible fine (Geis and Jesilow, 1993). It is even less likely that they will be prosecuted or convicted for when it comes to forms of economic crime the benefits of breaking the law far outweigh the costs. In Commonwealth Africa, for example, Coldham (1995) suggests that although the criminal law has been extensively used to combat corruption it has failed. Penal measures taken to sharpen the deterrent effect of the criminal law, such as the creation of new offenses, the presumption of corruption, severe penalties, and the introduction of special courts have had little effect on levels of corruption and economic crime. This, of course, is hardly surprising given that these criminal activities are an inherent and endemic feature of a criminogenic capitalist commercial order where perpetrators hold socio-economic and political power and are themselves responsible for initiating and implementing legislation.

Perhaps the last word on the undoubted seriousness of economic crime, and particularly commercial corruption, is best left to the 18th Century English writer, Jonathan Swift, author of Gulliver's Travels, who is quoted by Box (1983) thus: "The Lilliputians look upon fraud as a greater crime than theft, and therefore seldom fail to punish it with death; for they allege that care and vigiliance, with a very common understanding, may preserve a man's goods from theft, but honesty has no defence against superior cunning".

Bibliography

Aday, L.A. and Andersen, R. (1974), 'A Framework for the Study of Access to Medical Care', *Health Services Research*, Vol. 9, No. 4, pp. 208-20.

Addison, T. (1993), *A Review of the World Bank's Efforts to Assist African Governments in Reducing Poverty*, ESP Discussion Paper No. 10, World Bank: Washington, DC.

Adedeji, A. and Shaw, T.M. (eds.). (1985), *Economic Crisis in Africa: African Perspectives on Development Problems and Potentials*, Lynne Rienner: Boulder.

Adepoju, A. (1988). 'Overview of International Labour Migration in Africa', Paper Presented at the African Population Conference, Dakar, Senegal, November.

Adjei, M. (1994), *Death and Pain: Rawlings' Ghana: The Inside Story*, Black Line Publishing: London.

Africa Confidential. (1995), Vol. 36, No. 1, pp. 1-4.

Africa Institute. (1994), *South Africa in Sub-Equatorial Africa: Economic Interaction*, Africa Institute: Pretoria.

Ahamed, L. (1986), 'Stabilization Policies in Developing Countries', *The World Bank Research Observer*, Vol. 1, No. 1, pp. 59-80.

Aidoo, A. (1993), 'Africa: Democracy with Human Rights?', *Human Rights Quarterly*, Vol. 15, No. 4, pp. 703-15.

Alant, N.G. (1995), Presentation on the Issues of the Legal Duties of the South African Reserve Bank as an Administrator of Financial Systems with Specific Reference to the Prevention and Investigation of Economic Crime, First African Conference on Economic Crime, Bloemfontein, South Africa.

Amoaku-Adu, B. (1985), 'Economic Recovery Programme: Problems and Prospects', A Lecture Delivered at the Bank of Ghana, July.

Andreassen. B., Geister, G. and Jostensen, A. (1992), *Setting a Standard for Africa? Lessons From the 1991 Zambia Elections*, Michelsen Institute: Fantoft-Bergen.

Anyang Nyong'o, P. (1988), 'Political Instability and the Prospects for Democracy in Africa', *Africa Development*, Vol. 13, No. 1, pp. 71-86.

Arnold, G. (1992), 'Is Colonialism Returning to Africa?', *Africa Analysis*, No. 146, p. 15.

Austin, D. (1993), 'Reflections on African Politics: Prospero, Ariel and Caliban', *International Affairs*, Vol. 69, No. 2, pp. 203-21.

Ayittey, G.B.N. (1992), *Africa Betrayed*, St. Martin's Press: New York.

Bacon, R. and Eltis, W. (1975), *Britain's Economic Problems: Too Few Producers*, Macmillan: London.

Balassa, B. (1989), *A Conceptual Framework for Adjustment Policies*, Working Paper No. 139, World Bank: Washington, DC.

Baldwin, R.E. (1966), *Economic Development and Export Growth: A Study of Northern Rhodesia, 1920-60*, University of California Press: Berkeley.

Bates, R.H. and Collier, P. (1995), 'The Politics and Economics of Policy Reform in Zambia', *Journal of African Economies*, Vol. 4, No. 1, pp. 115-43.

Beckman, G. (1992), 'Empowerment or Repression?: The World Bank and the Politics of African Adjustment', in Gibbon, P., Bangura, Y. and Ofstad, A. (eds.), *Authoritarianism, Democracy and Adjustment: The Politics of Economic Reform in Africa*, The Nordic Africa Institute: Uppsala.

Behrman, J. (1988), 'The Impact of Economic Adjustment Programs', in Bell, D. and Reich, M. (eds.), *Health, Nutrition and Economic Crises: Approaches to Policy in the Third World*, Auburn House: New York.

Bell, S.W. (1995), *Sharing the Wealth: Privatization through Broad-Based Ownership Strategies*, Discussion Paper No. 285, World Bank: Washington, DC.

Berlage, L. and Stoke, O. (eds.). (1992), *Evaluating Development Assistance: Approaches and Methods*, Frank Cass: London.

Bernstein, B. and Boughton, J.M. (1993), *Adjusting to Development: The IMF and the Poor*, IMF: Washington, DC.

Bheenick, R. and Schapiro, M.O. (1989), 'Mauritius: A Case Study of the Export Processing Zone', in World Bank (ed.), *Successful Development in Africa*, World Bank: Washington, DC.

Boahen, A. (1992), *The Ghanaian Sphinx: Reflections on the Contemporary History of Ghana, 1972-1987*, Sankofa Educational Publishers: Accra.

Boston, J. (1992), 'New Zealand's Privatization Programme: Objectives, Principles, Problems, and Outcomes', *Annals of Public and Cooperative Economics*, Vol. 63, No. 4, pp. 555-600.

Bourguigon, F. and Morrison, C. (1992), *Adjustment and Equity in Developing Countries: A New Approach*, OECD: Paris.

Bourguigon, F., Branson, W.H. and de Melo, J. (1992), 'Adjustment and Income Distribution: A Micro-Macro Model for Counterfactual Analysis', *Journal of Development Economics*, Vol. 38, No. 1, pp. 17-39.

Box, S. (1983), *Power, Crime and Mystification*, Routledge: London.

Bradshaw, J. and Deacon, A. (1986), 'Social Security', in Wilding, P. (ed.), *In Defence of the Welfare State*, Manchester University Press: Manchester.

Brake, M. and Hale, C. (1992), *Public Order and Private Lives: The Politics of*

Law and Order, Routledge: London.
Brand, V., Mupedziswa, R. and Gumbo, P. (1993), 'Women Informal Sector Workers in Zimbabwe', in Gibbon, P. (ed.), *Social Change and Economic Reform in Africa*, The Nordic Africa Institute: Uppsala.
Bratton, M. and van de Walle, N. (1992), 'Popular Protest and Political Reform in Africa' *Comparative Politics*, Vol. 24, No. 4, pp. 419-42.
Burawoy, N. (1972), 'The Role of the University Student in the Zambian Social Structure', unpublished Master of Arts dissertation, University of Zambia: Lusaka.
Burdette, M.M. (1988), *Zambia: Between Two Worlds*, Westview Press: Boulder.
Business Day. (1995), October 4.
Callaghy, T.M. (1994), 'State, Choice, and Context: Comparative Reflections on Reform and Intractability', in Apter, D. and Rosberg, G. (eds), *Political Development and the New Realism in Sub-Saharan Africa*, University Press of Virginia: Charlottesville.
Campbell, B. and Parfitt, T. (1995), 'Virtual Adjustment: Whose Reality?', *Review of African Political Economy*, No. 63, pp. 3-8.
Centre for Social Research (CSR). (1990), *Report of the Workshop on the Effects of the Structural Adjustment Programme in Malawi*, Centre for Social Research, University of Malawi: Zomba.
Chakaodza, O. (1993), *Structural Adjustment in Zambia and Zimbabwe: Reconstructive or Destructive?*, Third World Publishing House: Harare.
Chambers, R. (1974), *Managing Rural Development: Ideas and Experience From East Africa*, The Nordic Africa Institute: Uppsala.
Chan, S. (1989), 'The Impossibility of Doing Good - The Desirability of Doing Bad: Some Notes on Community and Youth Development in Third World Nations', in Osei-Hwedie, K. and Ndulo, M. (eds.), *Studies in Youth and Development*, Multimedia Publications: Lusaka.
Chanda, D. (1990), 'Auctioning Revisited: A Re-Examination of Currency Auctioning in Zambia: 4th October 1985 - 1st May 1987', in Osei-Hwedie, K. and Ndulo, M. (eds.), *Development at Crossroads: An African Experience*, Brunswick Press: Lawrenceville.
Chazan, N., et al. (1992), *Politics and Society in Contemporary Africa*, Lynne Rienner: Boulder.
Chenery, H., Robinson, S. and Syrquin, M. (1986), *Industrialization and Growth*, Oxford University Press: New York.
Chidzonga, M. (1993), 'The Situation of Women in Agriculture in Communal Areas of Zimbabwe', in Mkandawire, R. and Matlosa, K. (eds.), *Food Policy and Agriculture in Southern Africa*, SAPES Books: Harare.
Chikulo, B.C. (1979), 'Elections in A One-Party State', in Turok, B. (ed.), *Development in Zambia*, Zed Press: London.
Chikulo, B.C. (1993), 'Democracy and Development in Africa: Problems and Prospects', Paper Presented at the African Studies Association of South Africa

Biennial Conference, Magaliesberg, June.
Chilowa, W., Kandoole, B., and Musukwa, L. (1990), 'Survival Mechanisms and Intervention for Food Deficit Rural Households', Paper Presented at the Workshop on Food Security, Socio-Economic Status and Nutrition of the Rural Population in Malawi, Zomba, December.
Chipeta, C. (1993), 'Malawi', in Adepoju, A. (ed.), *The Impact of Structural Adjustment on the Population of Africa*, James Currey: London.
Chisvo, M. and Munro, L.T. (1994), *A Review of the Social Dimensions of Adjustment in Zimbabwe, 1990-1994*, UNICEF: Harare.
Christiansen, R. and Southworth, V. (1988), 'Agricultural Pricing and Market Policy in Malawi: Implications for a Development Strategy', Paper Presented at the Symposium on Agricultural Policies for Growth and Development, Mangochi, November.
Cogill, B. and Zasa, M. (1990), *Report of the Pilot Nutrition Modules for CSO, National Food and Nutrition Commission, and UNICEF*, Central Statistical Office/National Food and Nutrition Commission/UNICEF: Lusaka.
Colclough, C. (1988), 'Zambian Adjustment Strategy-With and Without the IMF', *IDS Bulletin*, Vol. 19, No. 1, pp. 51-60.
Coldham, S. (1995), 'Legal Responses to State Corruption in Commonwealth Africa', *Journal of African Law*, Vol. 39, No. 2, pp. 115-26.
Commonwealth Observer Group. (1992), *Presidential and National Assembly Elections in Zambia, 31 October 1991*, Commonwealth Secretariat: London.
Commonwealth Secretariat. (1989), *Engendering Adjustment for the 1990s: Report of A Commonwealth Expert Group on Women and Structural Adjustment*, Commonwealth Secretariat: London.
Daniel, P. (1985), 'Zambia: Structural Adjustment or Downward Spiral?', *IDS Bulletin*, Vol. 16, No. 3, pp. 52-60.
Dava, G. (1993), 'Urban Poverty, Intervention Strategies and the Role of Social Work in the Framework of Structural Adjustment: Concepts, Approaches and Experiences', in *Proceedings of a Workshop on Social Development and Urban Poverty*, School of Social Work, University of Zimbabwe: Harare.
de Abreu, A. and Baltazar, R.A. (1994), *The Role of the State and its Fiscal and Monetary Policies in the Successful Implementation of Reform Programmes*, Konrad Andenauer Foundation: Harare.
Demery, L. (1994), 'Structural Adjustment: Its Origins, Rationale and Achievements', in Cornia, G.A. and Helleiner, G.K. (eds.), *From Adjustment to Development in Africa: Conflict, Controversy, Convergence, Consensus?*, St. Martin's Press: New York.
Demery, L. and Squire, L. (1996), 'Macroeconomic Adjustment and Poverty in Africa: An Emerging Picture', *The World Bank Research Observer*, Vol. 11, No. 1, pp. 39-59.
Dia, M. (1996), *Africa's Management in the 1990s and Beyond: Reconciling Indigenous and Transplanted Institutions*, World Bank: Washington, DC.

Diamond, L. (1994), 'Democracy and the New Wind', *Africa Report*, Vol. 39, No. 5, pp. 50-54.
Diamond, L., Linz, J. and Lipset, S.M. (eds.). (1988), *Democracy in Developing Countries: Volume 2: Africa*, Lynne Rienner: Boulder.
Dresang, D.L. (1994), 'Ethnic Politics, Representative Bureaucracy and Development Administration: The Zambian Case', *American Political Science Review*, Vol. 68, No. 4, pp. 1605-17.
Easterly, W. and Schmidt-Hebbel, K. (1994), 'Fiscal Adjustment and Macroeconomic Performance: A Synthesis', in Easterly, W., Rodríguez, C.A. and Schmidt-Hebbel, K. (eds.), *Public Sector Deficits and Macroeconomic Performance*, Oxford University Press: New York.
Economic Research Group (ERG). (1989), *Perspective on the Zambian Economy, No. 3*, Working Papers of the Economic Research Group, University of Zambia: Lusaka.
Economist Intelligence Unit. (1994), *Country Report: Zambia*, Economist Intelligence Unit: London.
Edgmand, M.R. 1983. *Macroeconomics: Theory and Policy*, Prentice-Hall: New Delhi.
Ekpo, A. (1992), 'Economic Development Under Structural Adjustment: Evidence from Selected West African Countries', *Journal of Social Development in Africa*, Vol. 7, No. 1, pp. 25-39.
Elliot, C. (1971), 'Introduction', in Elliot, C. (ed.), *Constraints on the Economic Development of Zambia*, Oxford University Press: Nairobi.
Endale, D. (1995), *Changing Patterns of Employment and Unemployment in Africa*, World Development Studies 7, World Institute for Development Economics Research, United Nations University: Helsinki.
Fardi, M.A. (1991), 'Zambia: Reform and Reversal', in Thomas, V., et al. (eds.), *Restructuring Economics in Distress*, Oxford University Press: New York.
Findley, S.E. (1993), 'The Third World City: Development Policy and Issues', in Kasarda, J.D. and Parnell, A.M. (eds.), *Third World Cities: Problems, Policies, and Prospects*, Sage: London.
Fontaine, J-M. (1993), *Reforming Public Enterprises and the Public Sector in Sub-Saharan Africa*, Discussion Paper No. 60, UNCTAD: Geneva.
Forensic Accounting. (1995), No. 3, p. 12.
Fortman, B. (1969), 'Humanism and the Zambian Economic Order', in Fortman, B. (ed.), *After Mulungushi: The Economics of Zambian Humanism*, East African Publishing House: Nairobi.
French, H.W. (1995), 'African Despots Changing the Rules for Democracy', *The Star*, October 25.
Friedman, M. (1973), 'The Quantity Theory of Money: A Restatement', in Clower, R.W. (ed.), *Monetary Theory*, Penguin: London.
Friedmann, J. (1992), *Empowerment: The Politics of Alternative Development*, Blackwell: Cambridge.

Frohlich, C. and Frayne, B. (1991), *Hawking: An 'Informal' Sector Activity in Katutura, Windhoek*, Namibian Institute for Social and Economic Research: Windhoek.

Fry, J. (1980), 'The Economy', in Tordoff, W. (ed.), *Administration in Zambia*, Manchester University Press: Manchester.

Geis, G. and Jesilow, P. (1993). 'White Collar Crime', *The Annals of the American Academy of Political and Social Science*, Vol. 25, Sage: London.

George, V. and Wilding, P. (1994), *Welfare and Ideology*, Harvester Wheatsheaf: New York.

Gerber, P.D., Nel, P.S. and van Dyk, P.S. (1995), *Human Resources Management*, Southern Book Publishers: Halfway House.

Gerschenkron, A. (1962), *Economic Backwardness in Historical Perspective*, Harvard University Press: Cambridge.

Gilmour, I. (1978), *Inside the Right*, Quartet: London.

Gilmour, I. (1983), *Britain Can Work*, Martin Robertson: London.

Government of Malawi. (1971), *Economic Report*, Economic Planning Division: Zomba.

Government of Malawi. (1977), *National Rural Development Programme: Policies, Strategy and General Features*, Ministry of Agriculture and Natural Resources: Lilongwe.

Government of Malawi. (1980), *Economic Report*, Department of Economic Planning and Development: Lilongwe.

Government of Malawi. (1986), *Annual Survey of Agriculture*, National Statistical Office: Zomba.

Government of Malawi. (1988), *Economic Report*, Department of Economic Planning and Development: Lilongwe.

Government of Malawi. (1989), *Guide to Agricultural Production*, Ministry of Agriculture: Lilongwe.

Government of Malawi. (1992), *Economic Report*, Department of Economic Planning and Development: Lilongwe.

Griffin, K. (1989), *Alternative Strategies for Development*, Macmillan: London.

Haddad, L., et al. (1995), 'The Gender Dimensions of Economic Adjustment Policies: Potential Interactions and Evidence to Date', *World Development*, Vol. 23, No. 6, pp. 881-96.

Hadjimichael, M.T., et al. (1995), *Sub-Saharan Africa: Growth, Savings, and Investment, 1986-93*, IMF: Washington, DC.

Haggard, S. and Webb, S.B. (1993), 'What Do We Know About the Political Economy of Economic Policy Reform?' *The World Bank Research Observer*, Vol. 8, No. 2, pp. 143-68.

Hall, R. (1969), *The High Price of Principles: Kaunda and the White South*, Hodder and Stoughton: London.

Hardy, C. (1990), 'The Prospects for Intra-regional Trade Growth in Africa', in Stewart, F., Lall, S. and Wangwe, S. (eds.), *Alternative Development Strategies*

in sub-Saharan Africa, Macmillan: London.
Harvey, C. (1991), 'On the Perverse Effects of Financial Sector Reform in Anglophone Africa', *South African Journal of Economics*, Vol. 59, No. 3, pp. 258-86.
Harvey, C. (1996), 'Introduction', in Harvey, C. (ed.), *Constraints on the Success of Structural Adjustment Programmes in Africa*, Macmillan: London.
Harsch, E. (1993), 'Accumulators and Democrats: Challenging State Corruption in Africa', *Journal of Modern African Studies*, Vol. 31, No. 1, pp. 31-48.
Hellinger, D. and Hammond, R. (1994), 'Structural Adjustment: Debunking', *Africa Report*, Vol. 39, No. 6, pp. 52-6.
Hemming, R. and Mansoor, A.M. (1988), *Privatization and Public Enterprises*, Occasional Paper 56, IMF: Washington, DC.
Hicks, J.R. (1965), *Capital and Growth*, Oxford University Press: Oxford.
Himbara, D. and Sultan, D. (1995), 'Reconstructing the Ugandan State and Economy: The Challenge of an International Bantustan', *Review of African Political Economy*, No. 63, pp. 85-93.
Hirschman, A. (1958), *The Strategy of Economic Development*, Yale University Press: New Haven.
Hope, K.R. Snr. (1983), 'Self-Reliance and Participation of the Poor in the Development Process in the Third World', *Futures*, Vol. 15, December, pp. 455-62.
Hope, K.R. Snr. (1984), 'Self-Reliance as a Development Strategy: A Conceptual Policy Analysis', *Scandinavian Journal of Development Alternatives*, Vol. 3, No. 4, pp. 17-27.
Hope, K.R. Snr. (1986), 'Urbanization and Economic Development in the Third World', *Cities*, Vol. 3, No. 2, pp. 41-57.
Hope, K.R. Snr. (1992), 'Development Theory and Policy in the Third World', *South African Journal of Economics*, Vol. 60, No. 4, pp. 333-53.
Hope, K.R. Snr. (1993a), 'The Growth and Impact of the Subterranean Economy in the Third World', *Futures*, Vol. 25, No. 8, pp. 864-76.
Hope, K.R. Snr. (1993b), 'The Subterranean Economy and the Role of Private Investment in Developing Countries', *Journal of Social, Political and Economic Studies*, Vol. 18, No. 2, pp. 181-95.
Hope, K.R. Snr. (1995a), 'Urbanization and Urban Management in the Third World', unpublished manuscript, University of Botswana: Gaborone.
Hope, K.R. Snr. (1995b), 'Managing the Public Sector in Botswana: Some Emerging Constraints and the Administrative Reform Responses', *International Journal of Public Sector Management*, Vol. 8, No. 6, pp. 51-62.
Hope, K.R. Snr. (1996a), 'Growth, Unemployment, and Poverty in Botswana', *Journal of Contemporary African Studies*, Vol. 14, No. 1, pp. 53-67.
Hope, K.R. Snr. (1996b), 'The Political Economy of Policy Reform and Change in Africa', unpublished manuscript, University of Botswana: Gaborone.
Hope, K.R. Snr. (1996c), *Development in the Third World: From Policy Failure*

to Policy Reform, M.E. Sharpe: London.

Hope, K.R. Snr. and Edge, W.A. (1996), 'Growth With Uneven Development: Urban-Rural Socio-Economic Disparities in Botswana', *Geoforum*, Vol. 27, No. 1, pp. 53-62.

Hunt, E.K. and Sherman, H.J. (1990), *Economics: An Introduction to Traditional and Radical Views*, Harper and Row: New York.

Huntington, S.P. (1968), *Political Order in Changing Societies*, Yale University Press: New Haven.

Huntington, S.P. (1994), 'What Price Freedom?' *Dialogue: The Economic Agenda*, No. 104, pp. 2-7.

Hyden, G. and Karlstrom, B. (1993), 'Structural Adjustment as a Policy Process: The Case of Tanzania', *World Development*, Vol. 21, No. 9, pp. 1395-1404.

Hyuha, M., Ndanshau, M.O. and Kipokola, J.P. (1993), *Scope, Structure and Policy Implications of Informal Financial Markets in Tanzania*, African Economic Research Consortium: Nairobi.

Institute of Statistical, Social and Economic Research (ISSER). (1994), *The State of the Ghanaian Economy in 1993*, ISSER, University of Ghana: Accra.

International Fund for Agricultural Development (IFAD). (1993), *The State of World Rural Poverty: A Profile of Africa*, IFAD: Rome.

International Labour Organization (ILO). (1981), *Zambia: Basic Needs in an Economy Under Pressure*, United Printers: Addis-Ababa.

International Monetary Fund (IMF). (1987), *Supplement to the Group of 24 Deputies' Report: IMF Survey*, IMF: Washington, DC.

International Monetary Fund (IMF). (1991), *Annual Report 1991*, IMF: Washington, DC.

International Monetary Fund (IMF). (1994a), *Financial Statistics Yearbook 1994*, IMF: Washington, DC.

International Monetary Fund (IMF). (1994b), *Direction of Trade Statistics Yearbook 1994*, IMF: Washington, DC.

International Monetary Fund (IMF). (1995), *Social Dimensions of the IMF Policy Dialogue*, Pamphlet Series No. 47, IMF: Washington, DC.

Johns, S. (1980), 'Parastatals in Zambia', in Tordoff, W. (ed.), *Administration in Zambia*, Manchester University Press: Manchester.

Johnson, H.G. (1973), 'Monetary Theory and Keynesian Economics', in Clower, R.W. (ed.), *Monetary Theory*, Penguin: London.

Jolly, R. (1971), 'The Skilled Manpower Constraint', in Elliot, C. (ed.), *Constraints on the Economic Development of Zambia*, Oxford University Press: Nairobi.

Jones, C. and Kiguel, M. (1994), 'Africa's Quest for Prosperity: Has Adjustment Helped?', *Finance and Development*, Vol. 31, No. 2, pp. 2-9.

Kadenge, P.G., Ndoro, H. and Zwizwai, B.M. (1992), 'Zimbabwe's Structural Adjustment Programme: The First Year Experience', in Mwanza, A.M. (ed.), *Structural Adjustment Programmes in SADC*, SAPES Books: Harare.

Kakwani, N. (1995), 'Structural Adjustment and Performance in Living Standards in Developing Countries', *Development and Change*, Vol. 26, No. 3, pp. 469-502.

Kalapula, E.S. (1985), 'Potentials and Limits of Agriculture Land Settlement Schemes as an Aspect of Rural Development: The Case of Zambia's Rural Reconstruction Centres', in Osei-Hwedie, K. and Ndulo, M. (eds.), *Issues in Zambian Development*, Omenana Press: Roxbury.

Kalapula, E.S. (1989), 'Agricultural Land Resettlement Schemes for Youths and the Role of Youth in Agriculture and Rural Development in Zambia', in Osei-Hwedie, K. and Ndulo, M. (eds.), *Studies in Youth and Development*, Multimedia Publications: Lusaka.

Kaluwa, B. (1990), 'Private Trader Response to Food Marketing Liberalization: Market Integration and Economic Efficiency', Paper Presented at the Workshop on Food Security, Socio-Economic Status and Nutrition of the Rural Population in Malawi, Zomba, December.

Kandoole, B. (1990), 'Structural Adjustment in Malawi: Short-run Gains and Long-run Losses', Paper Presented at the Effects of Structural Adjustment Programmes in Malawi, Mangochi.

Kasere, C. (1993), 'Structural Adjustment: Zimbabwe', in *Proceedings of a Workshop on Social Development and Urban Poverty*, School of Social Work, University of Zimbabwe: Harare.

Kashambuzi, E. (1995), 'Poverty Still Deepening in Zambia', *Africa Recovery*, Vol. 9, No. 1, p. 13.

Kaunda, K. (1968), *Speech to the UNIP Delegates at Mulungushi, 9 November*, Government Printer: Lusaka.

Kawonga, F. (1981), *Youth Development and Schemes for Youth Employment in Zambia*, ILO/JASPA: Lusaka.

Kayizzi-Mugerwa, S. and Levin, J. (1994), 'Adjustment and Poverty: A Review of the African Experience', *African Development Review*, Vol. 6, No. 2, pp. 1-39.

Kelso, B.J. (1994), 'Human Rights, A Sorry Record', *Africa Report*, Vol. 39, No. 5, pp. 59-63.

Khan, A.R. (1994), *Overcoming Unemployment*, International Labour Organization: Geneva.

Khan, M.S. (1987), 'Macroeconomic Adjustment in Developing Countries: A Policy Perspective', *The World Bank Research Observer*, Vol. 2, No. 1, pp. 23-42.

Kikeri, S., Nellis, J. and Shirley, M. (1992), *Privatization: The Lessons of Experience*, World Bank: Washington, DC.

Killick, T. (1993), *The Adaptive Economy: Adjustment Policies in Small, Low-Income Countries*, World Bank: Washington, DC.

Killick, T. (1995), 'Structural Adjustment and Poverty Alleviation: An Interpretative Essay', *Development and Change*, Vol. 26, No. 2, pp. 305-31.

Kirkpatrick, C. and Nixson, F. (1983), *The Industrialization of Less Developed Countries*, Manchester University Press: Manchester.

Kirkpatrick, C. and Weiss, J. (1995), 'Trade Policy Reforms and Performance in Africa in the 1980s', *Journal of Modern African Studies*, Vol. 33, No. 2, pp. 285-98.

Kiguel, M. and O'Connell, S.A. (1995), 'Parallel Exchange Rates in Developing Countries', *The World Bank Research Observer*, Vol. 10, No. 1, pp. 21-52.

Krueger, A. (1993), *Political Economy of Policy Reform in Developing Countries*, MIT Press: Cambridge.

Kutengule, M. (1993), 'The Structural Adjustment Economic Reform Programme and Urban Poverty in Malawi', in *Proceedings of a Workshop on Social Development and Urban Poverty*, School of Social Work, University of Zimbabwe: Harare.

Kydd, J. (1988), 'Coffee after Copper? Structural Adjustment, Liberalization and Agriculture in Zambia', *Journal of Modern African Studies*, Vol. 26, No. 2, pp. 227-51.

Kydd, J. and Christiansen, R. (1982), 'Structural Change in Malawi Since Independence: Consequences of a Development Strategy Based on Large Scale Agriculture', *World Development*, Vol. 10, No. 5, pp. 355-75.

Kyle, S. (1994), 'Structural Adjustment in a Country at War: The Case of Mozambique', in Sahn, D.E. (ed.), *Adjusting to Policy Failure in African Economics*, Cornell University Press: Ithaca.

Lall, S. (1990), 'Structural Problems of African Industry', in Stewart, F., Lall, S. and Wangwe, S. (eds.), *Alternative Development Strategies in sub-Saharan Africa*, Macmillan: London.

Lall, S. (1995), 'Structural Adjustment and African Industry', *World Development*, Vol. 23, No. 12, pp. 2019-31.

Landell-Mills, P. (1992), 'Governance, Cultural Change, and Empowerment', *Journal of Modern African Studies*, Vol. 30, No. 4, pp. 543-67.

Leftwich, A. (1996), 'Two Cheers for Democracy? Democracy and the Developmental State', in Leftwich, A. (ed.), *Democracy and Development: Theory and Practice*, Polity Press: Cambridge.

Le Grand, J. (1982), *The Strategy of Equality*, George Allen and Unwin: London.

Le Grand, J. (1995), 'The Strategy of Equality Revisited: A Reply', *Journal of Social Policy*, Vol. 24, No. 2, pp. 187-91.

Lele, U. (1975), *The Design of Rural Development: Lessons From Africa*, Johns Hopkins University Press: Baltimore.

Levi, M. (1987), *Regulating Fraud: White Collar Crime and the Criminal Process*, Tavistock: London.

Lindauer, D.L. Meesook, O.A. and Suebaseng, P. (1988), 'Government Wage Policies in Africa: Some Findings and Policy Issues', *The World Bank Research Observer*, Vol. 3, No. 1, pp. 1-25.

Lipumba, N.H. (1994), *Africa Beyond Adjustment*, Overseas Development Council: Washington, DC.

Liuksila, C. (ed.). *External Assistance and Policies for Growth in Africa*, IMF: Washington, DC.

Lowe, R. (1993), *The Welfare State in Britain Since 1945*, Macmillan: London.

Lulat, Y.G.M. (1981), 'Determinants of Third World Student Political Activism in the Seventies: The Case of Zambia', in Altbach, P. (ed.), *Student Politics: Perspectives for the Eighties*, Scarecrow Press: London.

Lundahl, M. and Moritz, L. (1993), 'Macroeconomic Stagnation and Structural Weaknesses in the South African Economy', in Blomstrom, M. and Lundahl, M. (eds.), *Economic Crisis in Africa: Perspectives on Policy Responses*, Routledge: London.

Magadlela, D. (1995), 'Smallholder-Big Dreams: Smallholder Irrigation Farmers' Perception of Subsistence and Commercial Production in Nyamaropa, Zimbabwe', Paper Presented at the ZIMWESI Seminar, University of Zimbabwe, June.

Magadzire, G. (1994). 'Smallholder Agriculture under ESAP: Challenges and Prospects', Paper presented at the Workshop on the Future of Smallholder Farming Under ESAP, Kadoma, November.

Mail and Guardian. (1996a), 9 February.

Mail and Guardian. (1996b), 29 March.

Maipose, G.S. (1989), 'Zambia's Economic and Unemployment Problems: An Analysis of Underlying Factors', in Osei-Hwedie, K. and Ndulo, M. (eds.), *Studies in Youth and Development*, Multimedia Publications: Lusaka.

Makgetla, N.S. (1986), 'Theoretical and Practical Implications of IMF Conditionality in Zambia', *Journal of Modern African Studies*, Vol. 24, No. 3, pp. 395-422.

Martin, A. (1972), *Minding Their Own Business: Zambia's Struggle Against Western Control*, Hutchinson: London.

Mashingaidze, K. (1994), 'Maize Research and Development', in Rukuni, M. and Eicher, C.K. (eds.), *Zimbabwe's Agricultural Revolution*, University of Zimbabwe Publications: Harare.

Masiye, G. (1993), 'An Analysis of the Impact of the Structural Adjustment Programme on Urban Poverty and Social Fieldwork in Zambia', in *Proceedings of a Workshop on Social Development and Urban Poverty*, School of Social Work, University of Zimbabwe: Harare.

Meijer, F. (1990), 'Structural Adjustment and Diversification in Zambia', *Development and Change*, Vol. 21, No. 4, pp. 657-92.

Mensah, S.N-A. (1993), 'Structural Adjustment Programmes in Africa: Lessons from Ghana and Nigeria', *Africa Insight*, Vol. 1, No. 2, pp. 72-8.

Mhone, G.C.Z. (1995), 'The Social Dimensions of Adjustment (SDA) Programme in Zimbabwe: A Critical Review and Assessment', *The European Journal of Development Research*, Vol. 7, No. 1, pp. 101-23.

Midgley, J. (1988), 'Sociology and Development Policy', in Hall, A. and Midgley, J. (eds.), *Development Policies: Sociological Perspectives*, Manchester University Press: Manchester.

Midgley, J. (1995), *Social Development: The Developmental Perspectives in Social Welfare*, Sage: London.

Mijere, N. (1989), 'Youth and the Development of Self-Reliance in Zambia' in Osei-Hwedie, K. and Ndulo, M. (eds.), *Studies in Youth and Development*, Multimedia Publications: Lusaka.

Mkandawire, T. (1989), *Structural Adjustment and Agrarian Crisis in Africa: A Research Agenda*, CODESRIA: Dakar.

Mkandawire, T. (1991), 'North-South Links and Democratization in Africa', *Development: Journal of the Society of International Development*, Nos. 3/4, pp. 39-41.

Mlambo, A.S. (1995), 'Towards an Analysis of IMF Structural Adjustment Programmes in Sub-Saharan Africa (SSA): The Case of Zimbabwe 1990-94', *African Development*, Vol. 20, No. 2, pp. 77-98.

Modigliani, F. (1977), 'The Monetarist Controversy or, Should We Forsake Stabilization Policies?' *American Economic Review*, No. 67, March, pp. 1-19.

Molteno, R. (1972), 'Zambia and the One-Party State', *East Africa Journal*, Vol. 9, No. 2, pp. 6-8.

Molteno, R. (1973), 'Zambian Humanism: The Way Ahead', *The African Review*, Vol. 3, No. 4, pp. 37-62.

Moody, J.A. (1989), *Research Notes and Comments*, Institute of African Studies: Lusaka.

Morandé, F. and Schmidt-Hebbel, K. (1994), 'Zimbabwe: Fiscal Disequilibria and Low Growth', in Easterly, W., Rodríguez, C.A. and Schmidt-Hebbel, K. (eds.), *Public Sector Deficits and Macroeconomic Performance*, Oxford University Press: New York.

Moshi, H.P.B. (1993), 'The Commercialization and Privatization of Public Enterprises in Tanzania', in Bagachwa, M.S.D. and Mbelle, A.V.Y. (eds.), *Economic Policy Under a Multi-Party System in Tanzania*, Dar es Salaam University Press: Dar es Salaam.

Moshi, H.P.B. (1994), 'Privatization and the Question of Economic Nationalism', Paper Presented at a Seminar on the Role of the Private Sector in the Enhancement of Indigenization of the Tanzanian Economy, Dar es Salaam.

Mosley, P. and Weeks, J. (1993), 'Has Recovery Begun? 'Africa's Adjustment in the 1980s' Revisited', *World Development*, Vol. 21, No. 10, pp. 1583-1606.

Mosley, P. and Weeks, J. (1994), 'Adjustment in Africa', unpublished manuscript, University of Reading: Reading.

Mosley, P., Subasat, T. and Weeks, J. (1995), 'Assessing Adjustment in Africa', *World Development*, Vol. 23, No. 9, pp. 1459-73.

Mrak, M. (1989), 'Role of the Informal Financial Sector in the Mobilization and Allocation of Household Savings: The Case of Zambia', *Savings and*

Development, Vol. 13, No. 1, pp. 65-85.
Mulengu, A.P. (1989), 'Youth Employment Problems in Zambia and the Role of Youth Skills Training Programmes', in Osei-Hwedie, K. and Ndulo, M. (eds.), *Studies in Youth and Development*, Multimedia Publications: Lusaka.
Mullei, A. (1994), 'Policies for Export Growth and Economic Development: The African Experience', mimeo.
Musgrave, R.A. and Musgrave, P.B. (1989), *Public Finance in Theory and Practice*, McGraw-Hill: New York.
Musokotwane, S. (1989), 'Structural Adjustment Programmes and Youth Development in Zambia', in Osei-Hwedie, K. and Ndulo, M. (eds.), *Studies in Youth and Development*, Multimedia Publications: Lusaka.
Musumali, C. (1992), 'A Testimony From Zambia', in *CCPD Debt Resource Material, No. 2*, World Council of Churches: Geneva.
Mwanawina, I. (1993), 'Zambia', in Adepoju, A. (ed.), *The Impact of Structural Adjustment on the Population of Africa*, James Currey: London.
Mwanza, A.M. (1992), 'Structural Adjustment Programmes in SADC: What Have We Learned?', in Mwanza, A.M. (ed.), *Structural Adjustment Programmes in SADC*, SAPES Books: Harare.
Mwanza, J. (1979), 'Rural-Urban Immigration in Zambia', in Turok, B. (ed.), *Development in Zambia*, Zed Press: London.
Mwase, N. (1995), 'Urbanization and Structural Adjustment Programmes: The Zambian Experience', *The Courier*, No. 149, January-February, pp. 64-5.
Naya, S. (1990), *Private Sector Development and Enterprise Reforms in Growing Asian Economies*, ICS Press: San Francisco.
Naya, S. and McCleery, R. (1994), *Relevance of Asian Development Experiences to African Problems*, ICS Press: San Francisco.
Ncube, P. Sakala, M. and Ndulo, M. (1987), 'The International Monetary Fund and the Zambian Economy', in Havenevik, K. (ed.), *The IMF and the World Bank in Africa*, Nordic Africa Institute: Uppsala.
Ndegwa, P. and Green, R.H. (1994), *Africa to 2000 and Beyond: Imperative Political and Economic Agenda*, East African Educational Publishers: Nairobi.
Nellis, J.R. (1994), 'Public Enterprises in Sub-Saharan Africa', in Grosh, B. and Mukandala, R.S. (eds.), *State-Owned Enterprises in Africa*, Lynne Rienner: Boulder.
New African. (1995), October.
Norval, D. and Namoya, R. (1992), *The Informal Sector Within Greater Windhoek*, Namibia Development Corporation: Windhoek.
Noula, A.G. (1995), 'Adjustment Structural et development en Afrique: L'experience des annees 80', *Africa Development*, Vol. 20, No. 1, pp. 5-36.
Nyerere, J.K. (1986), 'One-Party has Flaws', *Times of Zambia*, 10 June.
Obasango, O. (1991), 'Towards the New Age of Economic and Political Democratization in Africa', *Development: Journal of the Society of International Development*, Nos. 3/4, pp. 42-5.

O'Higgins, M. (1987), 'Egalitarians, Equalities and Welfare Evaluation', *Journal of Social Policy*, Vol. 16, No. 1, pp. 1-18.

Onimode, B. ed. (1989), *The IMF, The World Bank and the African Debt*, Zed Press: London.

Onimode, B. (1992), 'The Bretton Woods Institutions and Africa's Development', *Development: Journal of the Society for International Development*, No. 1, pp. 62-7.

Osei-Hwedie, K., Mwansa, L-K. and Mufune, P. (1991), *Rural Poverty Alleviation in the Commonwealth: The Case of Zambia*, Commonwealth Secretariat: London.

Osei-Hwedie, K., et al. (1992), *Towards Structural Adjustment in Zambia: An Overview*, UNRISD: Geneva.

Oucho, J. (1988), 'The Relationship Between Internal and International Migration: Concepts, Methodology and Interpretation', Paper Presented at the African Population Conference, Dakar, November.

Organization of African Unity (OAU). (1991), *The Lagos Plan of Action for the Economic Development of Africa, 1980-2000*, OAU: Addis Ababa.

Oxfam. (1991), *Africa - Make or Break: Action for Recovery*, Oxfam: London.

Oyowe, A. (1993), 'Economic Recovery Well Under Way', *The Courier*, No. 141, September-October, pp. 32-4.

Pachai, B. (1978), *Law and Politics in Malawi, 1875-1975*, Limestone Press: Kingston.

Pack, H. (1988), 'Industrialization and Trade', in Chenery, H. and Srinivasan, T. (eds.), *Handbook of Development Economics - Vol. 1*, North-Holland: Amsterdam.

Pack, H. and Westphal, L.E. (1986), 'Industrial Strategy and Technological Change: Theory Versus Reality', *Journal of Development Economics*, Vol. 22, No. 1, pp. 87-128.

Palmier, L. (1983), 'Bureaucratic Corruption and its Remedies', in Clarke, M. (ed.), *Corruption: Causes, Consequences and Control*, Frances Pinter: London.

Parfitt, T. (1995), 'Adjustment for Stabilization or Growth? Ghana and the Gambia', *Review of African Political Economy*, No. 63, pp. 55-72.

Parnwell, M. (1993), *Population Movements and the Third World*, Routledge: London.

Pasha Magazine. (1989), No. 8.

Patten, C. (1983), *The Tory Case*, Longman: London.

Paus, E. (1994), 'Economic Growth through Neo-Liberal Restructuring? Insights from the Chilean Experience', *Journal of Developing Areas*, Vol. 29, No. 1, pp. 31-56.

Pearce, F. (1976), *Crimes of the Powerful*, Pluto Press: London.

Petersson, L. (1993), 'Structural Adjustment and Economic Management in a Dependent Economy: The Case of Lesotho', in Blomstrom, M. and Lundahl, M. (eds.), *Economic Crisis in Africa: Perspectives on Policy Responses*, Routledge: London.

Phiri, M.J. (Zambian High Commissioner to Botswana), (1995), Speech on the Occasion of Zambia's 31st Independence Anniversary, Gaborone, Botswana.

Please, S. (1992), 'Beyond Structural Adjustment in Africa', *Development Policy Review*, Vol. 10, No. 3, pp. 289-307.

Prebisch, R. (1950), *The Economic Development of Latin America and Its Principal Problems*, United Nations: New York.

Prebisch, R. (1959), 'Commercial Policy in the Underdeveloped Countries', *American Economic Review*, Vol. 49, pp. 257-69.

Reinikka-Soininen, R. (1990), *Theory and Practice in Structural Adjustment: The Case of Zambia*, Helsingin Kauppakorkea-Koullin Julkaisuja: Helsinki.

Reisman, D. (1980), 'Galbraith and Social Welfare', in Timms, N. (ed.), *Social Welfare: Why and How*, Routledge and Kegan Paul: London.

Republic of Botswana. (1991), *National Development Plan 7: 1991-1997*, Government Printer: Gaborone.

Republic of Botswana. (1994), *1991 Population and Housing Census: Administrative Report*, Government Printer: Gaborone.

Republic of Zambia. (1964), *Economic Report: The Transitional Development Plan*, Central Planning Office: Lusaka.

Republic of Zambia. (1986), *Report of the Commission of Inquiry into the Affairs of the University of Zambia*, Government Printers: Lusaka.

Republic of Zambia. (1987), *New Economic Recovery Programme: Interim National Development Plan*, Government Printers: Lusaka.

Republic of Zambia. (1988), *New Economic Recovery Programme: Interim National Development Plan: Progress Report No. 2*, Government Printers: Lusaka.

Riddell, R., et al. (1994), *Manufacturing Africa*, James Currey: London.

Riley, S.P. (1992), 'Political Adjustment or Domestic Pressure: Democratic Politics and Political Choice in Africa', *Third World Quarterly*, Vol. 13, No. 3, pp. 539-51.

Rimmer, D. (1995), 'Development and Africa: Changing Perceptions', *Africa Insight*, Vol. 25, No. 2, pp. 122-28.

Robb, G. (1992), *White Collar Crime in Modern England: Financial Fraud and Business Morality, 1845-1929*, Cambridge University Press: Cambridge.

Robinson, D. (1990), *Civil Service Pay in Africa*, ILO: Geneva.

Roemer, M. and Radelet, S.C. (1991), 'Macroeconomic Reform in Developing Countries', in Perkins, D.H. and Roemer, M. (eds.), *Reforming Economic Systems in Developing Countries*, Harvard Institute for International Development: Cambridge.

Rohdewohld, R. (1993), 'Deregulating the Public Sector: Privatization and Commercialization in Nigeria', *Annals of Public and Cooperative Economics*, Vol. 64, No. 4, pp. 501-604.

Rohrbach, D.D. (1988), 'The Growth of Smallholder Maize Production in Zimbabwe, 1979-1985: Implications for Food Security', in Rukuni, M. and Bernstein, R.H. (eds.), *Southern Africa: Food Policy Options: Proceedings of*

the Third Annual Conference on Food Security Research in Southern Africa, Department of Agricultural Economics, University of Zimbabwe: Harare.
Rukuni, M. (1994), 'The Evolution of Agricultural Policy, 1890-1990', in Rukuni, M. and Eicher, C.K. (eds.), *Zimbabwe's Agricultural Revolution*, University of Zimbabwe Publications: Harare.
Rukuni, M., and Makadho, J. (1994), 'Irrigation Development', in Rukuni, M. and Eicher, C.K. (eds.), *Zimbabwe's Agricultural Revolution*, University of Zimbabwe Publications: Harare.
Sahn, D.E., Arulpragasam, J. and Merid, L. (1990), *Policy Reform and Poverty in Malawi: A Survey of a Decade of Experience*, Food and Nutrition Policy Program, Cornell University: Ithaca.
Salim, S. (1992), 'So Much Achieved but So Much More to Do', *Africa Analysis*, No. 148, p. 15.
Samboma, J. (1995), 'Africa's Crippling Debt Burden', *New African*, September, p. 23.
Samuelson, P.A. and Nordhaus, W.D. (1992), *Economics*, McGraw-Hill: New York.
Sandbrook, R. (1988), 'Liberal Democracy in Africa: A Socialist-Revisionist Perspective', *Canadian Journal of African Studies*, Vol. 22, No. 2, pp. 240-67.
Sandbrook, R. (1991), 'Economic Crisis, Structural Adjustment and the State in Sub-Saharan Africa', in Ghai, D. (ed.), *The IMF and the South: The Social Impact of Crisis and Adjustment*, Zed Books: London.
Sandbrook, R. (1993), *The Politics of Africa's Economic Recovery*, Cambridge University Press: Cambridge.
Sarris, A.H. and Van den Brink, R. (1994), 'From Forced Modernization to Perestroika: Crisis and Adjustment in Tanzania', in Sahn, D.E. (ed.), *Adjusting to Policy Failure in African Economies*, Cornell University Press: Ithaca.
Sawyer, A. (1990), *The Political Dimension of Structural Adjustment Programmes in Sub-Saharan Africa*, Ghana University Press: Accra.
Schatz, S.P. (1994), 'Structural Adjustment in Africa: A Failing Grade So Far', *Journal of Modern African Studies*, Vol. 32, No. 4, pp. 679-92.
Schumpeter, J.A. (1934), *The Theory of Economic Development*, Harvard University Press: Cambridge.
Schumpeter, J.A. (1942), *Capitalism, Socialism and Democracy*, Harper and Row: New York.
Scitovsky, T. (1954), 'Two Concepts of External Economies', *Journal of Political Economy*, Vol. 62, pp. 143-51.
Scott, I. (1980), 'Party and Administration Under the One-Party State', in Tordoff, W. (ed.), *Administration in Zambia*, Manchester University Press: Manchester.
Seshamani, V. (1992), 'The Economic Policies of Zambia in the 1980s: Towards Structural Transformation With a Human Face?', in Cornia, G.A., van der Hoeven, R. and Mkandawire, T. (eds.), *Africa's Recovery in the 1980s: From Stagnation and Adjustment to Human Development*, St. Martin's Press: New

York.
Shao, I., Kiwara, A. and Makusi, G. (1992), 'Structural Adjustment in a Socialist Country: The Case of Tanzania', in Mwanza, A. (ed.), *Structural Adjustment Programmes in SADC*, SAPES Books: Harare.
Shapiro, H. and Taylor, L. (1990), 'The State and Industrial Strategy', *World Development*, Vol. 18, No. 6, pp. 861-78.
Sharer, R.L., De Zoysa, R. and McDonald, C.A. (1995), *Uganda: Adjustment with Growth, 1987-94*, Occasional Paper 121, IMF: Washington, DC.
Shaw, T. (1992), 'Africa', in Hawkesworth, M. and Kogan, M. (eds.), Encyclopedia of Government and Politics - Vol. 2, London: Routledge.
Shirley, M. and Berg, E. (1987), *Divestiture in Developing Countries*, Discussion Paper No. 11, World Bank: Washington, DC.
Siegel, L.J. (1986), *Criminology*, West Publishing: St. Paul.
Silumbu, E. (1995), 'Money, Credit, Income and Prices in sub-Saharan Africa: Where Do We Stand?', *Development Southern Africa*, Vol. 12, No. 3, pp. 309-20.
Simson, H. (1985), *Zambia: A Country Study*, The Nordic Africa Institute: Uppsala.
Simukonda, P. (1994), 'Integrated Rural Development in Malawi and Socio-Economic Change: The Karonga Project', *Development Southern Africa*, Vol. 11, No. 3, pp. 283-300.
Simwinga, G. (1980), 'Corporate Autonomy and Government Control', in Tordoff, W. (ed.), *Administration in Zambia*, Manchester University Press: Manchester.
Singer, H. (1950), 'The Distribution of Gains Between Investing and Borrowing Countries', *American Economic Review*, Vol. 40, pp. 473-85.
Sirleaf, E.J., (1996), 'Challenges to Africa's Leadership', Statement to the Conference of African Ministers of Planning and UNDP Resident Representatives in the Africa Region, Ouagadougou, Burkina Faso, 30-31 January.
Sklar, R.L. (1996), 'Towards a Theory of Developmental Democracy', in Leftwich, A. (ed.), *Democracy and Development: Theory and Practice*, Polity Press: Cambridge.
Smith, J. (1996), 'All Eyes on Once-Humble Stokvels as the Informal Sector Begins to Flex its Multi-Million-Rand Financial Muscles', *The Sunday Independent*, 24 March, p. 16.
Southern African Political and Economic Monthly (SAPEM). (1995), June.
Steel, W.F. and Webster, L.M. (1992), 'How Small Enterprises in Ghana have Responded to Adjustment', *The World Bank Economic Review*, Vol. 6, No. 3, pp. 423-38.
Stevens, M. (1994), 'Public Expenditure and Civil Service Reform in Tanzania', in Lindauer, D.L. and Nunberg, B. (eds.), *Rehabilitating Government: Pay and Employment Reform in Africa*, World Bank: Washington, DC.
Stevens, M., and Gnanaselvam, S. (1995), 'The World Bank and Governance', *IDS*

Bulletin, Vol. 26, No. 2, pp. 97-105.

Streeten, P. (1987), 'Structural Adjustment: A Survey of the Issues and Options', *World Development*, Vol. 15, No. 12, pp. 1469-82.

Strydom, P.D.F. and Fiser, F.H. (1995), 'Structural Adjustment Programmes', *Development Southern Africa*, Vol, 12, No. 3, pp. 321-32.

Sunday Times. (1995), 10 October.

Sunday Times. (1996a), 12 May.

Sunday Times. (1996b), 18 February.

Szeftel, M. (1983), 'Corruption and the Spoils System in Zambia', in Clarke, M. (ed.), *Corruption: Causes, Consequences and Control*, Frances Pinter: London.

Tambunan, T. (1993), 'Some Issues with Respect to the Relative Efficiency of Public Enterprises', *Annals of Public and Cooperative Economics*, Vol. 64, No. 3, pp. 450-62.

Tanzi, V. (1992), 'Structural Factors and Tax Revenue in Developing Countries: A Decade of Evidence', in Goldin, I. and Winters, L.A. (eds.), *Open Economies: Structural Adjustments and Agriculture*. Cambridge University Press: Cambridge.

Tarp, F. (1993), *Stabilization and Structural Adjustment: Macroeconomic Frameworks for Analyzing the Crisis in Sub-Saharan Africa*, Routledge: London.

Tawney, R.H. (1964), *Equality*, George Allen and Unwin: London.

Tembo, R. (1993), 'Structural Adjustment and Personal Social Services in Zambia: The Case of Urban Poverty', in *Proceedings of a Workshop on Social Development and Urban Poverty*, School of Social Work, University of Zimbabwe: Harare.

The Economist. (1994), 5 March.

The Economist. (1995), 29 July, 'Cities Survey'.

Theobald, R. (1990), *Corruption, Development and Underdevelopment*, Macmillan: London.

The Southern African Economist. (1995), June/July.

Thompson, C. (1992), *Harvests Under Fire*, Zed Books: London.

Times of Zambia. (1987), 5 November.

Times of Zambia. (1988), 18 July.

Times of Zambia. (1989), 31 December.

Todd, D.M. and Shaw, C. (1980), 'The Informal Sector and Zambia's Employment Crisis', *Journal of Modern African Studies*, Vol. 18, No. 3, pp. 411-25.

Tordoff, W. (1974), *Politics in Zambia*, Manchester University Press: Manchester.

Tordoff, W. (1993), *Government and Politics in Africa*, Macmillan: London.

Townsend, P. (1979), *Poverty in the United Kingdom*, Penguin: London.

Toye, J. (1992), *The Appraisal and Evaluation of Structural Adjustment Lending: Some Questions*, mimeo., Institute of Development Studies, University of Sussex: Brighton.

Toye, J. (1996), 'Structural Adjustment, Labour Markets and Employment Policy', in Harvey, C. (ed.), *Constraints on the Success of Structural Adjustment Programmes in Africa*, Macmillan: London.

Tungwarara, O. (1995), 'Human Rights in Africa', *Southern Africa Political and Economic Monthly*, Vol. 8, No. 10, pp. 5-7.

Turok, B. (1979), 'The Penalties of Zambia's Mixed Economy', in Turok, B. (ed.), *Development in Zambia: A Reader*, Zed Press: London.

United Nations. (1988), *International Migration Policies and Programmes: A World Survey*, United Nations: New York.

United Nations Children's Fund (UNICEF). (1986), *Situation Analysis of Children and Women in Zambia*, UNICEF: Lusaka.

UNICEF. (1992), *The State of the World's Children*, Oxford University Press: New York.

United Nations Conference on Trade and Development (UNCTAD). (1987), *Handbook of International Trade and Development Statistics 1986*, United Nations: New York.

United Nations Development Programme (UNDP). (1990), *Human Development Report 1990*, Oxford University Press: New York.

UNDP. (1993), *Human Development Report 1993*, Oxford University Press: New York.

UNDP. (1994), *Human Development Report 1994*, Oxford University Press: New York.

UNDP. (1995), *Human Development Report 1995*, Oxford University Press: New York.

United Nations Economic Commission for Africa (UNECA). (1989), *African Alternative Framework to Structural Adjustment Programmes for Socio-Economic Recovery and Transformation*, UNECA: Addis Ababa.

UNECA. (1994), *The Ecology of Public Administration and Management in Africa*, UNECA: Addis Ababa.

United Nations Industrial Development Organization (UNIDO). (1990), *Industry and Development Global Report 1990/91*, UNIDO: Vienna.

United Nations Interregional Crime and Justice Research Institute (UNICRI). (1993), *Understanding Crime: Experiences of Crime and Crime Control*, UNICRI: Rome.

UNICRI. (1995), *Criminal Victimization in the Developing World*, UNICRI: Rome.

Vandemoortele, J. (1991), 'Labour Market Informalization in sub-Saharan Africa', in Standing, G. and Tokman, V., (eds.), *Towards Social Adjustment: Labour Market Issues in Structural Adjustment*, ILO: Geneva.

Vandemoortele, J. (1994), 'Austerity: Does it Have a Human Face? A UNDP Note on Budgetary Expenditure and Recent Development in Malawi', mimeo.

van de Walle, N. (1994b), 'Review Essay: Adjustment Alternatives and Alternatives to Adjustment', *African Studies Review*, Vol. 37, No. 3, pp. 103-17.

Walker, P. (1987), *Trust the People: Selected Essays and Speeches*, Collins: London.
Weiss, J. (1988), *Industry in Developing Countries: Theory, Policy and Evidence*, Croom Helm: London.
Wellisz, S. and Findlay, R. (1988), 'The State and the Invisible Hand', *The World Bank Research Observer*, Vol. 3, No. 1, pp. 59-80.
Whitaker, C.S. (1991), 'Doctrines of Development and Precepts of the State: The World Bank and the Fifth Iteration of the African Case', in Sklar, R.L. and Whitaker, C.S. (eds.), *African Politics and Problems in Development*, Lynne Rienner: Boulder.
Wina, A.L. (1990), 'An Open Letter to the Fifth Zambia National Convention', mimeo.
World Bank. (1981), *Accelerated Development in Sub-Saharan Africa: An Agenda for Action*, World Bank: Washington, DC.
World Bank. (1983), *Annual Report, 1983*, World Bank: Washington, DC.
World Bank. (1984), *Zambia: Industrial Policy and Performance*, World Bank: Washington, DC.
World Bank. (1987), *World Development Report 1987*, Oxford University Press: New York.
World Bank. (1989a), *Sub-Saharan Africa: From Crisis to Sustainable Growth: A Long-term Perspective Study*, World Bank: Washington, DC.
World Bank. (1989b), *World Development Report 1989*, Oxford University Press: New York.
World Bank. (1989c), *Malawi Country Economic Memorandum: Growth through Poverty Reduction*, World Bank: Washington, DC.
World Bank. (1990), *World Development Report 1990: Poverty*, Oxford University Press: New York.
World Bank. (1991), *Managing Development: The Governance Dimension*, World Bank: Washington, DC.
World Bank. (1992a), *World Bank Structural and Sectoral Adjustment Operations: The Second OED Review*, World Bank: Washington, DC.
World Bank. (1992b), *Governance and Development*, World Bank: Washington, DC.
World Bank. (1993), *World Development Report 1993*, Oxford University Press: New York.
World Bank. (1994a), *Status Report on Poverty in Sub-Saharan Africa 1994: The Many Faces of Poverty*, World Bank: Washington, DC.
World Bank. (1994b), *Adjustment in Africa: Reforms, Results, and the Road Ahead*, Oxford University Press: New York.
World Bank. (1994c), *Trends in Developing Economies Extracts: Volume 3: Sub-Saharan Africa*, World Bank: Washington, DC.
World Bank. (1994d), *Governance: The World Bank's Experience*, World Bank: Washington, DC.

World Bank. (1994e), *Social Indicators of Development*, World Bank: Washington, DC.
World Bank. (1995a), *African Development Indicators 1994-95*, World Bank: Washington, DC.
World Bank. (1995b), *World Development Report 1995: Workers in an Integrating World*, Oxford University Press: New York.
World Bank. (1995c), *Labour and the Growth Crisis in Sub-Saharan Africa*, World Bank: Washington, DC.
World Bank. (1995d), *Bureaucrats in Business: The Economics and Politics of Government Ownership*, Oxford University Press: New York.
Zambia Daily Mail. (1989), 21 April.

Index

For Product Safety Concerns and Information please contact our EU representative GPSR@taylorandfrancis.com Taylor & Francis Verlag GmbH, Kaufingerstraße 24, 80331 München, Germany

Batch number: 10725923

Printed by Printforce, the Netherlands